Reinventing our nation's electric supply system is at the heart of solving our climate change and energy security problems. It is the key to extending energy efficiency all the way to the end of the wire. But as the authors of *Perfect Power* point out, today we are using World War II-era analog technology to power a network and devices that are increasingly digitized. If our economy is to remain the most successful and sustainable in the future, it must be the most energy-efficient. That means decarbonizing our electric generation fleet and moving transportation from fossil fuels to hybrid and all-electric technologies. This book underscores the urgency of modernizing our grid and our business models to meet this challenge for our future generations.

—*James E. Rogers*

The vulnerability of the nation's grid, particularly in this era of terrorism, is a serious source of concern. The advanced technologies recommended by these two highly-knowledgeable authors promise to reduce those vulnerabilities (and eventually to reduce power costs to boot). These proposals should be carefully investigated and, if they offer serious reductions in vulnerabilities, should be pressed by the federal government. Moreover, what the authors have to say about our complex and crippling regulatory mechanism is regrettably right on the mark.

—*James R. Schlesinger*

The current electricity supply system may well be the greatest engineering achievement of the 20th century, but it does not meet the standard for Perfect Power in the 21st century. This book describes the pathway from today to Perfect Power. Robert Galvin states in the introduction that "I envision Mr. Edison already on his way to the patent office...." As a former vice president of the Thomas Alva Edison Foundation, I think he would have been there already. Maybe it is time for the rest of us to catch up. Anyone expecting to be part of the electricity industry of the future needs to read *Perfect Power*.

—*Barry Worthington*
Executive Director
The United States Energy Association

PERFECT POWER

PERFECT POWER

HOW THE MICROGRID REVOLUTION WILL UNLEASH CLEANER, GREENER, AND MORE ABUNDANT ENERGY

ROBERT GALVIN AND **KURT YEAGER**
WITH JAY STULLER

New York Chicago San Francisco Lisbon London Madrid Mexico City
Milan New Delhi San Juan Seoul Singapore Sydney Toronto

ISBN: 978–0–07–154882–3
MHID: 0–07–154882–3

While the information in this book is believed to be accurate, it is not intended to be used as a guide to investing, and the authors make no guarantees that any investments based on the information contained herein will benefit you in specific applications, owing to the risk that is involved in investing of almost any kind. Thus neither the publisher nor the authors assume liability for any losses that may be sustained by the use of the advice described in this book, and any such liability is hereby expressly disclaimed.

McGraw-Hill books are available at special quantity discounts to use as premiums and sales promotions, or for use in corporate training programs. To contact a representative, please visit the Contact Us pages at www.mhprofessional.com.

This book is printed on acid-free paper.

Contents

Acknowledgments

With three authors, this book might seem to have more than enough cooks in the kitchen, but the fact is, we relied heavily on many very thoughtful, "outside-the-box" experts and leaders who graciously helped bring our original ideas to fruition.

Some colleagues contributed their expertise to establishing the technological basis for the Galvin Electricity Initiative and its path to Perfect Power. Others helped sharpen our reasoning on the need to fundamentally reinvent America's electricity systems, while defining the new value propositions and regulatory policy changes that influentials and all citizens need to broadly understand and embrace. Still others helped anticipate the crucial environmental, quality of life, and human prosperity issues that electricity must resolve in the 21st century. We are deeply grateful to these contributors for their inspiration and insights. Many are mentioned in the text but several are particularly deserving of special recognition.

In the early days of the Galvin Electricity Initiative, our vision of innovation nodes and smart microgrids as key enablers of a Perfect Power delivery system was fundamentally shaped by colleagues from the Electric Power Research Institute (EPRI), most notably vice president Clark Gellings, who served as our "alter-ego" throughout this period. Clark's superb power engineering wisdom was very creatively augmented by Dr. Massoud Amin, an EPRI alumnus and now professor at the University of Minnesota. A particularly important dimension of our quest for power perfection is the emphasis on quality leadership and training brought by Jim Buckman, head of the Joseph Juran Center for Leadership in Quality. Our team also could not have established a convincing entrepreneurial leadership game plan without the insights and guidance of GF Energy's president and CEO, Roger Gale and his senior strategist, Jean-Louis Poirier.

As our efforts to catalyze fundamental change in the electricity enterprise and infrastructure came into focus, stakeholder communications quickly took center stage. This outreach effort has been superbly led by Deanna Troust, vice president of Vanguard Communications and her predecessor Caren Benjamin. We are also particularly grateful to Leah Spiro, senior editor at McGraw-Hill, for her guidance and her unwavering faith in an unconventional concept that is not always easily described. Last but not least, this book literally would not have been possible without the dedicated assistance of Susan Towle, who patiently and repeatedly translated reams of hieroglyphic-like, handwritten notes into a cogent manuscript.

Above all, the authors offer heartfelt thanks to our dear wives and immediate family members for their unwavering support, forbearance and understanding as we debated and formulated our experience and perspectives into a manuscript at all hours of the day and night. In closing, we dedicate this book to our fathers, Paul Galvin and Joseph Yeager, for establishing a standard of unqualified excellence that has been our lifelong inspiration.

PERFECT POWER

Introduction
The Electric Imperative

The nonprofit, public interest Galvin Electricity Initiative advocates the reinvention of how we generate, deliver, and use electricity. Electricity is where the rubber meets the pavement in terms of converting the world's many underlying energy resources into all the goods and services needed worldwide, and in successfully addressing the three-pronged dilemma of population, poverty, and pollution threats to global sustainability in the 21st century.

This initiative, launched in 2005, is motivated by the conviction that the vitality of the United States and the world is fundamentally threatened by an obsolete and highly vulnerable electricity supply system that has been starved of innovation and renewal for decades. To carry out the ambitious goal of reinventing a trillion-dollar-per-year global industry that forms the backbone of the world's economy and quality of life, we are focused on achieving four distinct but interdependent goals:

1. To meet the energy reliability and quality needs of the Digital Age
2. To generate an entirely new sector of goods and services that creates jobs, empowers consumers, and lowers the cost of energy
3. To fundamentally reduce the impact of energy upon the environment
4. To facilitate local, regional, and ultimately even national energy independence

To turn these goals into reality, we have engaged and stimulated extraordinary, creative, big-picture thinking by electricity industry technologists and leaders. These individuals have developed a blueprint for literally reinventing our nation's electricity supply system. This system of tomorrow will enable consumers large and small to receive electricity service without the penalties of recurrent interruptions and the other inefficiencies levied by today's power system. The result will never fail to provide the exact quantity and quality of power required by each consumer—what we call *Perfect Power*.

I know from personal experience that striving for perfection pays off. During my five decades at Motorola, three decades as chairman and chief executive officer, I learned that costs always fell in the face of rising quality, and that striving for perfection ensures the lowest cost. We applied the now-famous Six-Sigma quality management program to everything we did and made. Six-Sigma means that 99.9999 percent of the time, we'd make no error in our processes, manufacturing, or products.

Today, America and the world needs and deserves an electricity system capable of providing *Nine-Sigma* service—a system that is smart and can automatically heal itself despite ice storms, hurricanes, lightning strikes, and even terrorist attacks. A Nine-Sigma electricity system can also produce an absolutely reliable stream of electricity that's pure and never interrupted for even a fraction of a second, which is essential to fully serve the highest levels of reliability needed by our Perfect Power–hungry digital economy and society.

THE GALVIN ELECTRICITY INITIATIVE

The technology to achieve electricity service perfection exists. But until now, we have not had the impetus of consumer discontent to overcome the barriers that stand in the way of renewal. We founded the Galvin Electricity Initiative to do our small part in catalyzing this urgent call for renewal. This book is the manifesto of this initiative.

I have spent much of my life changing the rules of the game and in so doing, solving "unsolvable problems." Given the free market opportunity, entrepreneurial innovators are the most effective change agents and creators of the goods and services that enhance human well-being. In virtually every situation during my eighty-plus years on this grand earth, obstacles have arisen from groups and individuals who opposed such changes—not out of mendacity, malice, or greed, but due to a comfortable belief in the value of the existing process or system and an uncomfortable fear of change. It has also been my experience that once the changes have occurred, the very institutions that offer the most initial resistance reap the greatest benefits.

I personally participated in a similar transformation of a monopoly industry in the 1970s and 1980s. Only a generation ago, the common hard-wired telephone was the predominant tool of personal communication over distances. The cell phone, invented and developed during my time at Motorola, was viewed as a serious threat by a strong and well-entrenched communications industry. The innovative developers of "decentralized" mobile telephones faced resistance from both the monopoly hard-line phone companies and their government regulators, who at first severely limited the frequencies available for cell phones. Thanks to consumer demand, cell phones ultimately ignited a telecommunications revolution, which in turn unleashed a landslide of invention and innovation that continues today, to the benefit of all consumers—the telecommunications industry and society alike.

Electricity, like communications, is a similar but even greater public good. Its value is clear and manifest, for with a fingertip and about an ounce of pressure, even a child can illuminate the darkest room. The lightest touch brings a television to life within seconds, and hundreds of programs on virtually every aspect of real and imaginative life flow into the home. A touch starts a fan that blows heat into a cold Minnesota home or cooling air into a sweltering Florida condo. The ease with which we use electricity to power intensive-care hospital equipment, computers, freezers, and traffic lights is perhaps the most remarkable—and underappreciated—accomplishment of our age. These unmatched attributes have literally made electricity the lifeblood of our economy and quality of life.

Electricity has three great advantages relative to any other form of energy. It is the equal opportunity user of all forms of raw energy including fossil, renewable, and nuclear. It can be the most efficient vehicle for transforming raw energy into useful goods and services. Above all, it enables the vast array of innovative technologies that continue to transform our world. This is why the American networks of electrification were heralded as "the greatest engineering achievements of the 20th century" by the United States National Academy of Engineering.

Unfortunately, this history of extraordinary achievement has also bred a subsequent culture of complacency. Dominated by aging equipment rapidly nearing the end of its long-extended useful life, the nation's electricity system is showing ever more signs of operational morbidity. Still controlled by analog, electromechanical switches and relays that have progressed very little in the past century, the nation's graying electrical infrastructure cannot keep pace with the quality and reliability demands of today's microprocessor-based devices in homes, offices, factories, hospitals, and even farms. Every day approximately half a million Americans experience blackouts of two hours or more, and power interruptions cost our nation's economy more than $100 billion each year. In many ways, the American electrical grid is regressing to the equivalent of muddy horse and buggy paths that are forced to carry the traffic-equivalent of the 21st century's freeways.

Other factors also conspire to lock the electricity industry into a 20th-century time warp. The two biggest hurdles are the regulated monopoly business model that underlies all electric utilities and the regulatory entities themselves. The revenues and profits of these monopoly utilities are still based on how much electricity they sell, rather than on the quality, reliability, and efficiency of service they provide. As a result, utilities have had little incentive to meet, let alone exceed, consumer quality expectations, improve reliability, or create new kinds of innovative products and services like those found in all other service sectors. It's also the primary reason that the electric utility industry has seen no significant efficiency and reliability improvements since the 1960s.

Our nation's electricity infrastructure cannot continue to survive on the life-support level of investment it has endured for the past 30 years. As the dawn of the 21st century approached, the opportunity for major modernization crystallized before my eyes. It was also evident to my co-author Kurt Yeager. As president of the Electric Power Research Institute (EPRI), he sat in a position that gave him an exceptionally close view of the industry's development and the mindset of its leaders. EPRI is the main research arm of the electrical utility industry. Since I was on EPRI's Advisory Council at the time, Kurt and I also began to share grave concerns about the declining quality of America's power system. We were convinced that if we adopted the proper spirit of constructive criticism and urgency, the looming crises of today could become the perfected services, lowered costs, and heightened values of tomorrow. The finest renewal is there simply waiting for dedicated leadership to make it happen.

Consumers frequently demand perfection from businesses. Consumers who buy televisions, automobiles, or MP3 players expect these items to work exactly as promised, or they return them for a replacement. An on-time Federal Express or UPS delivery is expected and is almost always delivered. During both my time and my son, Chris' time serving as CEOs of Motorola, we ran the company based on the fact that perfection was both reasonable and practical. To that end, Motorola was founded and managed by three generations of Galvins on two basic principles: First, the business must never be stagnant in its ideas and its growth must be based on a cycle of continuous renewal. Second, this vital process of shedding skins is most effectively accomplished by encouraging a healthy spirit of discontent that leads to the near-constant challenge of inadequacies. Together these principles breed private sector innovation that creates value and jobs and earns universal wealth.

So why then do consumers expect so little in the way of quality from their electric power service? They seem to shrug off as inevitable, the fact that ordinary thunderstorms and even errant squirrels falling on power lines regularly shut down the electricity consumers rely on for virtually every aspect of their lives. They tolerate the fact that they can't customize electricity service to suit their individual needs—though they are able to do so with home theaters, the telephone, and the Internet. This acceptance of the fallacy that perfection in electricity service is not possible has stifled the healthy spirit of constructive discontent with the status quo. As Kurt and I continued our conversations, it struck us that if the electricity enterprise could start over with a "clean sheet of paper," it would *focus first and foremost on the needs of the electricity consumer.* And the only acceptable performance standard would be *perfection.* Setting a lesser goal simply guarantees an unacceptably mediocre result.

Reflecting these priorities, Kurt led the development of two landmark EPRI reports before his retirement in 2004. The first was the *Electricity Technology Roadmap.* This report, reflecting the contributions of over 200 diverse organizations, focuses on the ways in which electricity and the technology it enables can help us meet the critical challenges of the 21st century. The second report was the *Electricity Sector Framework for the Future.* Commissioned by the EPRI board of directors in the wake of the severe economic pressures on the utility industry in 2001–2002, this report recommended a set of actions and accountabilities enabling the U.S. electricity sector to meet the rapidly escalating needs and aspirations of its customers, investors, and society.

These two reports underscored the fact that the innovative technologies needed to achieve a comprehensive quality transformation of the U.S. electricity system were available. Further, the economic benefits to the nation and its citizens alone would be orders of magnitude greater than the cost each year. These reports, and the research and development results they represent, provided a confident base from which to launch the nonprofit, public interest Galvin Electricity Initiative. There is no government money or direction involved in this initiative, just my resources and experience, and Kurt's knowledge and leadership. It is not our intention to be in the electricity business but rather to catalyze a process of productive change for our nation and all its citizens. We are offering the results of this initiative to all others who reject the status quo and, in so doing, opt to enter the next great growth industry.

THE SOLUTION: SMART MICROGRIDS

In order to most rapidly and efficiently achieve electricity service perfection, the Galvin Electricity Initiative is focusing its efforts on the development and implementation of decentralized "smart microgrids" that represent the consumer-focused leading edge of total power system modernization. Incorporating what is known as "distributed generation," these electronically controlled microgrids can immediately supply perfect power service to individual buildings, office complexes, industrial parks, and even entire communities. Smart microgrids use the utility bulk power supply to best advantage, but can operate independently when necessary to maintain perfect service, or to capitalize on energy cost-saving opportunities. These smart, decentralized microgrids are also what will enable cleaner alternative sources of energy, especially solar power with backup storage in homes and offices, to most rapidly reach their full potential. Woven together and managed by computerized controllers that—unlike human system operators—operate at the speed of light, this emerging web of smart microgrids is like a medieval knight's chain mail, a flexible array that's stronger than the sum of its parts. These smart microgrids will also increase energy efficiency while reducing the need for new, very expensive, large centralized power plants and their power delivery infrastructure.

There's another reason the Galvin Electricity Initiative is focusing on the smart microgrid approach. We recognize that the most rapid, confident, and sustainable engine for quality improvement is to enable innovative entrepreneurs to get involved in the electricity supply industry. What valiant entrepreneurs do is to find answers. Equally important is the fact that this approach will set the tone for comprehensive, creative solutions rather than timid patchwork answers. Everyone involved in the electricity enterprise—including consumers and utilities alike—will echo the call for comprehensive performance innovations that are nothing less than transformative.

This Perfect Power supply system, ironically enough, will look a bit like the distant past. A decentralized electricity model was originally proposed and championed more than a century ago by none other than Thomas Alva Edison. In the early years of electrification, this proved to be an effective and efficient method for initially electrifying small communities and individual factories. Above all, Edison saw electricity's primary value as the enabling vehicle for innovative consumer products and services, not as just another form of commodity energy. In fact, with his relentless drive to invent and develop technologies that created new enterprises and jobs that benefited society, Edison's vision for electricity is very similar to what we propose today with the Galvin Electricity Initiative.

Unfortunately, Edison's world of the late 1800s lacked the variety and sophistication of technologies needed to create such a sound, seamless, and economically decentralized system on a national basis. Rapid advances in technologies and economies of scale during the first half of the 20th century, when the United States was being electrified, made a centralized bulk electricity generation and delivery system more profitable to investors, more manageable for suppliers, and also more accessible and less costly for consumers whose service demands were very modest by today's standards.

This centralized, commodity electrification model has dominated the world ever since. As a result, however, consumers generally remain limited to purchasing electricity from one franchised monopoly utility supplier. In terms of service quality and

choices, what consumers have today is the electrical performance and choice equivalent of the old analog, black rotary-dial
telephone. However, technology has caught up with Edison and
we can move on to the digital cell-phone equivalent and beyond
in the world of electricity as well. Every commodity is a service
waiting to happen, and electricity has waited far too long.

Although most of the best and brightest engineering students
have avoided the stale and uninspiring electric utility business
since the 1970s, we believe that this new and revitalized electricity industry will attract dynamic young innovators who will lead
the quality transformation to levels even beyond our imagination.
I can easily envision the emergence and growth of local service
businesses, not unlike plumbing, heating, and electronic special-
ists, that install, maintain, and fine-tune the perfect power system
to the highest quality standards, while dramatically cutting costs
for all consumers. What's more, the new system will demand the
best work ever done by software programmers to control and coordinate both smart microgrids and their interactions with the bulk
power system. These new, prolific, high-quality job opportunities
will make a significant contribution to our nation's economy and
competitiveness.

This brings us to the Green Revolution, which is now sweep-
ing the world. The reinvention of the electrical system is an enormous and vital piece of this revolution. Electricity is arguably the
cleanest and greenest form of energy at its point of use. It provides
unique access to the emerging array of clean, renewable energy
resources while enabling maximum energy efficiency. Most
alternative and renewable energy systems eventually convert
something—be it the wind, waves, or solar radiation—into electricity. Electricity also empowers the technical innovation that is
essential to sustainable progress. And while green buildings have
numerous features and materials that are kind to the environment, they cannot function without electricity. In fact, because
the economics and practicality of most alternative green technologies ultimately depend upon this form of energy, it's essential for
the green and clean movement to incorporate better electrical use

into a holistic environmental strategy that converts our office buildings and homes into net energy producers rather than users.

MICROGRID ENTREPRENEURS

Several of the changes we suggest have already started. But instead of the idealists who talked about unrealistic forms of energy production in the 1970s, a group of flinty-eyed entrepreneurs is now emerging, a number of whom are featured in subsequent pages. They see ways to provide superior service that exceeds consumer expectations, yet still earn a profit. Microgrid entrepreneurs will work in conjunction with facility and land developers, advanced technology suppliers, and utilities alike. Their learning curve experiences will also stimulate continuous renewal. Certainly, some of their motivation comes from a desire to ameliorate man's effect upon the environment. Even more, I believe, their motivation comes from the drive to innovate, create, and sell products and services that benefit consumers in ways those consumers never before imagined.

With more than 6.5 billion people already on the planet, our earth will likely host at least 9 billion people by the middle of this century. Their collective struggle for a better quality of life will continue to put a heavy demand upon natural resources, including access to clean water and secure food supplies as well as energy. Without abundant energy—in a form that does not continue to alter the climate and degrade the environment—the future will certainly hold dismal choices and distasteful adjustments for the human species. Electricity is *the* energy key to a sustainable global future, despite its deeply flawed infrastructure.

Today, nearly two billion people still lack access to electricity and to the economic opportunities it enables. Under business-as-usual development conditions, the number of those who lack access to electricity will more than double by 2050. An amount of energy equivalent to no more than 10 percent of the world's electricity production would provide the basic level of electricity services needed by these impoverished people. Successful rural electrification programs, where the majority of those now denied access to electricity live, would also lighten the pressure to leave the countryside for cities unable to cope with the added population demands.

The ability of decentralized electricity microgrids to most quickly power and empower these impoverished people, while using locally available energy resources such as biomass and solar, is key to controlling the rising temperature of the world's human climate as well as the natural climate. Therefore, the urgent goal to which we all must commit is completing the electrification of the world. Indeed, the key global sustainability challenges can only be resolved through electricity, innovative technology, and the power of the free market.

Recognizing this reality, many countries in the developed world are applying the smart microgrid concept as an essential vehicle for accelerating the modernization of their electricity supply systems. The European Union's Parliament has, for example, called upon its members to make their national power grids smart and independent so that regions, cities, and citizens can produce and share energy in accordance with the same open-access principles that now apply to the Internet. For example, these efforts include converting individual sections of their bulk power systems into smart microgrids. This enables the essential intelligence to be added in a manner that avoids service disruptions while ensuring that the real savings to consumers and utilities alike are most quickly realized.

Despite this positive international experience, there are still significant policy barriers to improving the quality of our power systems. For example, there are laws in many jurisdictions around the world, including the United States, that allow only public utilities or governments to run wires that cross a public street or even to power remote villages. This limits the ability of entrepreneurs to implement superior solutions incorporating distributed generation and decentralized microgrids. Politicians, regulators, and utilities alike have generally been quite comfortable with the regulated monopoly status quo and it remains the conventional wisdom. Indeed, it is well known that human culture resists change at all cost.

Correcting an entrenched situation of this magnitude requires that the leaders of our "heretical" view take charge and demand positive and immediate change. To this end, the Galvin Electricity Initiative is also aggressively addressing the obsolete utility regulations and counterproductive financial incentive structures that must be dealt with on a nationwide policy level if quality transformation is to succeed. Recognition by influential leaders and consumers alike that our electricity supply system is dangerously unreliable, inefficient, and shockingly vulnerable to disruption and attack is the first and most important step in this transformation of electricity policy.

By opening this decentralized door to innovation in electricity and unleashing the creativity of thousands of self-organizing entrepreneurial, investors, and even established corporations, we can create a fundamentally better way of living for the United States and the entire world. We are limited only by our willpower and imagination. Were he still alive, I envision Mr. Edison already on his way to the U.S. Patent Office with his first dozen applications to deliver Perfect Power.

Bob Galvin

Guiding the Path to Perfect Power

THE WELCOME HERESIES OF QUALITY
Robert W. Galvin

A few years after Motorola Inc. became one of the first winners of the Malcolm Baldridge National Quality Award, Robert W. Galvin, then CEO of Motorola, wrote this document challenging commonly held assumptions regarding quality. These ideas on the importance of quality are particularly relevant to electricity today and have guided the Galvin Electricity Initiative.

Old Testament (OT): Quality control is an ordinary responsibility of the quality department.
New Truth (NT): Quality improvement is not just an institutional assignment; it is a daily personal priority and obligation for all.

OT: Training is overhead and costly.
NT: Training does not cost.

OT: New quality programs have high up-front costs.
NT: There is no up-front cost to high-quality "quality programs."

OT: Better quality costs more.
NT: You cannot raise cost by raising quality.

OT: Keep measurement data to a minimum.
NT: You cannot have too much relevant data.

OT: To err is human.
NT: Perfection is the standard—total customer satisfaction.

OT: Quality defects should be divided into major and minor categories.
NT: There is only one defect category—intolerable! A single standard is essential to unqualified dedication.

OT: Quality improvements come only from small continuous steps.
NT: Partially true—but radical, step-function improvements are essential and doable.

OT: It takes extra time to do things right.
NT: Quality doesn't take time; it saves time.

OT: Haste makes waste.
NT: (*Thoughtful*) Speed makes quality.

OT: Quality programs best fit products and manufacturing.
NT: Quality's most crying needs and promises are in administration and services.

OT: At a certain level, the customer no longer cares about better quality.
NT: The customer will differentiate. Incremental improvements drive better pricing, delivery and performance.

OT: Thou shalt not steal.
NT: Thou shalt steal (nonproprietary) ideas shamelessly.

OT: We take care of the company—our suppliers better beat the price.
NT: An essential to being a world-class company is to be a world-class customer.

1
The Heat Is On

While largely unrecognized by the public and government officials, North America's aging, inefficient, and dangerously unreliable electrical infrastructure is crumbling. In an era of precise digital power demands and serious environmental concerns, this system is also needlessly wasteful, bleeding energy throughout the creation, delivery, and use of that electricity. In short, our electric power infrastructure is as incompatible with the future as horse trails were to automobiles. If not urgently renewed and literally reinvented, North America's electrical grid is rapidly approaching a crisis point for which we are already paying an exorbitant price. The future is now.

A broad, swelling, and searing layer of atmospheric heat settled upon North America during the third week of July 2006, the stuff of an epic inquisition, a test of the continent's electrical grid and the will of its people. As the leading edge of the Digital Age met the Dark Ages, the damage stretched from coast to coast.

In temperatures exceeding 100 degrees F., New Yorkers desperate to cool off turned up air-conditioners and fans, putting an almost unprecedented load upon Consolidated Edison's electrical generation, transmission, and delivery systems. Under the strain, even heavy-duty circuits began to fail. At LaGuardia Airport, a power outage that shut down security screening in the morning grounded hundreds of outgoing passengers, and another nighttime blackout left travelers literally fumbling about in the pitch black restrooms of the main terminal.

A large portion of the borough of Queens went dark and remained so for nearly six days, through a series of electrical failures that left Consolidated Edison engineers flummoxed for an explanation. In other parts of the city, additional power outages brought subway trains to a halt. According to news reports, heavily sweating New Yorkers sat in the dark, whimpering.

Meanwhile on the West Coast, more than 5,000 Pacific Gas and Electric customers in Marin County were left in the dark overnight when, according to one early report, an owl "mislanded" on a 60,000-volt transmission line near the coastal town of Bolinas. Crews later determined that an old lightening strike on a utility pole had caused it to eventually fall. And while relatively few people were directly inconvenienced by the blackout, the entire south-central portion of the county faced an *indirect* threat when the failure took down a key water plant for 14 hours, a period during which water levels in the 130 holding tanks in the district's 147-square-mile service area precipitously dropped. Consumers were asked to curtail their water use for at least 24 hours as water district crews scrambled to get this electricity-dependent service back online.

From the Midwest, the Associated Press reported that nearly 700 laboratory mice and rats died when a power failure at Ohio State University cut off air-conditioning to six buildings at the school's medical campus. Temperatures in the labs rose from 80 degrees to as high as 105 degrees Fahrenheit. Even worse, about 20 projects involving critical research into epilepsy, multiple sclerosis, cancer, and cardiovascular disease were affected, including studies that researchers had been working on for years.

In the high desert of southern California, near the city of Palmdale, sits the Federal Aviation Administration's Los Angeles Air Route Traffic Control Center, a facility from which controllers manage flights on long-distance routes at 38,000 feet or higher, covering parts of Arizona, Nevada, Utah, and much of the Golden State. At 5:30 p.m. on July 18, the Center's electrical supply went dead, shutting down radar and communications. For some 90 minutes — until an emergency generator that was supposed to automatically start finally kicked on—the Los Angeles International Airport (LAX), the world's fifth-busiest passenger complex, was, as an airport spokesperson explained, "pretty much shut down."

Less than a week later, the 18th consecutive day of triple-digit heat continued in California, triggering still more power outages that eventually swept through downtown Los Angeles. The most acute problem occurred at the prestigious Garland Building on Wilshire Ave., a data center designed to maintain operations even in an 8.3 magnitude earthquake. The Garland facility provides housing for some of the leading Web hosting and home page companies, including Media Temple and the ubiquitous MySpace.com. But when the main incoming electrical power failed and the backup system couldn't keep the chillers cold, the servers went down, producing what could have been the most agonizing 24-hour disconnection in the history of Teenage America.

As the shock from the Great Heat Wave of 2006 finally subsided, something weird and dissonant happened in the world of electricity. In late July, a consortium that includes all of the nation's regional electrical grid operators—known as independent system operators, or ISOs, entities that coordinate electrical transmission between utilities and across state lines—issued a press release, noting that each operator handled record electricity demands and "met the challenge of record temperatures without incident."

Huh?

Utility executives and industry representatives appeared on National Public Radio, praising their overall reliability. And herein we find the catch: System data appear to conflict with human events.

Indeed, the Electric Reliability Council of Texas, which serves about 85 percent of the load in that state, did reliably produce more electricity than it had in the past, meeting a peak demand of 62,396 megawatts on July 17, exceeding the previous peak of 60,274 megawatts during the previous August.

The New York Independent System Operator, which serves 20 million people, met a record peak load of 32,624 megawatts, without enacting emergency procedures, breaking a record of 32,075 in July of 2005.

Moreover, the California Independent System Operator also handled a new record demand of 50,270 megawatts, up nearly 5,000 megawatts from the previous year's record peak, and a level that was not expected to be reached for another five years. "We plan operations for extreme scenarios and for a 1-in-10-year heat wave, but this was a 1-in-50-year heat storm," said California ISO President and CEO Yakout Mansour, in a press release. "Power plant operators responded to the challenge well ahead of the season and prepared their plants to withstand difficult conditions." The California ISO system, added the press release, held up throughout the heat wave.

In other words, virtually all of the nation's power outages during the summer of 2006 were localized—a fact that brings little comfort to the grounded airline passengers in the western United States, the people of Queens, and the many other cities that suffered blackouts. Apparently, anything less than a total power system collapse, such as California and the West Coast from British Columbia to Baja experienced in 1996, is considered a victory by the ISO. What *didn't* happen, and it's why utility operators were sounding a sigh of relief, was a reprise of the cascading and cataclysmic outage of August, 14, 2003, which blacked out more than 50 million people within eight minutes and conservatively cost the U.S. economy more than 10 billion dollars.

The Great Northeast Blackout began when an overheated and therefore sagging power line in Ohio made contact with a tree; tripping off more than 400 transmission lines and generating units at 261 power plants. The massive disruption threw most of New York and parts of Pennsylvania, Ohio, Michigan, and two Canadian provinces into darkness, an event that was the largest power loss in history. Considered a blunt wake-up call to the utility industry, this monumental power outage compelled grid operators to coordinate more closely, and spend more maintenance money on, not so ironically, trimming trees.

THE TRUTH AND NOTHING BUT THE TRUTH

So wherein lay the truth about the summer of 2006? Is it in the numbers compiled by the system operators? Are the anecdotes about outages just that, a random collection of isolated incidents? Perhaps a more important pair of questions follow: Was the heat wave of 2006 really just a 1-in-50-year event? Or, was it a portent of what North America faces in a climate that appears to be warming at an alarming rate?

In the wake of this failure, power system operators in the Northeast and Midwest made a number of changes in the way they monitor and control their related grids. And the grid's overall stalwart performance during the record heat wave was cited as a testament to the adaptations that were made. Just as all belief systems include a few bits of irrefutable fact, the same can be said of this somewhat self-serving operators' analysis of the nation's power system performance.

The independent system operators and their Canadian counterparts who manage regional electricity transmission throughout North America did prevent a cascading systemwide failure despite severe stress. But it also seems clear that even small blackouts and power interruptions have much greater health, social, and economic consequences than in decades past—simply because of our reliance on air conditioners, digital devices in hospital intensive care units, and the Internet. What *should* be apparent to grid operators, utility executives, government regulators, elected officials, business leaders, and even the public, is that the United States dodged a whole lot of bullets during a summer that in an age of a warming climate is very likely a harbinger of more to come.

The fragile condition of the U.S. power system was brought front-and-center again in February 2008 when a massive power outage in Florida suddenly left some three million people without electricity for several hours or more. The official cause of this major disruption was "human error." Because of the lack of electronic diagnostic capabilities, and associated automatic control systems, an engineer at Florida Power and Light, the state's largest utility, who was diagnosing a relatively minor substation problem inadvertently caused a short circuit that could not be contained. The problem instantly cascaded through 26 transmission lines and 38 substations. This forced the major Turkey Point nuclear power plant, as well as a number of other power plants across Florida, to shut down.

Indeed, the spotlight is now on a North American electricity system that is largely based on technologies developed prior to the 1950s. Most of its generation plants, millions of relays, controls, transformers, and power lines are 40 to 50 years old, nearing the end of their useful life. Even ordinary thunderstorms, much less blizzards, hurricanes, and heat waves, routinely bring down pieces of this increasingly precarious electrical infrastructure. Utilities that overlook the thousands of fragile points on the grid—while boasting about avoiding systemwide blackouts—suggest an industry in complete and utter denial.

The root cause of this denial can be traced to the fact that regulators for the most part remain unwilling to accept the reality that their short-sighted bureaucratic policies restricting electricity infrastructure investment have robbed the system of innovation and kept it on little more than a life-support level of infrastructure renewal and maintenance for several decades. This false economy has left the United States dependent on a dangerously vulnerable and highly obsolete power supply system to provide more than 40 percent of the nation's total energy needs (Figure 1–1). If even 10 percent of the $100 billion-plus national electricity reliability penalty we all pay each year were reinvested in revitalizing and modernizing the power delivery system, this penalty would soon be eliminated. Moreover, the productivity and global competitiveness advantages that would result would rapidly add thousands of dollars to every family's income. In spite of these achievable advantages, we continue

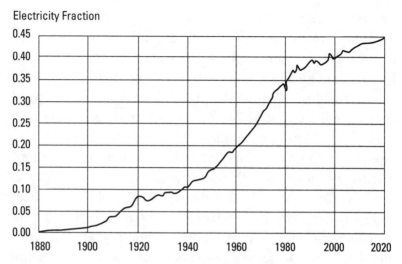

Figure 1-1 Fraction of U.S. Energy Needs Met by Electricity

to sustain the electrical equivalent of the "subprime mortgage" debacle in which a few are rewarded at the major long-term expense of the nation and the majority of its citizens.

The consequences of this unreliable electricity service grow greater with each passing day, since an electrical infrastructure inflection point is coming at a time when the very nature of electricity demand is undergoing a profound shift. While the current system was designed to serve analog devices such as lights, motors, pumps, and such—which work just fine despite varying electric loads—today's personal computers and other "smart" digital devices with microprocessors inside are highly sensitive to even the slightest disruption in power, as well as to variations in power quality due to voltage surges and sags and harmonic changes in the alternating electron flow. Such interruptions and disturbances—measuring less than one cycle, or less than 1/60th of a second—can crash assembly lines, computer servers, intensive care and life support machines, and other microprocessor-based equipment.

The electricity supply system's dangerous obsolescence is certainly not lost on the U.S. Defense Department. More than six years after the terrorist attacks on the Pentagon and World Trade

Center, the Defense Science Board warns that the U.S. electricity grid remains alarmingly vulnerable to attack. In a 2008 Board report entitled "More Fight—Less Fuel," former Secretary of Defense and CIA Director Dr. James Schlesinger and General Michael Carns conclude that, the "almost complete dependence of military installations on a fragile and vulnerable commercial power grid places critical military and homeland defense missions at an unacceptably high risk of extended disruption." The report goes on to state that physical or cyber sabotage—or even a simple capacity overload—could devastate U.S. military and homeland security installations and have a frightening ripple effect across the country. In order to most quickly eliminate this threat, the Defense Department has become a leading proponent of installing self-sufficient microgrids on military installations in the United States and around the world.

BLEEDING AT THE SPEED OF LIGHT

The enormous economic cost of the system's unreliability is only part of the downside of today's electrical system. Another revolves around wasted energy that starts during the generation of electricity, bleeds at the speed of light from transmission lines, and also leaks from household devices left on standby 24 hours a day. For example, as shown in Figure 1–2, 98 percent of the energy needed to illuminate a lightbulb is lost along the way primarily as heat. Carbon dioxide (CO_2) emissions and their implications for global warming are also a direct result of this wasted energy.

Simply start with coal-fired power plants, which produce about half of the electricity used in the United States. Some of these plants burn some 25 tons of pulverized coal per minute, blown into a box that contains a continuous fireball that superheats water that flows through a web of high-pressure steel tubes. As the water turns to steam, its pressure drives turbines that generate electricity. The thunderous sounds of such plants are an aural marvel, as is the product.

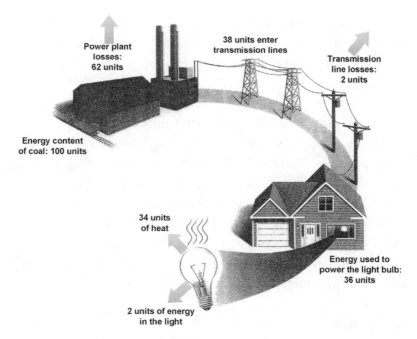

Figure 1–2 Energy Losses in Powering a Light Bulb

Alas, more than 60 percent of the energy in each and every ton of coal goes up into the atmosphere in smokestacks and cooling towers in the form of heat, emissions, or warm water that's ultimately discharged into a river, lake, or the ocean. These large power plants are also usually located a long way from where their electricity is ultimately used. The power must therefore travel over long-distance transmission wires, which creates another weak link in the chain of electricity reliability and efficiency losses.

Nearly all of the nation's transmission lines are made with copper cables, just as they have been for a hundred years. While these lines conduct electricity quite well, the electrons do meet resistance that causes at least some energy loss and always generates heat. When hot weather triggers an additional spike in electrical demand for air-conditioning, these steel core and copper wires heat up to an even greater degree, expand under the extra load, and start to sag. This thermal expansion is still limited by obsolete, slow, electromechanical controls that, as a result, seriously constrain the amount of electricity each transmission line can carry. The result creates the need for more and more lines in somebody's back yard.

The United States is hardly alone in this situation. Europe experiences periodic major blackouts that can be traced to obsolete controls on its transmission networks. Electrification in the developing world also is generally dependent on the same obsolete "low-cost" technology. For example, the surging economic powerhouse that is India has one of the weakest electrical grids in the world, with enormous infrastructure inefficiencies. Not surprisingly, its basic design is similar to that of North America's. According to India's Ministry of Power, transmission and distribution losses alone average 26 percent of total electricity production, and in some of India's states as much as 62 percent.

The inefficiencies continue right into the modern home, which is filled with what's known in the trade as *vampires*, or devices that leak electricity—again in the form of heat—without actually providing much service. These include phone chargers, instant-on televisions, computers that are left humming 24–7, and just about anything that can be observed as illuminated during the night. In fact, these electron-sucking vampires typically devour an average of nearly 7 percent of a home's total electricity consumption and in some cases as much as a quarter. In Europe, the International Energy Agency figures that about four major power plants are needed to supply the electricity that goes into the continent's so-called standby power. According to a piece in the *Pittsburgh Post-Gazette*, the agency also expects that the growth in such devices just here in the United States will require the power equivalent of *eight* major centralized plants by 2010.

Whether the vampires are instant-on televisions, computer printers, DVD players, home alert systems, and chargers feeding cell phones and personal digital assistants, such as Palm Pilots and Trios, much of the energy consumed seldom goes to an active and tangible benefit. Consumers see positives for these states of readiness, because they are a function of time and convenience. The technology and designs that provide it, however, are antiquated and woefully inefficient. In the electricity business these end uses are known as *loads*, and except for certain types of appliances most are dumb pieces of machinery.

Steve Pullins, the President of the Tennessee-based Horizon Energy Group, a consulting firm that works on smart-grid developments states the challenge well. "Until we have an electrical supply business that addresses the needs of consumers, and is regulated to meet those needs first and foremost, we won't have appliances that can interact with a new, modern, and different grid from what we now have. There are obviously problems with inefficiency and waste in the generation and transmission of electricity. But it will be difficult to deal with those elements if we don't first address the loads, getting appliance manufacturers to make devices that use power only intermittently, and which in turn enables consumers to ease the demand on wasted electricity."

To its credit, the U.S. government has leaned on manufacturers to make voluntary and active choices in the name of energy efficiency. In 1992, the U.S. Environmental Protection Agency introduced Energy Star as a discretionary program designed to identify and promote energy-efficient products, defined as models that are at least 10 to 50 percent more efficient in the use of energy and water when compared to standard models. This program, which is now a joint venture of the EPA and the U.S. Department of Energy, has more than 40 categories of products that can carry the Energy Star label, from major home appliances to office equipment, lighting, and even new homes and industrial buildings. While some 1,500 manufacturers have been allowed to place the label on more than 35,000 individual product models, these items often compete against less expensive appliances that don't have energy-saving features.

LET THERE BE LIGHT

Simple changes, if widely adopted, can make a significant difference. Consider, for example, the lighting that consumes nearly 25 percent of all electricity and the development and ramifications of the compact fluorescent lightbulb, or CFL, which could render the venerable incandescent bulb obsolete. Once again, it works thanks to a technology that reduces the production of heat, which in turn saves electricity.

Simply explained, regular incandescent bulbs give off light when electricity passes through the metal filament that's inside the vacuum-sealed bulb, and which heats up to about 2,300 degrees Celsius. A CFL is a glass tube that's filled with gas and a tiny bit of mercury and coated with phosphor. As electricity passes through electrodes on both ends of the tube it excites the molecules of mercury, which then give off ultraviolet light. In turn, the beams from this invisible part of the spectrum excite the phosphor, which emits visible light. The trick is that the CFL bulb gets only about a third as hot as an incandescent, but also produces about three times the amount of light per watt of power. In other words, it gives off as much light as an incandescent bulb while using only about a quarter of the energy. Improvements in light-emitting diodes, or LEDs, are another more efficient alternative illumination source that is rapidly gaining market acceptance. These white light LEDs use about half the energy consumed by a conventional bulb and last about a decade. Indeed, the city of Ann Arbor, Michigan, replaced its 1,400 street lights with LEDs and expects to save about $100,000 in electricity costs each year.

In a remarkable 4,400-word article that appeared in the September 2006 edition of *Fast Company* magazine, Senior Writer Charles Fishman suggested that if each one of America's 110 million households replaced just one incandescent bulb with a CFL, it would save enough electricity to power a city of 1.5 million. And since a typical home has more than 50 light sockets, the social and environmental savings from replacing all the bulbs is staggering. The issue is that at about 75 cents apiece, the incandescent bulbs cost about a quarter as much as the CFLs, even though the latter lasts much longer and would save an average household at least $25 in electricity costs over its operating life.

Of course, even the most efficient home appliance and lightbulb will do little good during a blackout. And the unreliability of the electrical infrastructure goes hand in hand with its inefficiency. Both are manifestations of the system's age and a lack of utility industry innovation. Even as this book goes to press, electric utilities and system operators in the United States still find themselves frantically attempting to maintain power, with no tools to "protect" their systems other than the intentional or accidental use of rolling blackouts and brownouts. Any jurisdiction that allows its utilities and regulators to maintain this state of affairs as "normal" when the benefit of the Perfect Power approach available today provides the means to avoid such catastrophes is, we believe, acting in an entirely negligent manner. It is, in effect, steering its citizens into an economic, environmental, and security backwater.

What's more, these unfortunate trends are converging in a socioeconomic, political, and environmental nexus that makes the reinvention of the electrical system a critical issue for society worldwide. If predictions of a warming climate bear out, stronger storms and heat waves far more intense than the one of 2006 will continue to apply stress to a balky system. Therefore, how we make and use this superb form of energy has profound impacts upon the environment, security, health, and well-being of a world that depends upon its lights remaining bright at all times.

INSTITUTIONS AND COMPANIES TO WATCH

Consolidated Edison (ConEd) (www.coned.com) provides electric service to approximately 3.2 million customers in New York City and Westchester County. ConEd is one of the largest investor-owned energy companies in the U.S., with $13 billion in annual revenues and $28 billion in assets. It also owns and operates the world's largest district steam system, providing service to most of Manhattan. ConEd has been supplying the energy that powers New York for more than 180 years.

Defense Science Board (DSB) (www.acq.ord.mil/dsb). The DSB was established in 1956, and is composed of 35 civilian members designated by the Undersecretary of Defense for Acquisition, Technology, and Logistics. The DSB advises the Secretary of Defense and the Joint Chiefs of Staff "on scientific, technical, manufacturing, acquisition process, and other matters of special interest to the Department of Defense." The DSB operates by forming task forces consisting of Board members and other experts to address those tasks formally referred to it.

Federal Energy Regulatory Commission (FERC) (www.ferc. gov). FERC is the independent U.S. government agency that regulates the interstate transmission of electricity, natural gas, and oil. FERC is also responsible for ensuring the reliability of the nation's high-voltage interstate transmission system. FERC's responsibilities do not include regulation of retail electricity to consumers or approval for electric generation, transmission, or distribution facilities. These are within the purview of state public utility commissions.

Horizon Energy Group LLC (www.horizonenergygroup.com) is a small company created to provide value-added services in the energy industry. These services include advanced control methodologies for distributed generation, demand response, and renewables aggregation. Horizon Energy Group services also include a variety of advanced power system asset intelligence and consumer portal projects supporting the modern grid. Horizon Energy Group is headquartered in Maryville, Tennessee, with a European division office in Riga, Latvia.

Independent System Operators (ISOs). Each ISO coordinates, controls, and monitors the operation of the electrical power system, usually within a single state, but often encompassing multiple states. Similar to an ISO is the regional transmission operator (RTO) which controls the operation of the electric power transmission system over wider areas. There are currently eight ISOs including Alberta, California, Florida, New England, New York, Ontario and Texas, plus four RTOs.

National Association of Regulatory Utility Commissioners (NARUC) (www.naruc.org). Founded in 1889, NARUC is the trade association representing the state public service commissioners who regulate electricity, natural gas, telecommunications, water, and transportation throughout the United States. These regulatory commissioners are charged with ensuring that the rates charged by regulated utilities are fair, just, and reasonable. NARUC's mission is to serve the public interest by improving the quality and effectiveness of public utility regulation.

North American Electric Reliability Council (NERC) (www. nerc.com). Created in 1962 and headquartered in Princeton, New Jersey., NERC's mission is to improve the reliability and security of the North American bulk power system. It establishes reliability standards for planning and operating this bulk power system. Since 2006, NERC is certified as the self-regulatory "electric reliability organization" for North America, subject to the authority of the U.S. Federal Energy Regulatory Commission and the Canadian government. NERC works through eight regional entities whose members account for virtually all the electricity supplied in North America.

2

The Grid

The electricity supply infrastructure today consists of various large sources of power generation, vast transmission networks, and local distribution systems. It is the most complex machine ever built, yet it depends on technologies that have changed very little in more than 50 years. As a result, electricity service reliability and efficiency are far less than perfect and continue to deteriorate in a world demanding digital-quality power. Major power outages that periodically occur worldwide affect millions of people and cost billions of dollars. These effects are just the tip of the imperfection iceberg that smart microgrids can most rapidly eliminate.

The delivery of electricity in the United States from some 16,000 power-generating plants to hundreds of millions of large and small consumers is arguably the least appreciated and most vulnerable part of our nation's infrastructure. It depends on a system of overhead wires and underground cables. This electricity delivery system is known as *the grid*, and it is graphically described in Figure 2–1. It is a $360 billion asset, which, in spite of its limitations, represents the essential connective tissue for both the nation's economy and the electric utility ecosystem.

Electricity is a miraculous natural phenomenon. The electricity that powers our lives is actually an invisible process that only exists in the infrastructure that produces, delivers, and uses it. *Elektron* was the Ancient Greek's word for amber which, when they rubbed it on fur, created an entertaining electric

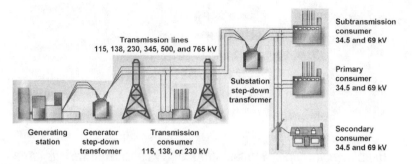

Figure 2–1 The Electric Grid

spark, the same static charge one occasionally feels when touching a doorknob, for example, and which can be observed in lightning. Electricity is simply the movement of tiny charged subatomic particles that are called *electrons*. Each electron flows only a short distance before transferring its energy to another, and another, and so on around a circuit, eventually leading back to the source. The energy transfer occurs at nearly the speed of light, or 186,000 miles per second. This invisible wonder occurs virtually everywhere in nature; it's even the mechanism that transmits our brain's signals through nerves to contract our muscles.

We see a few drops of gasoline when filling a car. We know when water comes out of a hose or faucet. A burning log that's producing heat has an obvious cause and effect. But because electricity is invisible, it's no surprise that most people have only a vague concept of what happens on the other side of a wall socket. In fact, electricity is only indirectly evident through the services that it enables. It is only when those services fail that we are reminded of how essential electricity is to our lives.

Electric current in a wire, measured in amperes, is the simultaneous motion in the same direction of enumerable electrons. These electrons are already in the wire, but their normal motion is random until electric energy pressure—called *voltage*—makes them all move in the same direction. This "electron theory" is the basis for all aspects of electricity. Just as a pump causes water to flow in a pipe, a generator or battery creates voltage and causes electrons to flow in a wire. But while gallons of water or gasoline are common measures, few people understand the obscure symbols in their electricity bill. The unit of electrical power is the watt, and it's equal to the amperage in the circuit, multiplied by the voltage applied to the circuit. Electrical power consumption is measured in terms of watt hours. This is equal to the watts being consumed multiplied by the number of hours they are consumed. The thousands of watt hours, or kilowatt hours (kWh), of electricity each of us use in a month are what the electric meter, essentially the utility company's cash register, measures and we all pay for in our electric bills.

Continuing the comparison with the flow of water, we can make a specific quantity of water move from one point to another in a couple of different manners. With one, we can use a large pipe with a thin wall and apply a low pressure to push the water. With the other, we can use a small pipe with a thicker wall and apply a higher pressure. The same rule applies to the movement of electric current. As voltage (pressure) is increased, amperage (current flow) can be correspondingly reduced to provide the same amount of power. As we will see later, this is the principle behind the movement of electricity over long distances, where voltage is first stepped up and then stepped down.

Materials having many free electrons, such as copper and aluminum, are good conductors and provide a relatively large current flow per unit of voltage. On the other hand, materials having few free electrons, such as glass, wood, and rubber, provide little or no current flow and therefore are used as insulators. Because the cost of copper or aluminum is relatively high compared to the insulating material, it is generally more economical to use high voltages in thinner, less expensive conductor wires, particularly for the predominant overhead transmission of power.

However, unlike water reservoirs and the pipes connecting them to our homes, electricity is still difficult to store in any large quantity. Once generated, electricity must therefore be able to instantaneously find an end use. The precise balancing act between creating electricity and getting it to the end user requires the ultimate just-in-time enterprise. This capability represents one of the most profound technical accomplishments of the electricity supply system, and it fundamentally differentiates the electricity supply system from other infrastructures, industries, and business supply chains.

STEAM POWER STILL REIGNS

In spite of the breadth of technical opportunity, the basic systems on which our electricity supply depends haven't basically changed, except in scale, since early in the 20th century. More than a century after it began, the electric utility industry still produces most of its electricity by boiling water to make pressurized steam. As shown in Figure 2–2, this steam turns a turbine-generator where the rotational energy of an armature in a magnetic field induces an electric current into the delivery wires. The industry then transmits this electric current from its centralized generating plants to load centers for ultimate distribution to individual consumers.

These complex electricity supply systems can be compared to trees. The roots represent the electricity generating plants supplying nourishment to all parts of the tree. The tree trunk, which carries the sap or lifeblood of the trees, is analogous to the

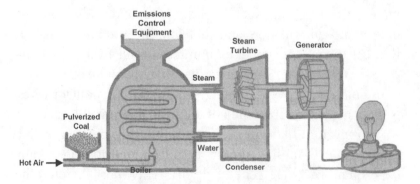

Figure 2–2   Steam Power System

transmission lines conducting bulk electricity from the generating plants. Finally, the branches represent the distribution system supplying electricity to each leaf which represents an individual consumer. The traditional electric utility consists of all four of these integrated functions: generation, transmission, distribution, and customer service.

Because bulk electricity cannot generally be produced in advance and stored for the moment it is needed, a utility must always have sufficient generating capacity available to meet the maximum demand on its system, whenever that occurs. Consumers, in effect, make two demands on the electricity supply system. One is for the generating capacity necessary to meet any level of total demand (measured in kilowatts), and one is for the electricity output to meet each consumer's needs (measured in kilowatt hours). This situation is one of the major challenges for the electric utility industry, which must always have the capacity required by the consumer available while realizing that the consumer's need for electricity at any given time may vary greatly.

The generation of electricity in the United States today involves some ten thousand power plants with a total generating capac-ity of more than a million megawatts, and producing over four trillion kilowatt hours of electricity each year. These power plants are a complex combination of engineered elements representing an investment of more than $500 billion. Replacement cost at today's prices would exceed $2 trillion. Most are large, centralized plants because utilizing the traditional concentrated aggregations of raw energy, such as coal seams and waterfalls, has always been easier and cheaper with large single power plants that can most effectively exploit the economies of scale. Natural gas, and more recently, renewable solar energy do not impose this constraint and thus encourage a more locally distributed electricity supply infrastructure.

As shown in Figure 2–3, the majority of these existing power plants obtain their heat from burning fossil fuels, primarily coal, or from the controlled fission of uranium atoms. The

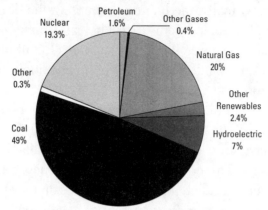

Energy sources used to generate electricity in the United States in 2006*

*Percentages do not sum to 100% due to independent rounding

Figure 2–3   Energy Sources Used to Generate Electricity in the United States in 2006 (Percentages do not sum to 100 percent due to rounding)

heat produced is then transferred through the furnace or nuclear reactor water tube walls to a steam generator. These electric utility steam generators can each produce as much as 10 million pounds of superheated steam at temperatures exceeding 1,000° F (540° C) at pressures exceeding 3,800 pounds per square inch (PSI). This is enough to produce 1,300 megawatts of electricity—power for a million or more people. Making electricity in such plants also releases enormous quantities of heat that if not captured and used is lost forever.

Historically, the cost of electricity production declined as the size and efficiency of these large generating units steadily grew. By the mid–1960s this economy of scale progress came to a screeching halt and there have been no further significant improvements in either the cost or the efficiency of power production from large steam-powered generators. In fact, both have regressed in the process of meeting subsequent environmental requirements.

However, we still depend on those same old plants, now approaching an average age of 40 years, because they produce power at significantly lower cost than any newer alternative.

The "rush to gas" in the late 1990s, stimulated by a combination of low natural gas prices and nonutility, independent power producers using lower-cost jet-engine-derived gas turbine power plants was, briefly, an encouraging exception. By 2001, however, the natural gas "bubble" predictably burst taking prices through the roof and bankrupting many of the independent power producers that had responded to the deregulation of wholesale electricity production in the 1990s.

Electricity is dispatched on the basis of its production cost, and gas generation went from first in line to last, further eroding its economics. Today, economies of scale in electricity generation have given way to the economies of precision and reliability. This has opened the door for distributed power generation in which small power units are advantageously located in microgrids designed to optimally serve the end user. This distributed capability supplements the large centralized power stations and also reduces the need for additional power delivery infrastructure.

THE ELECTRICITY RAILROAD

The traditional grid, the "railroad" system that actually delivers electricity to consumers today, is composed of two basic parts: high-voltage, long-distance transmission and lower-voltage, local distribution. Throughout this transmission and distribution of power, the electricity voltage, or pressure, must be raised and lowered to meet the particular delivery circumstances. The device that performs this function is called a *transformer*. The first function of the transmission system is to use "step-up transformers" to raise the voltage produced by the electricity generator, typically about 20,000 volts, to the levels required for long-distance transport, which is generally 230,000 volts or greater.

This high-voltage power is then conducted over the transmission lines to switching stations located at the major electricity load centers in each service territory. The distance between generating plants and these load centers can be quite large since the priority for locating generating plants is their proximity to fuel and water. By operating at ever-increasing voltages and by enabling interconnections among different power plants, transmission systems contributed significantly to providing lower electricity costs and more reliable service during the first half of the 20th century. Increasing voltage, like higher water pressure in a pipe, allows more electricity (watts) to pass through the transmission line. Doubling the voltage, for example, increases a line's capacity by a factor of four. Because of resistance to the flow of electrons, transmission lines grow hotter, expand, and sag as the amount of electricity they carry increases. As a result, they are thermally limited to only carrying a fraction of their full electrical capacity. These North American electricity transmission systems contain more than 300,000 miles of high-voltage lines serving more than 120 million customers. They are the backbone of the grid.

These transmission systems were designed decades ago to serve as private toll roads delivering a one-way flow of electricity from a central utility power plant to its end users. The designers never imagined the enormous quantities of electricity that are now being sold across state lines in competitive transactions, or that the lines would be used as open-access freeways by wholesale power producers. Consequently, these transmission lines are often overloaded and blackouts have become larger and more frequent. As a result, there is continued pressure to build new transmission lines but technology can dramatically reduce this requirement. What is also needed is an electronically controlled, nationwide "superhighway" for electricity transmission to enable the inter-regional transfer of bulk power while fundamentally increasing reliability and stability.

When the power reaches the transmission switching stations, "step-down transformers" reduce the voltage for transfer to the primary distribution substations in each service area. (Transformers do yeoman work; alas, the average in-service age of these oil-filled electromechanical devices now exceeds their

40-year operational design life.) At substations the incoming power is further stepped-down in voltage for local area distribution, typically within a radius of one to five miles. Finally, secondary distribution transformers bring the voltage down to 120 or 240 volts, which is the electricity service provided to consumers. Over 500,000 miles of distribution lines have been installed throughout the United States to provide this essential final delivery service.

SMALL BLIPS AND BIG CONSEQUENCES

In the digital world of the 21st century, ultrareliable electricity distribution is critical. This means not only eliminating interruptions but precisely maintaining the alternating current frequency as well. Even millisecond disturbances in the alternating current wave structure, which are invisible to traditional electric lights and motors, give electronic devices nervous breakdowns that can interrupt their operation for extended periods of time. This demand for ever-higher-quality power poses the greatest challenge to the electricity distribution system, which is artificially considered by utilities and regulators to stop at the meter rather than realistically and seamlessly incorporating the consumer's electrical end uses.

As a result, and in contrast to the many performance improvement opportunities available, power distribution reliability standards today remain egregiously lax. Indeed, power outages of less than five minutes are not even considered a reliability issue by many state regulatory authorities. These lax requirements further reduce the impetus for utilities to deploy modern technology including electronic control and advanced conductor materials. As a result, electricity service in the United States has become significantly less reliable than in many other countries worldwide, as shown in Figure 2–4. For example, the average electricity consumer in the United States is likely to suffer nearly 30 times more service interruptions each year than his or her counterpart

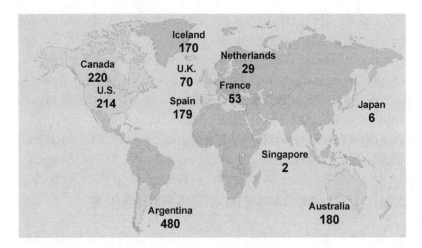

Figure 2–4   Worldwide Examples of Annual Outage Duration (in Minutes)

in Japan and Singapore. This unreliability adds up to more than 4 hours a year for the average consumer and cascades into ever-greater and more pervasive economic costs.

As shown in Figure 2–5, power interruptions are just the tip of the cost iceberg. The National Energy Technology Laboratory (NETL) in its recent report on "Barriers to Achieving the Modern Grid" underscored a host of robust trends reflecting the declining quality of the U.S. electricity delivery system. These trends include: increasing business losses from grid performance issues; increasing transmission curtailment actions; increasing numbers of small businesses and residences divorcing from the grid; and fewer engineers entering the power field. The result deprives each United States consumer thousands of dollars a year in wasted energy, lost productivity and reduced global competitiveness.

The resulting impact on the United States telecommunications industry alone is some two billion dollars each year just for backup power to compensate for grid deficiencies and to avoid essential service outages. This is just one example of consumers being forced to continuously treat the effects of poor power quality because the utility industry largely avoids correcting the root

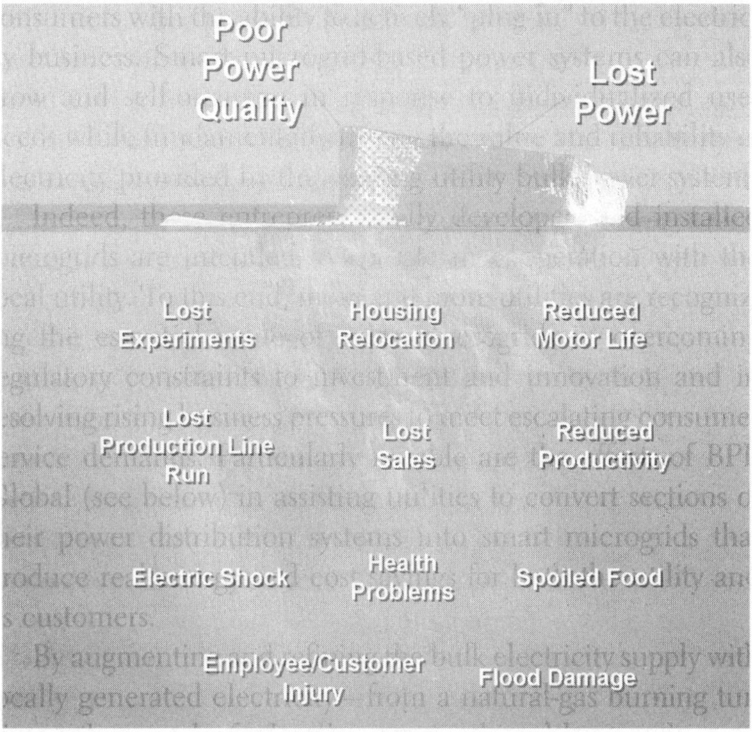

Poor Power Quality		Lost Power
Lost Experiments	Housing Relocation	Reduced Motor Life
Lost Production Line Run	Lost Sales	Reduced Productivity
Electric Shock	Health Problems	Spoiled Food
Employee/Customer Injury		Flood Damage

Figure 2–5 The Hidden Costs of Imperfect Power

causes. An Electric Power Research Institute (EPRI)-sponsored study in 2004 found that about a third of U.S. businesses would be willing to pay 5 percent more on their electricity bills to fund a more reliable power delivery system. Many others agreed in principle, but they doubted that utilities would use the funds for the needed system improvements.

The electricity system is at once remarkable and increasingly vulnerable. Its unreliability and inefficiency are obvious, and its dependency on cheap fossil fuels puts it squarely in the bull's-eye of potential climate change regulation. And there is yet another major expense that goes into the cost of electricity, albeit one that's fairly arcane for public discussions, but which cries out for correction. It is the equipment that's needed to produce enough power to meet peak demands.

Indeed, a quarter of the nation's power production capacity exists to produce power less than 10 percent of the time. Moreover, a small but still significant piece of this power reserve is actually used only a couple of days each year. We, the consumers, however, pay for that reserve every day. A truly smart power system would use efficiency "negawatts" rather than more megawatts to fill this need. In so doing, the costs involved would be largely eliminated.

The average total cost to produce and deliver a kilowatt hour (kWh) of electricity in the United States today is about 6.5 cents. This reflects the combined costs of fuel, operations, maintenance, and capital infrastructure required for power generation and delivery. In fossil fuel–fired power plants, which generate more than 70 percent of all U.S. electricity, fuel is the largest single cost factor. In nuclear power plants, which produce nearly 20 percent of the nation's electricity, fuel is a much smaller cost component. While the cost of fuel is eliminated in the case of hydroelectric plants, wind farms, and solar renewable power generation technologies, dams and windmills do have significant capital costs, including the energy needed to build them. Still, fuel is the major variable in electricity cost.

Consequently, a residential consumer in New York whose electricity service depends on natural gas or long-distance power transmission pays on average almost 16 cents for a kilowatt hour of electricity. This is nearly three times as much as an equivalent consumer in Kentucky or Washington State, for example, where local low-cost coal and hydro power predominate, respectively.

In addition to this fuel variability, the actual cost of electricity service changes considerably depending on *when* the electricity is actually consumed. For example, during the peak afternoon demand hours in the summer, the cost of providing electricity service is typically at least five times higher than during the rest of the 24-hour day. In spite of this variability in production cost, the regulated electricity rate structure in each utility service area still generally charges retail consumers an average electricity price. This effectively eliminates any incentive to cut back as costs rise during peak demand periods.

These electricity rates are based first on ensuring that the regulated monopoly utility recovers its costs and makes a profit under all operating conditions. This is the traditional regulatory quid pro quo for the utility's obligation to serve all present and future customers in its exclusive service territory. This electricity rate structure as determined by each state typically differentiates industrial, commercial, and residential consumer classes, but does not provide retail time-of-use electricity pricing. As a result, industrial consumers typically pay about 40 percent less per kilowatt hour of electricity than residential and commercial consumers who, in total, actually purchase 80 percent of all the electricity used in the United States, as shown in Figure 2–6.

Industrial consumers can extract these lower rates because they have competitive market power, by virtue of their much

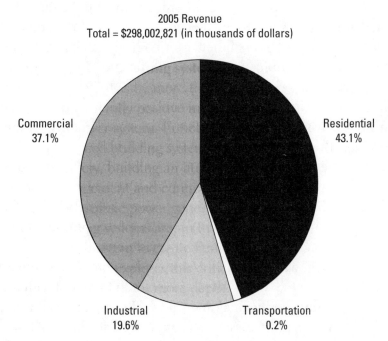

2005 Revenue
Total = $298,002,821 (in thousands of dollars)

Commercial
37.1%

Residential
43.1%

Industrial
19.6%

Transportation
0.2%

Figure 2–6   Electricity Supply Industry Revenue in the United States in 2005

larger power consumption demands. Individual residential and commercial consumers have no such influence on electricity prices. Today's regulations essentially give utility suppliers absolute market power over these retail consumers in a cost environment that also discourages innovation and is subject to manipulation. Market-based retail electricity pricing is therefore crucial to delivering 21st-century value and choice to consumers. Giving consumers the right and the ability to say "not at that price" is a powerful tool for both efficiency and equity. Indeed, if the electricity system was just 5 percent more efficient, we could save the equivalent of 40 large coal and nuclear power plants—and the costs and energy associated with building and operating these facilities.

Jim Rogers, CEO of Duke Energy and an outspoken proponent for technical and business model innovation in the utility industry, considers efficiency to be potentially the most important "electricity fuel" today. "I am currently being forced to consider making a multibillion-dollar, bet-the-company investment in a new nuclear power plant in order to meet the anticipated growth in Duke's electricity demand. In terms of risk-adjusted returns, it would be much better for both my stockholders and customers if I could invest first in efficiency improvements and renewable power production on the customers' side of the meter. **Unfortunately, current state regulations prohibit me from recovering those superior value investments simply because they are on the wrong side of the meter.**"

Utilities like Duke are being forced to spend a lot on waste right now which we all pay for. We can continue to pay for this waste, or we can make the improvements that eliminate the waste. Think of it as a one-time payment to the plumber to fix the leaky faucet that's driving up your water bill. If you don't fix it now you will be paying in drops until you do. Of course, the builders of today's electrical system didn't start out with the idea of creating inefficiency and waste. After all, these pioneers were delivering power based on a vision of perfection that transformed society, creating comfort, jobs, and wealth by literally making and controlling lightning. How the system grew, prospered, and turned south is a saga that's as American as apple pie and Thomas Edison, and one that has also proven equally important to the whole world.

INSTITUTIONS AND COMPANIES TO WATCH

American Electric Power (AEP) (www.aep.com). Headquartered in Columbus, Ohio, AEP is one of the largest electric utilities in the United States, delivering electricity to more than five million customers in 11 states. AEP owns nearly 38,000 megawatts of generating capacity and is the largest user of coal in the United States. It also owns the nation's largest electricity transmission system, a nearly 39,000-mile network. This network includes more than 765-kilovolt extra-high voltage lines than all other U.S. transmission systems combined.

Consolidated Edison (ConEd) (www.coned.com). ConEd provides electric service to approximately 3.2 million customers in New York City and Westchester County. ConEd is one of the largest investor-owned energy companies in the United States, with $13 billion in annual revenues and $28 billion in assets. It also owns and operates the world's largest district steam system, providing service to most of Manhattan. ConEd has been supplying the energy that powers New York for more than 180 years.

Duke Energy (www.duke-energy.com). Duke Energy is one of the largest electric utilities in the United States. Founded in 1904 and headquartered in Charlotte, North Carolina, Duke Energy has assets in the United States, Canada, and Latin America. With annual revenues exceeding $16 billion, Duke Energy owns and operates 36,000 megawatts of electricity generation that it distributes to its four million customers in North Carolina, South Carolina, Ohio, Kentucky, and Indiana. It is also sponsoring the Duke Energy Utility of the Future project to add intelligence and automation to the electricity grid.

Energy Information Administration (EIA) (www.eia.doe.gov). The EIA was created by the U.S. Congress in 1977 as a statistical agency of the Department of Energy. Its mission is to provide unbiased, policy-independent data, forecasts, and analyses to promote sound policy making, efficient markets, and public understanding regarding energy and its interaction with the economy and the environment. The EIA neither formulates nor advocates any policy conclusions. Its Annual Energy Outlook provides a summary of energy-related data and statistics.

National Energy Technology Laboratory (NETL) (www.netl. doe.gov). NETL is part of the Department of Energy's national laboratory system. NETL is devoted primarily to fossil energy research, and implements a broad spectrum of energy and environmental R&D programs. NETL maintains 14 major research facilities located in Morgantown, West Virginia, and in Pittsburgh and at five other sites across the United States. NETL programs include clean coal technology, carbon sequestration, hydrogen fuel cells, and critical infrastructure assurance.

Southern California Edison (SCE) (www.sce.com). Headquartered in Los Angeles, SCE is a subsidiary of Edison International, Inc. It operates nearly five thousand transmission and distribution circuits plus five nuclear, hydro and coal-fired power plants in California's open wholesale power market. The parent company, Edison International, also has a variety of power generation projects in Indonesia, Turkey, the Philippines, Thailand, Australia, South Africa, the Netherlands, and the United Kingdom, as well as in Illinois and Pennsylvania. SCE has consolidated assets of approximately $28 billion and 15,500 employees.

3

Electrifying the World

Throughout the past century, electricity has been the wellspring of technical innovation. It has been the basis for global economic progress and profound advancements in our quality of life. It is also the only hope for lifting the developing world out of poverty, where a quarter of the world's people survive without any electricity. Embracing smart microgrids holds the key to resolving this fundamental global challenge. While the cost to completely electrify the world is steep: $250 billion a year probably for the next 50 years, it could be financed by a global carbon trading market with economic dividends of at least 10 times the cost.

Since the dawn of the electrical age at the turn of the 20th century, electricity has literally enabled mankind to create modern civilization. To put this unprecedented progress in perspective, consider this scenario: You are driving your family car and briskly accelerate from 0 to 60 mph in 10 seconds. Suddenly, when you reach 60 mph, an astonishing burst of energy accelerates your car to 6,000 mph (Mach 10) in literally the blink of an eye! This is precisely the pace of change that has occurred over the past century relative to the entire prior history of mankind—and this amazing burst of creative capability was made possible at the dawn of the 20th century by the commercial conversion of raw energy into electricity, a fundamentally more perfect form of energy. This unprecedented human progress is certainly the defining event of our era in terms of its implications for all the world's inhabitants, human and otherwise.

When the U.S. National Academy of Engineering polled its members for the top 20 engineering achievements of the 20th century, and ranked them in terms of their impact on society, the number one achievement was the vast networks for electrification. The list of 20 reads like a recitation of top industries, from autos and TVs to computers and air-conditioning. Almost certainly, the reason that electricity ended up as number one is that none of the other profound engineering achievements of the 20th century would exist without electricity. Indeed electricity became an inventor's and toolmaker's dream. In the course of the first half of the 20th century, commercial electricity enabled mass transportation, mass production, and mass communications. More recently, it enabled the electronic revolution that begot broadcasting, computers, the Internet, and the information age. Figure 3–1 underscores this direct relationship between electric power and economic development.

Why was this profound progress possible? It was possible because in the physical sense, electricity was able to take the traditional energy forms from nature to unprecedented performance heights. It took the rough-and-tumble energy from coal combustion and falling water and converted it into a more perfect

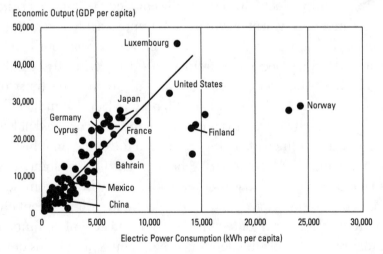

Figure 3–1 Electric Power Consumption per Capita versus Economic Output

high-tech form of energy, a form that was precise enough and flexible enough to run an integrated circuit, fast enough to send information around the world at the speed of light, and powerful enough to open the electromagnetic spectrum to practical use in science, medicine, and industry. The magnitude of this difference in energy form and capability can be brought home, with this example: Imagine trying to run your computer on a lump of burning coal instead of electricity.

ELECTRICITY: KEY TO THE REVOLUTION

Only through the continuous improvement capabilities made possible by electricity can we resolve our major 21st-century global challenges in a sustainable manner. The determining factor is whether the world will find the leadership, wisdom, and will to harness and expand electricity's unique abilities. Only electricity can accomplish the big three requirements for human progress: (1) transform the widest range of energy resources into useful goods and services; (2) facilitate maximum energy efficiency; and (3) enable the continued technological innovation essential to human progress. Unfortunately, on a regional and local basis, access to electricity still varies dramatically. As a result, mankind's 20th-century progress has also created a population, poverty, and pollution "trilemma" producing shock waves that reverberate throughout the world.

Climate change is now at the center of this trilemma as population pressures and economic aspirations combine to drive up greenhouse gas emissions, even as billions of people remain without access to electricity. The central role of electricity in climate change can be best understood by looking at the energy chain. At the end of the energy chain—at the point of consumption—electricity represents the cleanest and greenest of all forms of energy; it moves silently into your home and business, performs its service with no fumes or trace emissions (other than heat), and automatically returns to the source.

At the beginning of the energy chain, where energy is converted into electricity, the conversion process can be either dirty or clean depending upon the technology used. It is therefore not the source of energy for electricity production that should be condemned, but rather the poor quality of technology we choose to apply. Indeed, the world will need to wisely use all energy resources including coal, nuclear and solar if its people are to survive, let alone prosper through the 21st Century. As shown in Figure 3–2, electricity can be created from any and all sources of energy; and once created, it remains clean, flexible, and precise in every application.

As the green revolution of the 21st century unfolds, electricity's role will be no less profound than it was in the 20th century. It will become increasingly important because electricity is also the only practical way to deliver the clean natural sources of energy and transform them into useful goods and services. Indeed, electricity is the indispensable enabler for transforming the global energy system from one that is now responsible for nearly 90 percent of carbon dioxide (CO_2) emissions made by humans to one that can be effectively emissions-free.

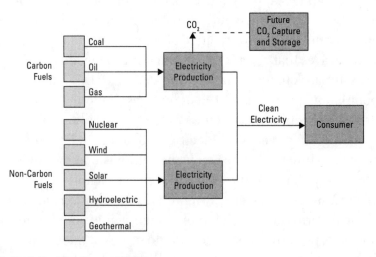

Figure 3–2 The Energy Chain

It is fair to say that without electricity, the green revolution would not be possible. Of equal importance to delivering energy cleanly is the fact that electricity use can be made smarter because of the inherent intelligence that comes from combining electricity, communication, and digital technology. Once electrified, any appliance, machine, or process can become more energy efficient—not once or twice, but continuously. This continuous improvement opportunity makes Perfect Power service an achievable goal for everyone.

DECLINING RETURNS FROM FOSSIL FUELS

Energy is the elemental force upon which all civilizations are built, and technology provides the means to harness that energy. Throughout history, society's ability to live in harmony with the natural environment and its resources has been dependent on the availability of energy. Decline sets in when a mature civilization reaches the point at which it is forced to spend more and more energy reserves just to maintain its social and political arrangements while experiencing diminishing productivity returns from the energy available per capita. As this occurs, the incentives to decompose the complex social order steadily increase, ultimately leading to collapse.

The major causes leading to the decline of civilizations have been either the gradual depletion of an essential energy resource base, often due to human mismanagement, or the more rapid loss of energy resources due to war or severe environmental fluctuation. Both cause societal unraveling through depletion of the resources on which a complex society depends. Today, the world is again facing this unraveling threat primarily because of the declining returns from its dependence on fossil fuels that provide over 90 percent of the world's energy. Remove fossil fuels from the human equation and today's modern societies would cease to exist.

With the world's energy appetite expected to increase by more than 50 percent by 2030, the days of this fossil energy "free lunch" are rapidly ending. As a result, the world finds itself precariously perched on an increasingly unsustainable energy structure that is producing diminishing returns at ever-greater economic, environmental, and security costs to all the world's people. Indeed, the 21st century represents a profound moment of truth for mankind's continued journey on this planet.

Ironically, the technological revolution that electricity has enabled over the past 50 years has largely been ignored by the electricity supply industry itself. Periodic blackouts around the world underscore the vulnerability of today's technically obsolete power supply systems. As discussed in Chapter 2, these events are only the tip of the iceberg. Dependable, let alone perfect, power service in the 21st century requires that power systems have the capability to reliably take up highly variable distributed renewable power generation, and at the same time, enable consumers to efficiently control their own use and production of electricity. As subsequent chapters will show, the technology to enable electricity to regain the high ground of service perfection is readily available for cost-effective global use.

To better understand the importance of this progress, we need to look beyond our national borders to the global stage. Every three years the world's population is growing by roughly the size of the United States, and 98 percent of that growth is in the poorest developing countries where 1.6 billion people lack access to electricity. With more than 30 of these developing countries on course to double their populations by 2050, while the developed countries are generally declining in population, the earth's profile promises to change dramatically as described in Figure 3–3. By 2050, today's developing nations are likely to account for 90 percent of the global energy footprint. Rapid population growth discourages developing regions from escaping poverty, and, as a result, nearly half the world's people continue to survive on the equivalent of less than $2 per day. In effect,

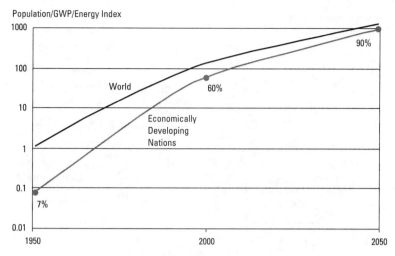

Figure 3–3 The Global Energy Footprint

these developing countries have been stuck in a pattern of growing bigger without growing richer. Since 1960, the resulting disparity in per capita income between the richest and poorest fifth of the world's nations has widened from 30 to 1 to 80 to 1.

CALLING FOR UNIVERSAL ACCESS TO ELECTRICITY

Lack of access to electricity is an essential factor creating this global poverty gap, as shown in Figure 3–4. For example, the United States, with less than 5 percent of the world's population, produces and consumes 24 percent of the world's electricity. This is more than Latin America, Africa, the Middle East, India, and Asia (other than China and Japan) combined. By 2050 the World Energy Council projects that electricity will provide more than half of all final energy in the developed nations, double current levels, while the developing world continues to lag farther and farther behind with only 10 percent of its energy in the form of electricity. Given electricity's critical role in accelerating productivity, improving living standards,

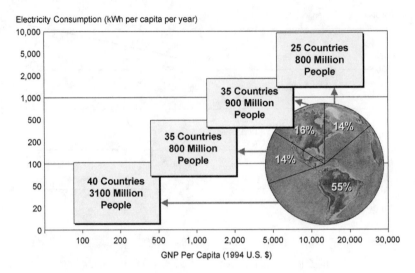

Electricity Consumption (kWh per capita per year)

Figure 3–4 Prosperity and Electricity Use Are Strongly Correlated

and enabling modern energy access, there needs to be much greater emphasis on achieving universal global electrification.

More than half the world's population still lives in these underdeveloped but often overpopulated regions, and they remain primarily dependent on the traditional fuels of wood, dung, and crop residue using primitive and inefficient technologies. This combination barely meets basic human survival needs, let alone the possibility of harnessing energy for productive uses that might begin to permit escape from the cycle of poverty. These people who lack even basic access to electricity are essentially the same people who lack access to education and sanitation, are condemned to extreme poverty, and are the remaining producers of global population growth. Roughly 7 percent of the world's electricity production today would be sufficient to break this destructive cycle for those currently without access to electricity. Unfortunately, this relatively modest challenge remains unanswered.

Only through universal global access to electricity, using a comprehensive portfolio of energy resources made available by advances in electrotechnology, can this demographic upheaval underway in the developing world, and the resulting threats to global welfare, environment, and security, be resolved. This imperative has been translated by the U.S. National Research Council, for example, into four "inextricably linked global needs" in the 21st century: restore and protect the integrity of the earth's life-support systems, manage the resources crucial to human welfare, eliminate poverty, and stabilize population.

Fortunately, these global needs can be met this century, and society's prospects significantly improved if universal electricity access, and the economic opportunity it brings, is achieved. The global average birthrate has declined from 3.8 in 1980 to 2.8 today, and the United Nations now projects that fertility rates in the developed and developing worlds will likely converge and stabilize by midcentury. However, the energy gap limiting economic opportunity in the least developed regions must be closed or their decline in fertility rate from the current level will be dangerously slowed, or it will be replaced with nature's more drastic control mechanisms including disease, famine, and war.

Population growth brings with it the pressure to create jobs. As a result, the world economy is now adding about 40 million workers a year—25 times the rate of U.S. workforce growth. At average levels of gross domestic product (GDP) per worker, this means that the world economy must generate at least $500 billion more each and every year. Since current economic growth rates are nowhere near this level, not only will tens of millions of people remain unemployed, but the ones who do get jobs are going to put increasing pressure on everyone else's standard of living. We can project that at least a 2 to 3 percent annual improvement in global rates of productivity and resource efficiency growth will be required over at least the next 50 years to close this gap between population growth and economic growth, and enable universal well-being. This is sometimes referred to by economists as the "2 percent solution," and it is more than twice the current rate of worldwide progress as shown in Figure 3–5.

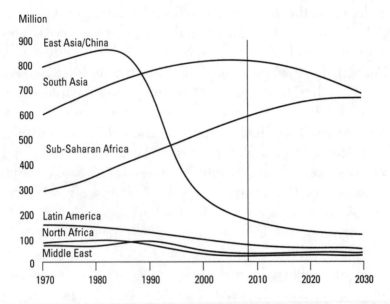

Figure 3–5 Households without Access to Electricity, 1970–2030

SETTING THE FLOOR AT 1,000 KILOWATT HOURS PER YEAR FOR EVERYONE

In order to achieve the 2 percent solution, we must first ensure that everyone in the world has access to a basic level of electricity service—at least 1,000 kilowatt hours per year. This is less than 10 percent of per capita electricity consumption today in the United States, for example. But in order to achieve even this modest goal for the world's growing population, electricity must reach at least an additional 80 million people per year for at least the next 50 years. Figure 3–6 indicates the opportunity for developing countries to use advanced electrotechnologies to leapfrog the inefficient, earlier development pathways followed by today's developed countries. In spite of these opportunities, the share of the world's population lacking access to electricity has remained constant at about one third since 1980. While the challenge is huge, the potential benefits resulting from doubling the rate of global electrification are equally staggering and include a 50 percent increase

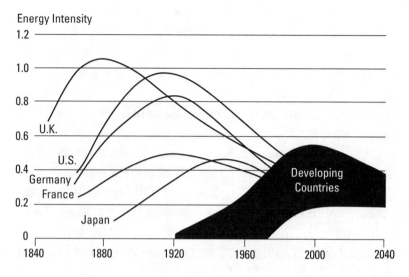

Figure 3–6 Advanced Electrotechnologies Enable Developing Countries to Leapfrog Over Historical Pathways

in economic output by the developing world, a 33 percent decrease in global carbon emissions, and a 12 percent decrease in the world's total energy use.

Where will the energy to produce the 13 million megawatts of electricity generation the world needs by 2050 come from? The short answer is a comprehensive portfolio including every fossil, nuclear, and renewable energy resource. No single source will be sufficient and the technology now used in each case is seriously deficient. Failure to commit to the development of this innovative energy resource and technology portfolio is a self-fulfilling prophecy that an electrified world will remain beyond our reach. A net doubling in the world's use of coal, for example, is forecast over the next 30 years. The technology to "refine" this coal, and capture and sequester the CO_2 produced is available but lacks the necessary commitment to its large-scale use. The cost of delay is already evident in headlines around the world.

The technology gap is also evident in the growing need for clean nuclear power to sustainably meet the world's 21st-century energy needs. Nuclear power is the only large-scale, zero carbon emitting energy resource that can confidently fill the world's growing energy gap in the coming decades. Here a variety of advanced system designs promises safe solutions to the waste and proliferation issues now limiting nuclear power expansion. Unfortunately this critically important energy resource also remains trapped behind an obsolete technology barrier which we can and must remove now.

While the various renewable energy alternatives are strategically attractive, their diffuse and intermittent nature remains a daunting technical and economic challenge in the context of today's obsolete electric power system design. The solution to this challenge rests with available smart-grid technology and its urgent use in microgrids incorporating renewable energy resources worldwide.

The dramatic relationship between electricity and human development, as evaluated by the United Nations, is highlighted in Figure 3–7. The benefits accruing from access to

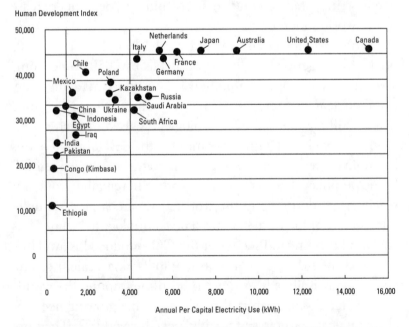

Figure 3–7 Correlation between Human Development and Electricity Consumption

electricity, beyond creating economic opportunity and more efficient use of natural resources, are broadly twofold: First, a fundamental reduction in levels of pollution, both indoor and outdoor; and second, the freeing up of time through the substitution of commercial energy for manual labor. The latter is particularly notable for women whose manual labor provides a disproportionate share of the energy in developing countries.

One of the greatest threats resulting from our continued failure to electrify the world is the reduced viability of the world's cities, particularly in developing nations. Lack of opportunity is leading to mass migrations from rural to urban areas where infrastructure development is not keeping pace. The result is an unsustainable global economic and environmental burden. According to the United Nations, 60 percent of the world will live in cities by 2030 and their electricity demand is expected to grow by more than 75 percent during that time frame. In 1950 there were only five megacities (population exceeding 10 million) in the world, and they were all in developed nations. By 2050, under business-as-usual projections, there will be over 50 such megacities and all but the original five will be in today's developing countries that lack the essential infrastructure to support these urban concentrations. This also does not bode well for the world's environment or the security of its people.

Water is a particularly urgent issue. By 2025 some 3 billion people will live in regions that are experiencing serious water scarcity that is now crossing international boundaries via the intensive grain trade. These regions are also generally underserved, if at all, by electricity. Because it takes roughly a thousand tons of water to produce a ton of grain, countries are incented to divert irrigation water from agriculture to satisfy the needs of their rapid urbanization, and to import grain to offset the loss. Unless rapidly corrected, this is a short-sighted, self-defeating expediency. Moreover without adequate electricity, efforts to ease these acute water shortages including irrigation, desalinization and more efficient agriculture are simply not possible. The alternative is increased mass migration and conflict as more and more countries compete for limited water.

VILLAGE-SCALE MICROGRIDS RUNNING ON RENEWABLE ENERGY

As recognition of these benefits grows, "bottom-up" electrification initiatives are emerging in the developing world. These are proving to be particularly efficient and cost-effective "entry-level" approaches to meeting the global electrification challenge. In this bottom-up approach, electrification is being achieved through village-scale, distributed, and renewable energy-powered microgrids under local leadership. These microgrids are well matched to the low population density and relatively low consumption of the communities they serve. They also provide the basic building blocks for future power system expansion. It is notable that these developing world microgrids are typically quite modern in design, using electronic controls and power converters that enable the seamless deployment of a variety of distributed generation and storage devices.

These local microgrid power cooperatives provide the direct consumer access and market transparency that traditional top-down, centralized utility power systems generally lack and have great difficulty in achieving. In Cambodia, for example, rural electrification already comes primarily from local electricity entrepreneurs that run microgrids and battery-charging stations. This process of connecting microgrids in a network the way we do PCs in an office is also a fertile opportunity for extending locally established market cultures. All other factors being equal, perhaps the most important advantage in building electricity networks and markets from the ground up using microgrids, relative to extending the top-down centralized status quo, is the more encouraging environment they produce for both innovation and investment throughout the world.

CLEAN ELECTRIFICATION—ONE OF THE WORLD'S LARGEST GROWTH INDUSTRIES

This effort to electrify the world likely will require a global investment rate in the developing world's electricity infrastructure of at least $250 billion per year for at least the next 50 years. This capital investment requirement, which is about half the total required worldwide for electricity infrastructure expansion and improvement, would be about equally divided between new generating capacity and power delivery. The International Energy Agency's (IEA) World Energy Outloon estimates that over the next 25 years alone China's power sector investment needs will be nearly $3 trillion, while other developing East Asian countries will need $800 billion, India $1 trillion, Latin America $750 billion, and Africa $500 billion. This is a considerable sum of money but less, for example, than the world spends each year on just tobacco products. Unfortunately, today's short-term investment climate does very little to encourage this strategic progress.

A potentially attractive approach for stimulating investment in global electrification is based on the concept of a global carbon-trading market mechanism that responds to the growing worldwide consensus for action on climate change. In such a system, the use of fossil fuels would require emitters around the world to purchase allowances in proportion to their CO_2 emissions. The market incentives for the purchase of these allowances would be designed to implement a least-cost global policy that takes advantage of flexibility in both time and location to achieve its CO_2 reduction goal. Such a post-Kyoto global protocol must first resolve a host of international equity, monitoring and enforcement challenges, but its positive development potential is profound. This mechanism could systematically address the global trilemma of population, poverty, and pollution by creating an efficient market and incentive system to spur developing world electricity infrastructure investment while simultaneously reducing global CO_2 emissions.

Using an expanded United Nations Clean Development Mechanism (CDM), in which industrialized countries can get credit for investing in CO_2-reducing projects in developing countries, a significant portion of these proceeds could be immediately reinvested in the clean electrification of the developing world. This would also provide the most cost-effective initial leverage on global carbon emission reductions. The result could steadily reduce global CO_2 emissions per unit of GDP by as much as a factor of three between now and 2050, and ultimately achieve a minimal global carbon economy this century. Only in this manner will it be feasible to keep atmospheric concentrations of CO_2 below the Intergovernmental Panel on Climate Change (IPCC) provisional limit of 500 ppm (parts per million). This contrasts with the business-as-usual emission projection which is expected to result in an atmospheric CO_2 concentration of 800 ppm this century, more than twice the current level.

In addition to the environmental benefits, a sustained global electrification investment would produce major economic advantages. For example, the resulting improvements in global productivity, efficiency, and new market creation could easily achieve a value that is 10 times greater than the cost. As Nicholas Stern points out in his October 2006 report, "Stern Review on the Economics of Climate Change" commissioned by the United Kingdom Chancellor of the Exchequer, reducing carbon emissions and increasing the sustainable use of natural resources is likely to become one of the world's largest growth industries. Indeed, the market for carbon emission reduction allowances and credits promises to spearhead the largest and fastest-growing commodity market in the world, ultimately worth hundreds of billions of dollars each year. Market management and support firms around the world, such as APX in the United States, are already jockeying for position in this rapidly expanding environmental market space.

It's been said that civilizations decline when they stop applying their economic surplus to new ways of doing things.

In modern terms we say the rate of investment decreases. This happens because those who control the surplus have a vested interest in using it for self-gratifying consumption without providing more efficient and effective methods of production. The 20th century was characterized by the success of an economic development model based on the mass production of relatively low-cost, short-lifetime products. This model has enabled rapid economic expansion in many parts of the world, but it has also depended on the unsustainable consumption of natural resources, including fossil-fuel–based energy. The fundamental challenge this century is to achieve a global electricity-based development model where producers of more efficient, less resource-intensive products and services prosper as consumers worldwide learn to embrace and use these more perfect products and services.

If the benefits of sustainable electricity access and economic progress do not reach those at the bottom of society, a much grimmer version of the future may prevail. In such a world, even prosperous regions would fear for their security, for when all else fails, the poor will learn to export their misery and anger. Enlightened self-interest therefore argues strongly for global attention and cooperation to closing the electricity gap that fundamentally excludes nearly a third of the world's population from the opportunity for individual well-being by any standard. If we fail to meet the global electrification challenge in this century, we will considerably increase the risk of going down in history as the latest in the progression of civilizations whose pivotal generations were unwilling or unable to meet their energy needs in a sustainable manner.

But if we succeed, we will have created the most profound legacy in history—demonstrating our enduring faith in the future and our dedication to all those generations that follow. As important as electricity was to the 20th Century, it can and must be even more important to the 21st Century—if we seize the opportunities it presents for fundamental improvement in our global energy system.

COMPANIES AND INSTITUTIONS TO WATCH

APX (www.apx.com) is an independent technology and service provider serving environmental and energy markets. APX is policy-neutral; it does not take positions in the markets, and its revenues are unrelated to the market prices for the environmental and cap-and-trade market certificates its system creates. The APX Environmental Market Depository creates, tracks, manages, and retires renewable energy certificates (RECs), carbon offset credits, and greenhouse gas emission allowances.

Intergovernmental Panel on Climate Change (IPCC) (www.ipcc.ch). The IPCC is a scientific intergovernmental organization established in 1988 by the World Meteorological Organization and the United Nations Environmental Program. Headquartered in Geneva, Switzerland, the IPCC provides an objective source of information and assessments to decision makers and others interested in climate change issues. Its constituency is made up of all UN member governments and scientists worldwide.

International Energy Agency (IEA) (www.iea.org). Headquartered in Paris, the IEA was founded during the 1973–1974 oil crisis by the Organization for Economic Co-operation and Development (OECD), which represents the major developed nations of the world. The IEA acts as an energy policy advisor to its 27 member countries with the goal of ensuring affordable and clean energy for their citizens. Current efforts focus on climate change policies, market reform, energy technology collaboration, and outreach to the rest of the world.

National Academy of Engineering (NAE) (www.nae.edu). Founded in 1964, NAE is a private, independent, nonprofit institution in Washington, D.C.; the NAE operates under the congressional act of incorporation that established the National Academy of Sciences in 1863. The NAE mission is to provide engineering leadership and promote the technological welfare of the United States by marshalling the knowledge and insights of leading members of the engineering profession. It has more than 2,000 peer-elected members and foreign associates in business, academia, and government.

National Research Council (NRC) (www.nationalacademies. org/nrc). The NRC was established in 1916 as the nonprofit, working arm of the U.S. National Academy of Sciences. The NRC mission is to improve government decision making and public policy, and to promote the acquisition of knowledge in matters of science, engineering, technology, and health. Individual NRC projects are funded by federal agencies, foundations, and the NRC's endowment fund. Its work is conducted by 6,000 of the world's top scientists, engineers, and professionals on a voluntary basis. The NRC is administered jointly by the National Academy of Sciences, the National Academy of Engineering, and the Institute of Medicine.

United Nations Clean Development Mechanism (CDM) (described at http://unfccc.int/2860.php). The CDM was created in 1998 by the Third Conference of the Partners to the UN Framework Convention on Climate Change as a potential means for achieving greenhouse gas (GHG) emission reduction partnerships between developed and developing nations. The CDM is a market-based concept which enables developing (non-Annex 1) countries to benefit from GHG-reduction project investments used by developed (Annex I) countries to comply with the Kyoto Protocol.

World Alliance for Decentralized Energy (WADE). Formed in 1997, WADE is a nonprofit research and advocacy organization representing global companies as well as industry and environmental groups. WADE's goal is to create more cost-effective, robust, and sustainable electricity supply systems by eliminating barriers to, and increasing the market share of, decentralized energy. WADE maintains offices in Canada, Egypt, India, Peru, the United Kingdom, and the United States (www.localpower.org).

World Energy Council (WEC) (www.worldenergy.org). The WEC was founded in 1924 to promote the sustainable supply and use of energy for the greatest benefit of all people. The WEC is a nonprofit organization headquartered in London made up of member committees from 94 countries. Each national committee represents the broadest possible range of energy and energy-related interests in its country. Through these member committees, the WEC develops and publishes analyses, projections, and policy recommendations spanning the entire energy spectrum.

4

The Edison Paradox

Born out of a competitive fight between Thomas Edison and several of his equally legendary contemporaries, the nascent electrical industry of the late 1800s could have gone in an entirely different direction. Edison's ideas for distributed power generation lost out at the time to centralized plants and long-distance transmission grids. These worked well for a century but devolved into the wasteful and inefficient system we have today. But with modern technologies, a resurrection of Edison's original decentralized vision would bring renewed innovation and competition to bear on regulated utilities and the electricity infrastructure.

An utterly shameless self-promoter, Thomas Alva Edison went so far as to publicly electrocute an elephant just to make a point. It is not the most flattering episode in the life of an icon, a singular character who even in his lifetime was known as "America's Greatest Inventor," the "Napoleon of Science," and the "Purveyor of Light." But with the filmed execution of Topsy, a three-ton Coney Island elephant that had killed three people, Edison tried to convince the public to accept his patented direct current (DC) electricity using locally distributed power generation in microgrids by equating the competition, alternating current (AC) from ever-larger centralized power systems, with instant death.

At the close of the 19th century when the composition of America's electrical infrastructure was up for grabs, Edison figured electrocuting an elephant with alternating current would make for a macabre and yet spectacular exhibition of its dangers. Although the jolt worked—Topsy dropped stone dead after a mere 10 seconds—the demonstration had little impact and America accepted AC from ever-larger centralized systems as the standard of the land.

The paradox of all this is that Edison had much of it right, especially with his notion of a distributed system of electrical generation and control for businesses and communities alike. The problem was that the technologies to make the system smart and competitive did not exist at that time, although that certainly wasn't for lack of effort or creativity on Edison's part.

Holding an amazing 1,093 patents, including the invention of the stock ticker, the phonograph, a motion picture camera, the industrial research laboratory, and, of course, the electric light bulb, Edison certainly had his share of other long-lasting influences. In July 1879, while traveling across the western United States by train, it occurred to Edison that the dark towns he passed through could be lit by electricity. He envisioned a new electricity distribution industry that would earn enough money to support his burgeoning "invention factory".

By October 1879, Edison had a working incandescent lamp, and within months had patented the direct current electric distribution system. To put his vision into place—and in a place where it would draw the immediate and direct attention of financial investors and the media—the great self-promoter opened the first American electricity-generation station at 257 Pearl Street in the heart of Manhattan's financial and news district.

On September 4, 1882, six coal-fired dynamos were switched on, and initially supplied direct current to 85 customers with enough energy to illuminate 400 light bulbs. Each bulb burned more white and steady than any kind of gas lamp and as Edison boasted, without the noxious fumes and smoke that typically blackened ceilings and furniture. For individuals in the Wall Street offices of financier J.P. Morgan—then one of the richest men in the nation and one of Edison's primary investors—the editorial department of *The New York Times*, and 40 other establishments within a one-square-mile area, it was the first glimpse into the 20th century.

While Pearl Street was a combined heat and power facility, making it *the* original cogeneration unit, it also was a dirty, loud, and ungainly cluster of machines. As Jeff Goodell recounts in his book, *Big Coal*, the primary fuel was brought to metal doors on the sidewalk and dumped into a shoot. "Conveyors then carried it up one floor, where filthy, soot-covered workers shoveled the coal into one of the four Babcock and Wilcox boilers, which fed the heat into the six steam engines one floor above," writes Goodell. Engine shafts were connected to generators with leather straps. "Black smoke and soot exited through a couple of makeshift chimneys in the roof, blackening the entire neighborhood."

Edison's choice of direct current, which maintained a low voltage from the power station to the consumer, meant that generating plants had to be within a mile or so of the end users. It was a concept suited for the United States in the 1880s and especially for heavily populated urban areas. Edison's generation stations were extremely small compared to today's central power plants and produced just a few megawatts. He also built many smaller isolated plants, essentially micropower facilities that were used in factories, department stores, hotels, and apartment buildings. By 1886, Edison's firm had installed 58 power stations and some 500 isolated lighting plants in the United States, Russia, Chile, and Australia.

Edison was hardly alone in making electricity. Indeed, in the late 1800s there were more than 20 telegraph, telephone, and electric light companies operating just in Manhattan, each with their own wires and poles, which made the city's skyline as unsightly as the horse manure–covered streets. By the last decade of that century, numerous small companies marketed and built power plants that not only made electricity but fed the plant's waste heat into pipes that brought warmth to nearby factories, offices, and neighborhoods. By 1900, around half of the electricity produced in the United States came from such small and isolated units.

THE TESLA ALTERNATIVE

Alas, while Thomas Edison's vision was ahead of its time, the technologies at his disposal were not. For one thing, the electricity-generating dynamos of the 1890s were loud and dirty, and not very amenable next-door neighbors. For another, there emerged a bright young Serbian with a different idea about electrical currents. In 1884, the 27-year-old Nikola Tesla traveled from Europe to New York bearing a letter of recommendation, just to meet Thomas Edison, with the hope of working for his idol. Edison hired the handsome, charismatic, and brilliant Serb on that same day.

Assigned to rather routine electrical work, Tesla nonetheless managed to solve some of the more difficult challenges faced in Edison's lab. But more than anything, Tesla wanted Edison's backing and approval to develop a device that did not yet exist—a practical motor generator that produced alternating current. As noted earlier, an alternating current surges back and forth, with voltages that are easily regulated up and down with transformers. Also, when sending electricity over long distances, losses are more limited when the voltage is high and the current is low, something that could be done with alternative current but not with direct current. But in an often-cited and thoroughly dismissive statement, Edison told his young colleague to put a sock in it, saying, "We're set up for direct current in America. People like it, and it's all I'll ever fool with. Spare me that nonsense. It [alternating current] is dangerous."

After four years of working for Edison, Tesla found another backer for alternating current, a Pittsburgh businessman named George Westinghouse. The inventor of the railroad air brake, Westinghouse envisioned the advantages of scale in building large central generation plants near the source or delivery point for coal or water for hydroelectric power. The power could then be shipped great distances over wires at high voltage, electricity that would then be stepped down in transformers to a voltage appropriate for distribution and end use. One generator, which could supplant hundreds of the smaller Edison-style units, raised the possibility of needing only one wiring grid, and in theory, it confined pollution from burning coal to a more limited area. Also, such a system had the diversity to handle the power drained by streetcars during rush hours, lighting in the evening, and factory motors during the times between.

With the technical battle over Tesla's alternating current system and Edison's direct current system settled in favor of the former, the fledging electricity business was about to enter its second stage of development, a period that has ringing echoes even today. At its center was another Edison disciple, Samuel Insull. After serving as Edison's secretary, managing his investments and handling many operations for the Edison Electric Company, Insull was promoted to take over the firm's manufacturing operations, and move it to Schenectady, New York. Insull oversaw huge growth, with the number of employees rising from 200 to some 6,000 in six years. He then got a job as the leader of Chicago Edison.

A nimble and gifted businessman, Insull understood that if Chicago Edison were to truly prosper, it must somehow reduce the number of small and aggressive firms offering competing supplies of electricity. In turn, it was in his company's best interests to also stimulate demand, which Insull did by offering "off-peak" discounts to farmers and other new consumers. Meanwhile, he purchased almost two dozen utilities, and he took to public pulpits, arguing that electricity was a "natural monopoly," so vital to homes and factories that it should come from one guaranteed source.

After all, the electricity business was in many ways as capital intensive as railroads. That meant high barriers to entry, and few if any new competitors to bother the monopolist. Insull argued that it would be "economically wrong" to see the rise of duplicate power plants and wires, and that states should regulate all the providers of power. And while it sounds counterintuitive, Insull used his monopoly utility status to lower, rather than increase, prices, which won great favor with consumers and elected officials and rapidly expanded the demand for electricity.

Indeed, while centralized utility power plants are expensive to build, they are relatively inexpensive to run on hydropower or coal. Thus, it benefited power generators to attract as many customers as possible through lower prices, convincing industrial customers to retire their own plants, and homeowners to install electrical outlets that brought forth innovations such as electric refrigerators, washing machines, fans, toasters, dishwashers, portable heaters, and other appliances. Insull built his enterprise by acquiring dozens of smaller firms and making their owners shareholders in his enterprise, eventually renamed Commonwealth Edison.

While arguing that public utilities were natural monopolies that needed government oversight, what Insull actually wanted was to deal with one regulatory agency in each state in which he operated, instead of many hundreds of municipal governments. States began to pass laws, upheld by the U.S. Supreme Court, that allowed regulators to award monopoly electricity service franchises and set rates that earned these monopoly investor-owned utilities "fair returns" on their investments. Such was born the declining cost commodity business model based on the economies of increasing scale and demand. This model still dominates the electric utility landscape even though electricity costs ceased to decline 40 years ago, and the model is being sustained by self-serving policies that create a much larger economic burden on businesses and consumers alike.

Insull built a terrifically efficient, near-perfect system for its time, but he fell from grace because of overreach, corruption, and greed. In the two years after the great stock market crash of 1929, American consumers still purchased more than two million refrigerators, almost doubling the nation's residential power consumption. But Insull had also built vast holding companies and investment trusts that eventually watered down the value of investor stock. His empire collapsed. Today, Samuel Insull might be the most influential and least remembered individual in American business.

THE LINGERING LEGACY

Throughout its regulated history since Insull's day, electricity has not been a "business" in the usual sense. That is, it has not engaged buyers and sellers in any two-way discussion of what is offered for sale or at what price. In this regulated monopoly system it is the captive customer who bears the risks and pays all costs. If you want electricity, take it or leave it on the conditions the utility dictates. Nevertheless, this state-regulated system Insull left behind continues unabated. It is an institution that, above all, serves the status quo and offers minimal incentives to resolve service deficiencies, or make investments in innovation. In this context, regulation is best understood as a political settlement intended to keep immediate peace within the state's political jurisdiction irrespective of the resulting cost to its citizens.

The state-regulated monopoly stranglehold on the nation's electricity supply was challenged by Congress in the Energy Policy Act of 1992. This legislation recognized that the regulated monopoly business model was no longer keeping pace with the growing power quantity and quality demands on the electricity infrastructure. The Energy Policy Act required that the Federal Energy Regulatory Commission (FERC) force transmission-owning utilities to open their systems to independent power producers at reasonable, nondiscriminatory, cost-based prices. As state regulatory commissions digested this new requirement, their emphasis was predictably on transferring only the responsibility while still retaining authority over the market. This economic contradiction predictably, and most notably, led to the California "restructuring" disaster and the Enron debacle. The limited federal efforts to relax government's grip on electricity also left resolution of the resulting uncompetitive utility generation assets issue to the individual states. Whether by accident or design, most states proceeded to disastrously mismanage this financial challenge. Consumer/voter unhappiness with the resulting utility "bail-out" at the consumers' total expense has largely stymied further efforts at utility deregulation and electricity market liberalization.

It is critically important that consumers reject such artificial and over-simplified blanket indictments of deregulation. Above all, do not let the special interests guarding the status quo use it to throw out the very promising retail competition baby with the poisoned political bathwater of misguided wholesale electricity restructuring. There is no reason that the existing electric utility distribution infrastructure would be stranded by competitive retail electricity service markets. Quite the contrary, competitive retail markets depend on these distribution systems as their primary energy source. In fact, retail competition would likely lead to private sector investments to help upgrade these seriously overstressed systems.

Thomas Edison understood this reality very well. If what you are selling is illumination, and competition forces you to make it as economical as possible, you have to optimize the entire system—the power generation, the delivery grid and the light bulb—because it all works together at the speed of light. Fortunately, Edison's path to perfection was not constrained by short-sighted regulatory roadblocks or we might still be depending on candles.

In the same manner today, innovative entrepreneurs focus on converting bulk electricity into the higher value, electricity-based services that consumers actually want: illumination, comfort, refrigeration, entertainment, security, and so on. Over time, entrepreneurs, given free rein, will design and provide Perfect Power services that satisfy even the most demanding consumer. Others including supermarkets, big box retail outlets, and affinity groups such as trade unions can be expected to also offer innovative electricity service propositions that are intended to best meet the desires of their customers. In all these cases, competitive retail markets will encourage the array of technical innovations that are largely being blocked by today's status quo regulated monopoly market place.

Regardless of these electricity value-enhancing opportunities, the opening of retail electricity service markets to competition continues to make monopoly distribution utilities who are resistant to change very uneasy. They have never had to deal with customers who are free to take their business elsewhere. What's more, so long as they avoid public criticism over blackouts, most regulated monopolies consider themselves bulletproof. Despite the growing unreliability of the aging infrastructure and environmental concerns driving new companies into the solar, wind, and microgrid businesses, most utility companies are remarkably complacent about future competition. The well-respected, Washington, D.C.-based electricity consulting firm, GF Energy, found that the "new electricity industry gestalt," after an unsettling flirtation with deregulation, is now "the belief that business-as-once-was-usual is resuming until further notice."

In a 2006 survey of U.S. and Canadian utility executives, GF Energy reports that 93 percent of them do not expect new competitive entrants into retail electricity markets within the next decade. Nearly 90 percent of the executives believe that it is the utility companies that will be introducing end-user electricity controls, rather than independent entrepreneurs. And some 88 percent believe that new assets will be constructed on the basis of regulated and set rates of return. In a very large sense, the prevailing sentiment in the regulated utility business is that it's still 1948 and happy days are here again, in spite of the fact that electricity costs are steadily rising while service quality declines.

"This year's Outlook results portray an industry that believes that the ultimate litmus test issue—retail choice—is dead," stated the GF Energy report. "After a recent past characterized by fear, whether of new entrants, of each other, of being driven over the edge by competition, or of living fast and loose in the market lane, there is a definite sense that utilities—and using that ancient word to describe them says a lot in itself—are in charge again."

The guaranteed cost-recovery business model, irrespective of service quality and value, is one of those legacy issues that makes the utility industry feel "future-proof" and rewarded for maintaining the status quo. The future, of course, will include public policy changes that enable those who invest in electricity innovation to recover their costs, in part, through efficiency and quality benefits, and to be rewarded for superior management that leads to lower expenses. But as long as the legacy rules are not changed, the game will be played in the same way that it has been since the 1890s. As a result, the grid's ability to control the flow of electricity has steadily deteriorated.

Even as this book goes to press, your local utility still finds itself frantically trying to maintain power with no tools to "protect" its system other than the one that Edison had at the Pearl Street Station—rolling brownouts or blackouts. Running today's digital economy with this outmoded electricity delivery system is equivalent to running the Internet through an old-fashioned telephone switchboard.

Utilities may be in charge of today's electrical supply side. But the demand side—the side of the light socket familiar to most of us—is for them foreign territory from which they are "protected" by regulators. What's more, no monopoly utility has ever introduced a product or service beyond commodity electricity that surprised and delighted a customer. Edison made his living by not only thinking up devices that people didn't really even know they wanted or needed, be it the phonograph or motion pictures, but entire systems built around those devices. "I never perfected an invention that I did not think about in terms of the service it might give others." Edison's entrepreneurial service-based business model remains just as valid today.

Edison produced his inventions during one of the most innovative periods in history. Modern innovators working on microprocessor-based power system intelligence and controls, distributed electrical generation and storage, and other ways to efficiently produce and use electricity are following his example in today's equally innovative world. The systems thinking behind microgrids are very much aligned with Edison's vision for power generation and use, and those investors and entrepreneurs on the leading edge will bring competition back into the reinvented electricity enterprise. Indeed, much of the same innovative technology that transformed the monopoly telecommunications industry 30 years ago has been standing ready ever since to do the same for electricity.

Today, there is no technical limitation to creating much more reliable and efficient local participating electricity networks where consumers can actually "plug in" to the electricity business. This can include installing solar panels on homes and businesses, hooking into small gas turbines with smart, real-time controls, and ultimately even using hybrid electric cars to gain valuable consumer leverage over the monopoly bulk power grids. The result will complement the bulk power grid by perfecting the quality of service to all consumers.

"A high-tech world can no longer afford a low-tech electricity grid. We must together build the smart electricity grid of the future," says John Bryson, CEO and president of Edison International, the parent company of the regulated utility Southern California Edison. "This will require substantial capital investment in the modernization of our transmission and distribution system and in the replacement of the dinosaurs of our industry—analog household electricity meters—with state-of-the-art smart digital meters."

The term "smart grid" can be best understood as the overlaying of a comprehensive electronics control and communications system on the electricity grid. The smart grid provides an instantaneous accurate flow of information and energy that eliminates the performance limiting barriers in today's obsolete electricity grid. As a result, the cumbersome layers of slow, manual decision-making required by today's grid operators are no longer needed. In effect, a smart grid enables the complex multitude of devices in the power system to work together for the first time as a finely tuned orchestra rather than a cacophony of disorganized instruments. The smart grid is indeed the conductor of the "electricity orchestra."

Implementing this self-healing system, capable of automatically anticipating and correcting disturbances while continually optimizing its own performance and sending time-of-use electricity price signals to each consumer's end-use devices (Prices-to-Devices), will be critical in meeting the needs of 21st-century consumers and society. This local "smart grid" modernization will enable electricity to be delivered with fundamentally greater reliability, efficiency, and security while facilitating the use of clean, renewable, and distributed power generation. Indeed, a smart grid is also a green grid.

As the following chapters will show, there are major business opportunities here for large innovative corporations and small independent entrepreneurs alike to develop smart appliances and cost-effective household electricity management systems. As Edison's original vision comes to fruition— albeit reinvented with a whole new range of technologies including solar power generation, smart microgrids, and homes adapted for the digital age—there will be much well-paying work to be done, labor with a positive economic, social, and environmental impact.

For those regulators and utilities who can't see the elephant in the living room, it may mean that they are simply failing to recognize the ghost of Topsy.

COMPANIES TO WATCH (AND SOME TO REMEMBER)

ABB (www.abb.com). Headquartered in Switzerland, ABB is a global supplier of products for transmitting and distributing electricity. Originally established as the Brown Boveri Corporation early in the 20th century, it manufactures high-voltage and medium-voltage products including transformers, switchgear, and circuit breakers. It also offers turnkey systems and services for power transmission and distribution grids, and electronic power solutions to improve power flows, such as flexible AC transmission systems (FACTS) and high-voltage direct-current (HVDC) systems.

Babcock and Wilcox (www.babcock.com). Headquartered in Barberton, Ohio, Babcock and Wilcox is an international provider of energy products and services. Boilers have been at the heart of B&W's business since its founding in 1867. The company also provides environmental control equipment and nuclear plant components, including reactor vessels and steam generators. B&W is now a subsidiary of McDermott International in Houston, Texas.

Combustion Engineering (www.namfg.com) of Stamford, Connecticut, was once an innovative engineering company involved in power system development with peak employment of 40,000. The company was acquired by Asea Brown Boveri, a Swiss-Swedish multinational conglomerate in the late 1980s. CE's former boiler and fossil fuel business was purchased by Alstom in 2000.

General Electric (GE) (http://geopower.com). Headquartered in New Jersey, GE was founded in 1892 based principally on a variety of Thomas Edison's business offerings including electric lighting, appliances, and power transmission. Today, GE is the world's second largest corporation and remains a world leader in these original energy business areas as well as in combustion turbine, wind energy, power distribution, and advanced metering. Since its first steam turbine in 1901, GE's installed base of steam and combustion turbines has grown to more than one million megawatts in over 120 countries. GE's energy activities produce over $20 billion in annual revenues, but this is only about 12 percent of total GE corporate revenues today.

Siemens (www.siemens.com). Headquartered in Germany, Siemens has been a major electricity technology and equipment supplier since the 19th century. It remains a leading engineering company helping utility customers to produce and deliver electric power more efficiently and effectively, and industrial customers to increase productivity. Siemens Distribution specializes in the automation, protection, and control of electricity distribution networks and substations. In 2007, Siemens generated over 68 billion euros in sales.

Westinghouse Electric (www.westinghouse.com). The Westinghouse Electricity Corporation was founded in 1886 by George Westinghouse in Pittsburgh, and it went out of business in 1999 when it was sold to Viacom, which still manages the Westinghouse brand. The company pioneered long-distance, high-voltage alternating current transmission. However, it sold its power distribution and control business unit to Eaton Corp. in 1994 and purchased the CBS broadcasting company. The last Westinghouse manufacturing asset, its nuclear energy business, was sold in 1998 and is now owned by Toshiba in Japan.

5

The Path to Perfect Power

*Achieving Perfect Power—an electricity system that is trouble-free
and never fails the user—depends on empowering consumers and
eliminating the dangerous and expensive vulnerabilities inherent in
today's outmoded power grid. The most expeditious and advantageous
way to achieve this performance transformation is by incorporating the
essential technology innovations in smart, local microgrids that enable
entrepreneurial change agents to rapidly transform electricity service,
quality, and value. True retail competition is the key to most effectively
meeting every consumer's power needs.*

Modern society is increasingly dependent on electricity.
The world expects higher-quality and more individualized service that keeps pace with the digital revolution. Consumers need to have more friendly and intelligent
control of electricity consumption that is reliable, responsive, and
environmentally sound. Over the next 25 years, an estimated
$6 trillion will be needed just to renew and expand the world's
aging power delivery grids. As a result, there is belated but growing recognition by the electricity sector that it needs to modern-
ize its aging infrastructure and its business model to affordably
meet these even larger and more stringent service expectations.

To this end, the Department of Energy, the Electric Power
Research Institute, and other organizations in the United States
and overseas are pursuing a series of complementary smart-grid
initiatives. The common goal is to achieve the grid performance
characteristics outlined in the sidebar, "Key Characteristics of

Smart-Grid Initiatives," by modernizing the electricity supply system principally within the current regulated utility structure. Unfortunately, the electric utility industry has a very poor track record of proactive infrastructure investment and innovation. This is underscored by the fact that the utility regulatory commissions in only 17 states consider a smart grid as fundamental to their energy future, and only a handful have provided even qualified support (for example, California, Colorado, Pennsylvania, Texas, and Washington).

Key Characteristics of Smart-Grid Initiatives

- **Self-healing.** Grid rapidly detects, analyzes, responds, and restores.
- **Empowers and incorporates the consumer.** Ability to incorporate consumer equipment and behavior in grid design and operation.
- **Tolerant of attack.** Grid mitigates and is resilient to physical and cyber attacks.
- **Provides power quality needed by 21st-century users.** Grid provides quality power consistent with consumer and industry needs.
- **Accommodates wide variety of supply and demand.** Grid accommodates variety of resources (including demand response, combined heat and power, wind, photovoltaics, and end-use efficiency).
- **Fully enables and is supported by competitive electricity markets.**

As a result, the traditional top-down approach to modernization promises to be a very expensive, a long-term, and an uncertain undertaking. Under business as usual, the U.S. electric utility industry will need nearly a trillion dollars in capital over the next 20 years for the long-overdue replacement of spent infrastructure and to build urgently needed new capacity and capabilities. The potential costs of carbon dioxide emission controls may add an additional half trillion dollars to this capital requirement.

In today's bureaucratically regulated monopoly utility business world, there is very little likelihood that such sums of money can be raised unless there is either a massive power crisis or a fundamental change in the electricity value proposition to the consumer. Telling the public that "we are doubling your electricity rates, but we aren't going to improve the quality of your service or your ability to control your monthly electricity bill," is most certainly dead on arrival. Several utility jurisdictions have already experienced this political and public relations "third rail" the hard way.

In the meantime, the nation and all its citizens are being held captive to an obsolete and very vulnerable power supply system that threatens the viability of every city and state. In today's highly competitive global marketplace where capital, labor, and technology can flow freely to any corner of the world, a deficient infrastructure is an intolerable disadvantage. Indeed, the U.S. electricity sector is at a critical "fork in the road," as shown in Figure 5–1, in terms of its value and viability. Only a comprehensive technological and business transformation can rescue it from continued decay at the major expense of the nation and all its citizens. Even in the more progressive states such as California, so-called smart-grid implementation is leaving the utility, not the retail consumer, in control and will therefore impose unnecessary future expenses on those same consumers.

REFOCUSING ON CONSUMER SERVICE QUALITY

Wall Street has been acutely aware of the deficiencies in the U.S. electricity system and its governing policies for many years. After the August 2003 northeast blackout, Standard and Poor's analyst Peter Rigby wrote the following assessment:

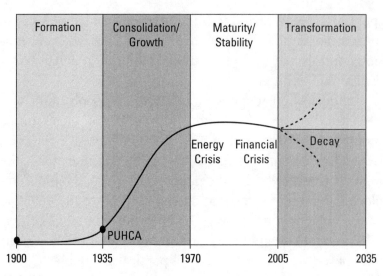

Figure 5–1 Electricity Sector Life-Cycle Fork in the Road

"While the blackout creates a sense of political urgency, addressing the problems of the nation's grid and, indeed, the regulation of the entire U.S. electricity industry, will be no simple matter. The politics of power are divisive and little consensus exists. … And even if policy-makers succeed in crafting a comprehensive solution to the problems of the nation's electricity grid, the regulatory treatment of the costs needed to upgrade the infrastructure remains uncertain.…Gaining consensus among industry participants and stakeholders looms as a Herculean task."

This is why the Galvin Electricity Initiative is pursing a fundamentally different approach in the United States. The initiative intends to bring consumer service quality in the electricity industry front and center as a mainstream issue. That's because an informed and empowered citizenry is essential to mobilizing change in a massive national institution that remains so deeply entrenched in the status quo and protected by outmoded regulations that it reflexively thwarts modernization. The Galvin Electricity Initiative seeks to transcend these largely artificial constraints, and the investment disincentives they generate, by focusing first and foremost on the consumer rather than the utility supplier.

This approach also recognizes that an activist citizenry is essential to achieving a power system that is consumer-focused and encourages entrepreneurial innovation to disrupt the status quo and most quickly demonstrate the advantages of providing more perfect electricity service. That's the fastest and most effective way to solve the growing problem of declining reliability of electricity service and its rising cost.

Enabling this future requires a substantial overhaul in how we think about electricity. In broad strokes, we need an adaptive, electronically controlled electricity supply system of extreme resiliency and responsiveness, one that is fully capable of "self-healing" under duress while responding in real time to the billions of decisions made by consumers and their increasingly sophisticated electronic microprocessor agents. This is not wishful thinking or science fiction. In the same way that the Internet changed the way that people exchange information, the technology exists to create a power system that provides the same reliability, efficiency, precision, and interconnectivity as the billions of electronic microprocessors it already powers. In many ways, this system will mimic not only the human autonomic nervous system, but the human brain and senses.

We have brought together dozens of leading experts in electrical engineering, digital technology, communications, environmental issues, public policy, and total quality management, along with a diverse group of entrepreneurs and financiers. The express idea is to apply state-of-the-art quality principles to transform how we generate, deliver, and use electricity. This independent and creative expert team has defined the architectural and technological building blocks of the Perfect Power system, and it has addressed how to overcome the obstacles in its path. In order to assure that the system is infallible, the expert team has considered and embraced all the elements in the technology and value chain for electricity production, delivery, and use across the entire range of consumer applications.

Much has been written about optimizing power systems. But the traditional thinking is generally limited by two anchors: the existing system design and the assumption that solutions are bounded by central generation on one end and the meter at the consumer's facility at the other. As a result, even less perfection is evident in the end uses of the system—the energy-consuming devices and appliances that convert electricity into heat, light, entertainment, refrigeration, and such. Indeed, to achieve perfection, the most efficient and environmentally friendly devices must be integrated with buildings and seamlessly connected to the power system in order for perfection to extend to the point of use.

The design of the Perfect Power system starts with the consumer's needs and provides absolute confidence, convenience, and choice in the services provided so as to delight the consumer. Perfection, based on the consumer's perspective, is the fundamental design principle guiding the Galvin Electricity Initiative. The focus is not on electricity for its own sake, but on the functionality and services that electricity can ultimately provide. To this end, the initiative has thoroughly examined the consumer and technology factors that are expected to have the greatest impact on 21st-century electricity use.

These factors derive from two underlying trends that dominate the foreseeable electricity service environment: first is the comprehensive transformation of the U.S. economy and society from an analog mechanical to a digital electronic enabling structure; and second is the rapidly rising cost of energy in a carbon- and fuel-constrained world. Power prices have jumped considerably just this summer, by 60 to 120 percent in different regions, and this might be just the beginning according to the Federal Energy Regulatory Commission.

This path to perfection embraces several overarching consumer goals. These include both the ability of the power system to be automatically self-correcting without interrupting service, and its ability to focus on specific local needs while improving economic productivity with minimal environmental impact.

Meeting these goals will require a fundamental change from the electric utility industry's traditional emphasis on supply-side technology and infrastructure which ends at the meter to one that embraces the numerous opportunities for individualized services and products on the consumer's side of the meter. Indeed, in the 21st century the opportunities for innovation on the consumer demand side are much greater than on the utility supply side, where there are no transformative "silver bullets" on the horizon.

TECHNICAL KEYS TO PERFECT POWER

The four fundamental technical areas of innovation that are making Perfect Power possible are:

- Digitally controlling and automating the power delivery system by replacing today's relatively slow analog, electromechanical switches with smart, real-time, electronic controls that can direct the flow of power with pinpoint precision, and are actually able to anticipate disturbances and correct them before they occur.
- Merging electricity and communications to create a dynamic and interactive, "smart infrastructure" that automates the distribution system and will enable today's digital electronic end-use devices and appliances to instantaneously exchange information and electricity with the supply market.
- Transforming today's "dumb" electric meter into a smart consumer portal that allows price signals, decisions, communications, and network intelligence to flow back and forth through the two-way energy/information portal. This is key to achieving consumer control of electricity costs and consumption.
- Seamlessly integrating an array of locally distributed power resources, including clean renewable solar sources and storage, in quantities far beyond what is

possible with today's power system. This plug-and-play capability that enables consumers to supply as well as purchase power will also dramatically help states to confidently meet their clean energy portfolio standards now being promulgated throughout the United States.

The Galvin Electricity Initiative is incorporating these technologies into comprehensive Perfect Power prototype projects, some of which are profiled in later chapters. The basic philosophy is to increase intelligence, independence, and flexibility for optimal energy management while using the least complex system configuration.

The primary system architecture for these prototypes, as shown in Figure 5–2, is the distributed microgrid power system or "smart microgrid," a small, local modernized version of the huge electricity grid that carries bulk power throughout the nation. These local participating networks indeed provide

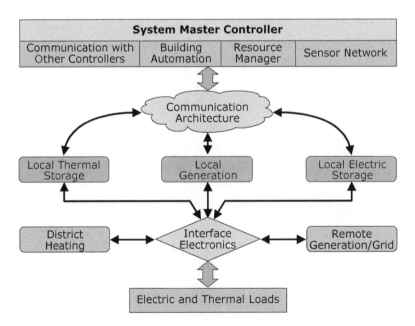

Figure 5–2   Distributed Microgrid Power Systems

consumers with the ability to actively "plug-in" to the electricity business. Smart microgrid-based power systems can also grow and self-organize in response to individualized user needs while fundamentally raising the value and reliability of electricity provided by the existing utility bulk power system.

Indeed, these entrepreneurially developed and installed microgrids are intended to operate in cooperation with the local utility. To this end, more and more utilities are recognizing the essential value of smart microgrids in overcoming regulatory constraints to investment and innovation and in resolving rising business pressures to meet escalating consumer service demands. Particularly notable are the efforts of BPL Global (see below) in assisting utilities to convert sections of their power distribution systems into smart microgrids that produce real energy and cost savings for both the utility and its customers.

By augmenting and refining the bulk electricity supply with locally generated electricity—from a natural-gas burning turbine, solar panels, fuel cells, or a combined heat and power generator—a microgrid may serve a single large building, a factory, or a cluster of buildings. Larger microgrids may serve an entire community. Clusters of overlapping microgrids can share power with each other, as well as sell excess power to the bulk electricity grid. The bottom line is lower cost to consumers. By taking advantage of the highly variable time-of-use cost of electricity throughout the day as well as absolutely eliminating expensive power interruptions regardless of duration, these smart microgrids are essential to Perfect Power. So too are an array of enabling technologies including the following:

- **Power electronics control** is the cornerstone of the Perfect Power system. Based on semiconductor switching technology, these solid state devices provide control of the power delivery system with the speed and accuracy of a microprocessor, but at a power level 500 million times higher.

- **Distributed generation** can augment or even replace the large central power generators of today's electricity grid. The portfolio of distributed generation technologies includes small combustion turbines (microturbines), solar photovoltaics, and various types of fuel cells in addition to today's mainstay diesel engines. These devices put generation closer to the end uses, and they are capable of improving power reliability and security for entire communities or individual residences and businesses.

- **Electric energy storage** can increase the value of electricity by enabling it to be used whenever and wherever needed. Electric energy storage also increases the tolerance of sensitive electrical equipment and end-use devices to withstand the frequent power quality variations in the electrical environment. The most common form of electric energy storage is the battery, a device for which we willingly pay more than $100 per kilowatt hour (roughly 1,000 times the cost of bulk power) because of the unique convenience it provides in terms of power portability.

- **Wireless power distribution** significantly expands the advantages of power portability. Emerging wireless power technology provides a much more flexible and consumer-friendly method of charging and powering mobile devices such as laptops and cell phones today, and its ultimate potential to power our homes and businesses is profound. This new local power delivery capability is being enabled by the use of magnetic resonance as a means of wireless electricity transfer. Magnetic fields travel freely through air yet have minimal effect on the environment or on living beings.

- **Integrated communications** put the intelligence into the smart grid and provide its enabling communication platform. The Perfect Power system requires instantaneous communications among all critical devices to allow continuous monitoring, control, and correction. It is now possible and practical to superimpose large quantities of digital information on power distribution lines themselves as well as to use cable or wireless networks into the home or office. This enables a single communications platform to support diverse, but significantly more reliable and efficient, electricity service capabilities.

- **Sensors** provide the means to continuously monitor the performance and conditions of every critical device in the Perfect Power system. Performance sensors en masse are becoming cheaper, more sensitive, and much smaller through advances in nanotechnology materials. This allows them to be ubiquitously located throughout the smart power system. These advanced sensors also incorporate optical fiber, wireless, or power line communication links that enable convenient integration with the smart grid control system. They are also capable of self-configuration into sensor networks that automatically adapt to meet changing requirements.

- **Advanced building systems** can reduce energy requirements by more than 50 percent, thereby having a significantly positive impact on the performance of the power system. Functional dimensions of these advanced building systems include waste heat recovery, building air automation, including data management and control, and integrated solar photovoltaic power generation systems. These efficient building systems are, in turn, integrated with the power supply system to create Perfect Power microgrids. Chapter 6 explores this critical aspect of achieving Perfect Power in more depth.

- **Efficient appliances and devices** are at least as important in achieving a Perfect Power system as the generation and delivery of the electric energy on which they operate. Efficient appliances and devices that can be networked via the Internet also play a key role in optimizing the energy requirements of all buildings in response to price signals. In addition to more efficient lighting, heating, and cooling, great strides can be made in reducing the energy requirements of electronic devices and appliances which are rapidly dominating the world market. Consider that 70 percent of the electricity they consume is now lost just in converting conventional alternating current (AC) to direct current (DC). Since these smart devices and appliances operate on DC, the Perfect Power system incorporates DC currents to eliminate the unnecessary energy and reliability losses.

These positively "disruptive" technologies can produce a power system that is robust under all conditions, allows technology breakthroughs to be exploited rapidly and effectively, enables differentiated price/performance-based electricity markets, and aligns economically and politically so as to provide simultaneous incentives for all stakeholders. In each case, the Galvin Electric Initiative has identified performance gaps and specific technology developments that can close those gaps within the coming decade.

COST IN PENNIES, VALUE IN DOLLARS

The fundamental value proposition of the Galvin Electricity Initiative is that Perfect Power (trouble-free and does not fail) creates value for consumers measurable in dollars per kilowatt hour. This value is many times the price in cents per kilowatt hour that consumers pay for electricity from the socket: Value is ultimately created by the array of electricity-powered devices, appliances, and processes that deliver comfort, convenience, security, enhanced quality of life, and a means of economic production. The role of the smart microgrid is to optimally provide these services at the maximum value to each consumer. It does so by enabling consumers to manage their electricity use so as to optimize the convenience, cost, and reliability of electricity service at all times.

Site-specific cost/benefit assessments indicate that a Perfect Power microgrid will generally pay for itself within three to five years on a purely economic basis without consideration of the additional convenience, security, and environmental benefits. These microgrids are designed to be interconnected with the local utility power distribution system, and they are able to automatically and instantaneously disconnect from, or provide support to, the bulk power grid during disturbances. Smart microgrids can also take advantage of waste heat from local distributed power generation to heat and cool buildings, thus doubling the overall efficiency of the power generation system.

The Galvin Electricity Initiative also illuminates the work of kindred spirits around the world by sharing technical progress and results with various industry and government-sponsored grid modernization programs, including Intelligrid, Gridwise, and the Modern Grid Initiative. Since the system transformation is certain to meet with opposition from interests heavily invested in the status quo, the initiative includes the public policy educational efforts needed to honorably change the rules of the game for the benefit of all the nation's stakeholders. There is no government money or direction involved in the Galvin Electricity Initiative. Rather, the initiative's results are available to any individual, nonprofit, or corporation that is committed to building what promises to be the greatest of all growth industries.

This reflects an additional principle guiding the Galvin Electricity Initiative. That innovative, self-organizing entrepreneurs guided by new consumer service opportunities—rather than by government prescriptions and regulations—provide the most effective engine for transforming the nation's electricity supply system. The initiative therefore includes innovative business models that encourage the success of these new entrepreneurial entrants. Equally important, these business models enable the existing regulated utilities to prosper in the reinvented system by fostering innovative ideas and investments. In emphasizing opportunities that yield maximum consumer value as quickly as possible, we will in subsequent chapters, highlight companies, communities, and other entities large and small, which already are on the forefront of their electricity system renewal.

A consumer-focused quality approach, as we know from the experience of Motorola, Toyota, General Electric, Honeywell, and other progressive corporations, is best able to generate sustained innovation and investment. Technology alone is insufficient to achieve and maintain absolute quality. As many companies have learned through Six-Sigma and similar quality programs, success demands that the human dimension be given equal attention. Therefore, in conjunction with the Juran Center for Leadership in Quality at the University of Minnesota, we have developed quality leadership and management guides, plus implementation courses for electricity entrepreneurs and their partners. Perhaps the most important tenet of the initiative is the conviction that it is quality, above all, that spurs innovation.

Today's bulk power system typically provides what quality students call "three-nines reliability," which is power generally delivered 99.9 percent of the time. While on the surface that may sound excellent, it actually translates into an average of nine hours of disruptions each year for every consumer, distributed intermittently over periods lasting nanoseconds to hours. Feeding this unstable power to today's warp-speed digital electronic world is like pouring crude oil into the gas tank of a Ferrari. And it's why the spaces under our desks have to be cluttered with a variety of expensive and energy-intensive power-conditioning devices, including transformers, converters, and surge suppressors.

In the concept of Perfect Power, uninterrupted quantities of electricity are selectively available with up to "nine-sigma," or 99.9999999 percent reliability. We believe that this is a standard that opens doors to innovation, just as the original cell phone paved the way for a telecommunications revolution that now includes wireless e-mail, pod-casts, and text-messaging and how basic cable television spawned hundreds of new channels of original programming, high-speed Internet, and more.

Another attribute of the new Perfect Power microgrid system is the ability to more easily incorporate DC circuits. Much of the hardware in the digital equipment and appliances we buy today exists just to invert and condition the incoming AC and its imperfections to the smooth direct current that the digital equipment requires. However, over time it is likely that the overwhelming advantages of DC in a digital world will ultimately supplant AC for essentially all end uses. That is already the case for very large digital quality power consumers such as electronic data centers and Internet "hotels." Smart buildings, as well as efficient appliances and devices, will follow their lead as soon as the electricity delivery system permits. Renewable solar energy technologies also naturally produce DC power. Reducing and ultimately eliminating the need for AC will significantly reduce both the cost and complexity of using this clean energy source. Perfect Power microgrids will be prepared for, and will enable, this power quality, efficiency, environmental and service cost transformation.

The twirling dials on the electric meter in homes and business buildings are another classic example of an interface that displays information that consumers cannot act on. As Alan Greenspan told Congress in 1999, the defining business model of our age allows providers to "detect and respond to finely calibrated nuances in consumer demand." This is how Wal-Mart, for example, uses an intricate inventory and sales data base to measure prices and purchase and swiftly resupply items that are pleasing shoppers and generating profit. But without feedback loops hardwired into the power grid—so that consumers know as much as the meter reader and also on a daily and hourly basis—the entire electrical infrastructure is a one-way ticket to a dead-end station.

A NEIGHBORHOOD OF SMART APPLIANCES

In contrast, imagine an air conditioner that receives constantly updated market signals about the price of electricity and knows what the other air conditioners in the vicinity are doing. Such smart devices and appliances could work together with the other smart appliances in the neighborhood to reduce demand when electricity is expensive, or provide micropower reserves when the bulk power grid is peaking out. As previously noted, the massive reserve power generation equipment needed for those rare times of peak demand is perhaps the most expensive insurance paid by American consumers; doing away with that costly premium is yet another facet of the Galvin Electricity Initiative.

Such smart, automatic control capabilities can be easily expanded to all appliances and devices that do not need to be maintained at a constant electricity demand level in order to perform their functions. This includes water heaters, thermostats, and the huge banks of lights in warehouses and malls. Likewise, envision millions of cheap miniature sensors fastened everywhere, feeding the electricity network data about temperature, light, and moisture—a precise real-time data stream about the state of the world and its implications for power system reliability. Imagine millions of home appliances that can sense when the grid is straining and can reduce their demand momentarily until the grid restabilizes. Ironically, none of these appliances and devices would have to be very intelligent on their own. But every node in the smart network would be awake, responsive, and most importantly, interconnected with everything else. In short, a new smart energy net, following the lead of the Internet, would be created.

This intelligent electricity system will automatically recognize problems, instantaneously find solutions, and continuously optimize performance to meet the expectations of each consumer. After extensive stakeholder discussions, consumers have made it clear that they increasingly expect, and are hungry for, higher-quality and more flexible levels of electric service that they can control. Consumers are also generally willing to pay accordingly if they can be assured of this service level. In the end, citizens want to better control their monthly electricity bill based on the value they receive. When electricity and information are combined, consumers can thus create customized services that are tailored to best meet their individual needs.

In open markets, the comprehensive technical and business opportunity roadmap being developed by the Galvin Electricity Initiative would be an entrepreneur's dream, promising rich commercial opportunities. Unfortunately, current power industry policies and governance impede such value propositions. The key to change is free enterprise, with industry exposed to market forces. As any economist would explain, this means no barriers to entry, the availability of clear and accurate price signals, an absence of subsidies, and the elimination of predatory practices.

One of the most significant barriers to smart microgrids is the legal prohibition against private electric lines crossing public streets. This ban is a result of the 20th-century argument that consumers are best served by giving one organization an electricity distribution monopoly in each geographic service area—the living ghost of Sam Insull. While modern technology has rendered this archaic rationale obsolete, the authority of local distribution monopolies, or DISCOs as they are called, remains alive and well with the support of most state regulatory commissions who ostensibly "represent the consumer."

As veteran electricity entrepreneur Tom Casten notes, monopoly protected wires are perhaps the last vestige of failed governmental central planning. Oddly enough, the ban on private local distribution wires, which is supposed to reduce societal costs by preventing wasteful duplication, actually increases the requirements for overall investment in wires. The local generation of electricity, or distributed power in smart microgrids, needs no new wires to deliver power to on-site consumers, while excess power could simply flow across the street to neighboring consumers. Competition would work its magic, reducing consumer prices while wringing inefficiencies out of the system.

REAL-TIME PRICING TO PUT CONSUMERS IN CONTROL

Functioning markets also depend on accurate and timely price signals, but bulk electricity is typically sold by utilities at average prices, even though marginal costs can be up to 10 times higher during peak hours. Real-time pricing would create incentives for consumers to shift some power use to off-peak periods, thus reducing system peak loads while reducing the cost of electricity. For example, Chicago's Community Energy Cooperative initiated a demand response program that saved the residential consumers an average of 19.6 percent on their electricity bills in 2003. We estimate that widespread national use of demand response would save U.S. consumers at least $30 billion a year. For years, Electricity de France (EDF), the French national utility, has enabled its customers to automatically conserve during peak rate periods. Ten million of EDF's 32 million customers have chosen this option and each saves several hundred dollars per year in electricity costs while reducing EDF's peak load by 10 percent.

As viewed through the lens of the Galvin Electricity Initiative, the picture of a vastly more reliable, efficient, secure, and environmentally responsive electricity system is coming into focus. The Perfect Power payoff will quickly reach more than a hundred billion dollars a year in power system reliability savings, as shown in Figure 5–3. This new, smart system is harnessing an amazing array of innovative technologies, many already in use to achieve other goals such as security and Web-connectivity to enable automatic control of electricity on a real-time basis.

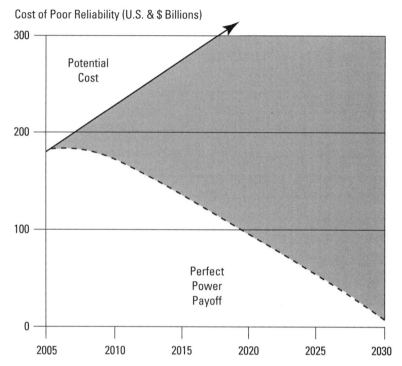

Figure 5–3 The Perfect Power Payoff from Improved Power System Reliability

The brain and nerve center of the Perfect Power system is its highly distributed electronic control capability. In effect, this provides the consumer with an automatic decentralized decision-making capability that instantaneously balances electricity demand and supply coming from both the distributed generation and storage within the local microgrid and the bulk power distribution feeder. This virtual brain is responsible for enabling the functionality advantages of Perfect Power in order to both maximize consumer value and optimize the microgrid's operation. By applying breakthrough software, this electronic control capability uses the time-of-use market prices of electricity to determine the amount of power that the microgrid should draw from the bulk power distribution feeder and to deal with utility requests to reduce demand. It also stabilizes the voltage and frequency of power during transient conditions, thus ensuring absolute reliability and Perfect Power quality at all times.

As discussed in Chapters 10 and 11, a number of commercial suppliers are already prepared to provide these smart, automatic energy management capabilities and services to consumers on a shared-savings basis.

Building on the Internet revolution, electricity consumers will finally be able to instantaneously know how they are using electricity, and to manage it more wisely and efficiently with price incentives. For the first time, consumers will have the oppurtunity to help choose the songs that their electricity qrenestia plays. Commercial experience around the world confirms that when consumers are aware of how much electricity they are using at any given time and how much it costs, they make behavioral changes that stick. Like cell phones and other must-haves in today's world, consumer control of electricity will be quickly embraced. Consumers today want more choices about the energy they buy, and they want to be able to actively control its cost and reduce its environmental impact.

INSTITUTIONS AND COMPANIES TO WATCH

AGM Batteries Ltd (www.agmbatteries.com) is a joint-venture company, located in Scotland, manufacturing lithium-ion cells. Its joint-venture partners include AEA Technology, Japan Storage Battery Co., and Mitsubishi Materials Corp. In 2002, AEA Technology was awarded a multi-million-pound contract to supply batteries and chargers to the UK's new Bowman battlefield communication system based upon AGM's world-leading cell.

Arcadian Networks Inc. (www.arcadiannetworks.com). Arcadian Networks provides "last mile" wireless carrier services to the energy sector (electric, water, and gas utilities and oil and gas companies). The company's 700-MHz licensed spectrum delivers a converged IP network with voice and data com munications for fixed and mobile applications. The real-time broadband communications platform reduces operational costs, improves resiliency, and transforms electric grids into efficient "smart grids" and oil fields into optimized "smart fields."

Ballard (www.ballard.com), located in Burnaby, British Columbia, is a global leader in the design, development, and manufacture of hydrogen fuel cells for cogeneration, backup power and transportation. It is partnered with the automotive industry through AFCC, owned by Daimler AG, Ford Motor Company, and Ballard. In the cogeneration area, it is involved in a joint venture with Ebara Ballard Corp. in Japan. 2007 revenues reached $65 million.

Beacon Power (BCON) (www.beaconpower.com) designs and develops sustainable energy storage and power conversion technology. Products include solar photovoltaic inverters and flywheel-based energy storage systems, designed to deliver instantaneous power from solar energy systems or battery backup in the event of a power outage. The company's patented advanced composite flywheel technology can provide megawatt-level energy storage.

BPL Global, Ltd. (BPLG) (www.bplglobal.net). BPLG is a smart-grid technology company founded in 2004 dedicated to leading the global energy and information and delivery transformation. BPLG partners with utilities, equipment suppliers, and financiers in joint ventures to provide the foundation for a coordinated, intelligent grid that delivers energy more efficiently for a greener environment. BPLG is headquartered near Pittsburgh and its eight regional offices are in France, Kuwait, Brazil, and China.

Capstone Turbine Corp. (www.microturbine.com), founded in 1988, is a leading producer of low-emission microturbine systems. Their products are compact, turbine generators suitable for applications ranging from remote locations to city centers, delivering high-quality power from a variety of fuels. In 2007, Capstone shipped its 4,000th unit, and reached $21 million in sales. Capstone, headquartered in Chatsworth, California, is listed on the NASDAQ exchange as CPST.

Cooper Power Systems (http://www.cooperpower.com) in Minneapolis, MN manufactures a wide range of medium- and high-voltage electrical equipment for the utility and industrial markets. Its Cannon Technologies Yukon® Advanced Energy Services Platform provides automated meter reading, demand response, plus distribution and substation automation capabilities to about 450 utility customers.

Department of Energy (DOE) (www.doe.gov) is a cabinet-level department of the federal government responsible for energy technology, energy innovation and R&D, energy information, and weapons-related energy development. DOE manages the nation's national laboratories, including the Lawrence Livermore, Oak Ridge, Sandia, Los Alamos, Argonne, Idaho, Renewable Energy, Brookhaven, and the Pacific Northwest National Laboratories.

Echelon (ELON) (www.echelon.com), headquartered in San Jose, California, is a world leader in control networks that connect machines and other electronic devices. Echelon's embedded control networks inside machines connect tiny sensors and actuators that govern the operation of machines. Echelon's smart metering hardware is the core of a next-generation utility infrastructure. Echelon revenues for 2007 were $138 million.

The Electric Power Research Institute (EPRI) (www.epri.com), founded in 1973, is a voluntary, nonprofit organization managing a collaborative R&D program on electric power generation, delivery and end-use technologies, as well as a variety of energy-related environmental issues. EPRI members represent more than 90 percent of the electricity generated in the United States. International participation includes 40 countries.

Elliot Energy Systems (www.elliotmicroturbines.com), located in Stuart, Florida, is a leading manufacturer of microturbines for use in distributed electricity generation and combined heat and power (CHP) applications. Their 100-kW turbine is designed for industrial and commercial applications and represents over 10 years of research, development, and testing. The optional remote monitoring system allows the turbine to be integrated with building controls system.

Enerpro-Inc.com (www.enerpro-inc.com), founded in 1983, has become a leading manufacturer of power electronics control products, including firing boards, regulators, control assemblies, battery charger systems, and customized power supply solutions. Applications extend from wind power applications to electric vehicles and industrial rectifiers. Customers include GE Wind, TM GE, Westinghouse, Xantrex, Northrop-Grumman, and General Atomics.

Harbor Research, Inc. (www.harborresearch.com). Founded in 1983, Harbor Research, Inc. has established a unique competence in developing business strategies for the convergence of pervasive computing and global networking. This Pervasive Internet is unleashing an age of "living intelligence" enabled by networked devices. The challenges and opportunities presented by the Pervasive Internet are profound and go to the heart of how companies perceive the markets they are in, how they organize themselves, and how they approach business opportunities.

Honeywell Automation and Control Solutions (ACS) (www.honeywell.com), a part of Honeywell International, is a diversified technology and manufacturing company employing more than 100,000 people in 95 countries. ACS is an $11 billion strategic business group applying sensing and control expertise to diverse markets. ACS technology is at work in 100 million homes and 5 million buildings worldwide, as well as in transportation. The future will involve wireless sensing, connecting, and communicating increasing amounts of data for processing.

Omron Corp. (www.omron.com), located in Kyoto, Japan, is a global supplier of advanced sensors, switches, relays, and control equipment that serve a wide array of industries. Omron's sensing and control technology is their core competency and their R&D is focused on going beyond the traditional data input function to integrate sensing and control into high-value information for subsequent systems processing.

Pacific Northwest National Laboratory (PNNL) (www.pnl.gov). Located in Richland, Washington, PNNL is one of the Department of Energy's (DOE) ten national laboratories. Battelle has operated PNNL for DOE since 1965. PNNL focuses on reducing the effects of energy generation and use on the environment, and on reducing dependence on imported oil through research on hydrogen and biomass-based fuels. It also performs applied research on cyber security of the nonproliferation of weapons of mass destruction.

Power Semiconductors (PSI) (www.powersemiconductors. com), founded in 1902, is a leading supplier of high-performance semiconductors including phase control SCR thyristors, fast recovery thyristors, and standard recovery diode rectifiers. PSI offers a wide selection of solutions for high-voltage, high-current industrial applications, such as welding, battery chargers, and high-power converters.

Rockwell Automation, Inc. (www.rockwellautomation.com), located in Milwaukee, Wisconsin, is a global leader in advanced automation, power control, and conversion products and services. Their Allen-Bradley condition-sensing product line supplies intelligence at important process points and communicates this information to automatically sequence equipment or processes. The company was voted the best supplier of process control automation by *Control Magazine*. The company is listed on the NYSE as ROK.

Silicon Power Company (www.siliconpower.com), located in Malvern, Pennsylvania, designs and fabricates a wide variety of power semiconductor devices for pulse power and power flow applications. It is the oldest continuously operating semiconductor engineering and manufacturing facility in the world, and was owned by GE until 1994. The company produces thyristors up to 9 kV and silicon diameters in 100-mm and 125-mm sizes.

Silver Spring Networks (www.silverspringnetworks), founded in 2002, develops intelligent, IP-addressable products and networks based upon open standards that provide customers with insight and control, and ensure the reliable delivery of low-cost products. Their approach provides value by supporting a broad range of utility applications that reach the entire delivery system. Silver Springs Networks software allows utilities to support billing, dynamic rate structures, demand response programs, and customer service. The company is located in Redwood City, California.

Tendril Networks Inc. (www.tendrilinc.com). The Tendril Energy Management System enables consumers to understand and control consumption and allows suppliers to deploy smart energy conservation programs. Tendril believes that sustained energy efficiency and awareness will only be realized by working hard to engage the consumer in the process.

UCA® International Users Group (www.ucausersgroup.org). The UCA® International Users Group is a not-for-profit corporation consisting of utility user and supplier companies that is dedicated to promoting the integration and interoperability of electric/gas/water utility systems through the use of international standards-based technology.

UTC Power (www.utcpower.com), located in South Windsor, Connecticut, is part of the $48 billion United Technologies Corporation. With 50 years experience, UTC Power is a world leader in developing and producing fuel cells for on-site power, transportation, space, and defense applications. The company is also a leader in renewable energy solutions and combined cooling, heating, and power for the distributed energy market.

Yamatake (www.yamatakeusa.com), established in 1906, is a leading manufacturer in the field of measuring and control technology for building and industrial automation. The product line of Yamatake Sensing and Control Ltd includes photoelectric sensors, proximity sensors, laser sensors, and fiber optic cables, as well as a complete line of process and power controls.

6

Smarter Than the Average Building and Car

The vast majority of global energy production is consumed by our dwellings and vehicles. The pivotal feature of today's most valuable and energy-efficient real estate properties is connectivity. That is, the ability to optimize energy management within and among buildings using innovative digital infrastructure. These real estate properties become, in effect, self-contained smart microgrids that form the "building blocks" of the Perfect Power system. Similarly, plug-in hybrid vehicles could become mobile microgrids that economically transfer stored electricity between commercial buildings and homes and the bulk power grid.

T he largest component of America's wealth is the nation's 110 million households, 5 million commercial buildings, and some 16 trillion square feet of industrial floor space. These structures also use more than two-thirds of all the electricity produced in the nation, and they account for 40 percent of both total energy consumption and carbon emissions. Most energy is consumed by equipment that transforms electricity into light, heat, chilled air, hot water, and electronic devices that manage information and provide entertainment. Although few homeowners or building operators fully realize it, they hold the collective key to becoming the most influential energy-use decision maker in the world and enabling perfection in electricity services.

In fact, the array of smart technologies described in Chapter 5, which transform electricity service reliability, efficiency, cost, and cleanliness, are most effectively applied in the homes, offices, and properties now held captive behind the "iron curtain" electric meter. The path to perfection depends on breaking this artificial barrier and giving all consumers the smart microgrid capability to control their own electrical service destiny to best advantage.

REMOVING THE OBSTACLES TO ENERGY-EFFICIENT BUILDINGS

The money, opportunity, and impact are manifest since the commercial real estate business in the United States alone produces revenues of more than a trillion dollars each year. After all, to build a new power plant costs over $2,000 per each kilowatt it can produce. By comparison, each kilowatt saved by an investment in an energy-efficient building costs only about $300. Despite the spread of green technologies and general agreement that such structures are a good thing, surprising obstacles remain in the path of energy-efficient building development.

One of these obstacles, oddly enough, is building codes ostensibly intended to ensure that structures are safe and sound and in compliance with modern standards. Alas, the localized nature of building regulations in the United States has created literally several thousand *different* code specifications, which in essence fragment the construction market, contribute to manufacturing inefficiencies, and increase costs. Because codes and standards take a long time to adopt and modify, they also tend to inhibit innovation and encourage the use of approved-but-obsolete technology. In terms of buildings and electrical use, these barriers stand in the way of swift and significant change.

Indeed, by 2010 advances in building design, equipment, and systems integration could lead to a 50 percent reduction in the energy requirements of a new building, relative to one built a mere decade before. When augmented by on-site power generation, be it from solar panels or gas-fired turbines, these buildings could reduce their net energy requirements from the bulk power grid by as much as 75 percent. The incremental cost of the energy-saving innovations—about 5 percent of the construction price—would be recovered from reduced energy bills in less than five years. What's more, many of the improvements can also be retrofitted to existing buildings.

But that's not how most buildings are now constructed, thanks to an investment climate driven by decision making that is focused on achieving the lowest initial construction cost irrespective of the longer-term costs to the owner and tenants. It is also based on the assumption that commercial structures are cost centers disconnected from employee motivation, productivity, and health. This weak investment climate is further encouraged by the common commercial construction business model of "flipping." The builder's goal here is to sell the building immediately after construction for the highest profit margin. As a result, American designers and engineers are encouraged to produce unresponsive buildings with inefficient space conditioning—meaning room temperature and the quality of air and light—plus controls that are static, hardwired, and inaccessibly embedded in building walls and floors. Such systems are unable to learn and adapt to differing application objectives and to integrate new technologies as they emerge. The result is that they severely restrict the management of energy as part of a coordinated green building system.

It is frankly baffling that, in light of today's economic and environmental reality, so many new structures do not allow for natural ventilation, rely totally on artificial illumination, and ignore or even fight the climate. Overheating in summer creates enormous and quite unnecessary cooling loads. To make matters worse, all too many buildings require both daily heating and then cooling power during the transitional seasons of spring and fall. Current building technology also remains vulnerable to chemical and biological attack through centralized air supply systems. Despite the tremendous investment in commercial real estate, numerous studies have shown that most buildings neither meet occupant needs nor function as long-term economic assets. But they could accomplish these tasks, and they could do it with surprising ease.

Even ordinary buildings can be "trained," if you will, to behave in a more energy-efficient manner. And when groups of these buildings are aggregated and operated in concert, they can begin to respond to market fluctuations in electrical use and price—the so-called demand response realm—and start cutting power use and utility costs. One company that's currently helping more than 900 buildings to do so is EnergyConnect.

Headquartered in Portland, Oregon, the company works mostly with buildings in Pennsylvania, Illinois, Maryland, and Virginia, parts of a bulk power grid region managed by the eponymous independent system operator, PJM Interconnection. "What we have here is primarily a technology play," explains CEO Rod Boucher. "Thanks to PJM, the buildings that are in our system, and our proprietary software we link consumers with the grid through automation and make many small decisions and transactions that add up to substantial power savings and payments to our clients. We often use the thermal properties inherent in large buildings just like batteries." EnergyConnect puts together groups of buildings based on their capabilities—including distributed power generation and their needs and preferences—and then shifts power loads in the most timely and cost-effective way.

EnergyConnect targets a $12 billion segment of the $380-plus billion electricity market. However, less that 1 percent of that market is currently served by this firm or its several competitors. "We still face policy limitations restricting where we're able to operate," explains Boucher. "And we must also manage resistance to change. Often the person this all comes down to is the building's engineer, the person who is responsible for the operations and environment of the building. If we can show the engineer how we can help reduce costs and improve relations, we'll get that client."

How much energy can a firm like EnergyConnect save? "Well, if you give us one million square feet, we generally have about one megawatt to work with," says Boucher. "And a megawatt in our hands can typically produce $100,000." "During one week last summer," he adds, "PJM paid $5 million for demand response, and estimated the benefits for that week at $230 million. For an average office building of 600,000 square feet, we currently cut power costs by at least 5 percent. In the future, as we put together more collections of smarter buildings, we expect at least 15 percent." And this is only the beginning. The exciting part is that as more technologies such as smart meters, distributed solar power and storage, and enhanced software platforms enter the market, the opportunities for demand response and other market-driven opportunities will increase dramatically, and many more energy consumers will be able to participate economically. With the right technology and universal access to real time electricity pricing, the door will open to a recovery of "doing electricity."

DESIGNING SMART OFFICES AND HOMES

The Carnegie Mellon University Center for Building Performance and Diagnostics (CBPD) in Pittsburgh has been at the forefront of showing how the United States can catch up with and lead other parts of the world in putting up more energy-efficient structures. For example, current U.S. building designs require, on average, about double the energy to condition a square meter of building space when compared to those in Europe. In addition, practices that even today are economically and technically feasible could reduce the amount of electricity needed from the grid to heat and cool that square meter from 1,000 kilowatt hours per year to only 100 kilowatt hours per year. In order to develop these sustainable practices, the building envelope—its facade and roofs—has to become dynamic, akin to a living membrane that harvests sun, water, and air.

Turning the concept of traditional energy management and use on its head in this manner is a primary CBPD effort. Called the Building as Power Plant (BAPP) initiative, it is led by the dynamic duo of Dr. Volker Hartkopf and Professor Vivian Loftness. The program demonstrates what's possible when advanced energy-efficient building technologies and practices are combined with innovative distributed power generation and storage systems. In this scenario, essentially all energy needs for heating, cooling, ventilating, and lighting are met on-site while also fulfilling user comfort requirements. In the BAPP initiative, an intelligent building does more than save energy; its design actually stands on the three pillars of (1) human needs for healthful, safe, and productive environments, (2) societal needs for secure and affordable energy resources, and (3) environmental needs for healthy and diverse ecological systems. These pillars are also reflected in the "intelligent" electric house portrayed in Figure 6–1.

As the BAPP initiative demonstrates, roof-top solar installations can fill the heating and cooling requirements while exporting significant electricity to the bulk power grid. In conjunction with these direct current (DC) solar installations, power conversion electronics enable these buildings to take advantage of local DC distribution circuits to power the rapidly expanding array of DC consumer electronic devices and

Figure 6–1 The "Intelligent" House

appliances. This dramatically improves the reliability and energy efficiency of these electronic end uses while still providing access to the alternating current needed by conventional appliances and other devices.

A crucial piece of an advanced building design is the integration of the diverse service functions that have traditionally operated in separate silos. These include ventilation, thermal conditioning, electricity, as well as data, voice, and video networks. These traditional stand-alone building control systems can now be integrated into a common information technology (IT) infrastructure that allows all functions and appliances to "talk" to one another and automatically coordinate their activities for the greatest efficiency. This ability to imbed intelligence into the physical fabric of each building is the core capability enabling smart and dynamic buildings. This intelligence, in the form of advanced plug-and-play sensing and control systems, enables every fixture to generate real-time operating data and make automated decisions regarding weather changes, occupancy patterns, and specific company requirements. Available through current technology, this intelligence also enables numerous interconnected buildings to share power generation and storage capabilities; thus turning a cluster of buildings into a smart microgrid.

Yet another revolutionary initiative is underway at Siemens Building Technology, which is developing a micro-electro-mechanical system, or MEMS. Imagine arriving at your workspace and being able to automatically control every aspect of your work environment to your personal criteria, a capability that contrasts starkly with present practices. While a car has hundreds of control points for just one or two people, buildings typically have only one thermostat for 10 or more workstations; it's no wonder occupants consistently report that their workspace is too hot, too cold, stuffy, drafty, too bright, or too dark. Through a wireless system, MEMS controls the variety of energy-using devices around an individual's space with sensors activated by occupant presence that automatically provide personal choice or respond to environmentally strategic commands. Residential markets for similar automation systems are also rapidly growing.

On the national level, the American Society of Heating, Refrigeration and Air-Conditioning Engineers (ASHRAE) reports that their energy standards have reduced commercial building energy consumption by nearly 30 percent since 1975 with a goal of at least a 70 percent reduction by 2020. Another important step is the move to Zero Energy Homes (ZEH) led by the Department of Energy's Building America Program. The goal is residential energy savings of 60 to 70 percent plus 30 to 40 percent on-site renewable power generation. More and more home builders are using off-the-shelf components to develop their own brands for these smart, solar-efficient homes. These home designs, with federal and local tax incentives, can create a positive cash-flow to homeowners between their mortgage and utility bills. The result not only sells better but can reverse the long-standing upward trend in U.S. home energy consumption.

Efforts to further contain the energy consumption of buildings are being most notably led through the United States Green Building Council (USGBC) with their LEED (leadership in energy and environmental design) initiative. This rating system is a voluntary, consensus-based national approach for developing high-performance, sustainable green buildings. The goal is to transform the way buildings and communities are designed, built, and operated, and thus improve the quality of life. The LEED rating system provides a framework for assessing building performance and meeting sustainability goals via state-of-the-art strategies encompassing sustainable site selection, energy efficiency, water efficiency, materials use and reuse, indoor environmental quality, and design innovation. The annual U.S. market in green building products and services is at least $12 billion and is growing rapidly. One indication of this growth is the fact that some 55,000 designers, builders, suppliers, and managers have attended USGBC educational programs.

The highest-rated level of LEED certification is platinum certified. Buildings that have reached this level include the University of California's Santa Barbara Business School facility, the Yale School of Forestry and Environmental Studies building, and the Chesapeake Bay Foundation headquarters. The first net-zero electric energy commercial building in the United States, the headquarters of Ferreira Construction in New Jersey, became operational in 2007. Notable international LEED certification examples include the Chinese Ministry of Science and Technology Agenda 21 Building (the first LEED gold-certified building in China), the Electricite de France Laboratory for the Design of Cognition in Paris, the Malaysian Energy Centre, and the Alcoa Fjardaal aluminum smelter in Iceland. LEED-certified residential developments are also expanding rapidly. The LEED principles are also applicable to existing buildings as demonstrated, for example, by the thirty-plus-year-old Center for Neighborhood Technology headquarters building in Chicago. The retrofit importance is underscored by the fact that the existing building market accounts for 85 percent of all construction dollars.

PLUG-IN HYBRID VEHICLES

Interconnected homes, office buildings, and factories are the most critical elements of a microgrid's architecture; however, the potential incorporation of mobile electricity storage systems in the form of automobiles is also feasible. Most Americans spend a considerable amount of time each day in these mobile "buildings," whether it's commuting to a workplace or shuttling children to school and activities. Today there are 215 million vehicles on U.S. roads, the vast majority of which are passenger cars and light trucks. These vehicles account for 85 percent of the miles traveled in the nation and consume some 10 million barrels of oil per day—more than 10 percent of the world's daily petroleum production—and emit about 30 percent of the nation's CO_2 emissions. Indeed, the United States consumes more gasoline each year than the next 20 countries combined.

However, if electricity is our energy end game based on its precision, flexibility, and cleanliness at the point of use, why not design vehicles that will plug directly into the electricity grid? In contrast to current hybrid vehicles on the market—which have batteries and electric motors energized by a gasoline-powered engine that operates as the ultimate source for most of the energy needed by the vehicle—a plug-in hybrid gains most of its energy from the electricity grid, using gasoline only for long distances. This serves to maximize the advantages of electric motor power versus the traditional internal-combustion engine, as displayed in Figure 6–2. What could this mean for the consumer? With the cost of gasoline reaching $5 per gallon and the national average price of residential electricity at about 11 cents per kilowatt hour, a plug-in hybrid will run on the equivalent of 75 cents per gallon and would reduce gasoline consumption by about 60 percent. Given the high efficiency of these vehicles, net CO_2 emissions are also reduced even when the electricity generation mix is based primarily on coal.

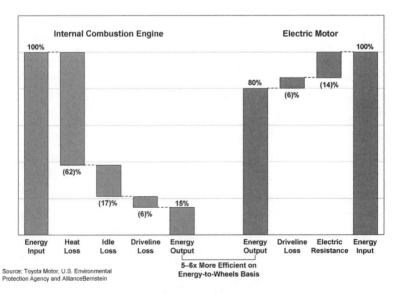

Figure 6–2 Efficiency of Electric Motors versus Mechanical Engines

The introduction of plug-in hybrid electric vehicles (PHEVs), moreover, shows a clear technological synergy between the technologies used in automobiles and smart electricity microgrids. For example, the plug-in hybrid automobile can be used as an electricity storage facility, able to provide power back to the grid during peak demand periods. This "vehicle to grid" (V2G) strategy could significantly improve grid reliability while reducing costs. In turn, this mobile storage system benefits from the bulk power system by recharging its batteries during periods of low-cost, off-peak electricity, assuming consumers have access to time-of-use electricity pricing. Time-of-use pricing is therefore essential if plug-in hybrids are to be an asset to the grid.

Plug-in hybrids will initially be able to run on electricity for up to 50 miles per charge—beyond the daily commute of the average American. The gasoline engine will only be used when a more extended range is needed. Concerned about looming energy crises and global warming, the U.S. House of Representatives introduced an amendment to the Internal Revenue Code in March 2007 providing tax credits for plug-in hybrid motor vehicles. However, to think about these cars simply as transportation is missing their holistic impact, especially if their capabilities are figured into the workings of utilities and the broad application of smart electricity metering and time-of-use pricing.

BUILDING A GROUNDSWELL OF DEMAND

Today, the plug-in hybrid is attracting the attention of both automobile manufacturers and municipalities concerned about reducing fuel costs and urban pollutants. According to Will Wynn, mayor of Austin, Texas, and current chairman of the U.S. Conference of Mayors, "We believe that the 50 largest cities in this country, united in purpose, can build a groundswell of demand sufficient to entice carmakers to mass produce what is the logical near-term step toward the critical goal of energy independence. And we intend to set the example right here." For starters, the city of Austin is setting aside a million dollars for rebates to help local businesses and citizens acquire plug-in hybrids when they become available. The local municipal utility, Austin Energy, is also moving toward the creation of a city-wide smart grid to take best advantage of the PHEV revolution.

From the perspective of the automobile manufacturers, General Motors has, for example, committed to initially producing Chevrolet Volt plug-in hybrid cars by 2010. Toyota claims to be the first automaker to have a PHEV certified for highway use, in Japan, and is planning tests in Europe and the United States as well. Toyota also expects to introduce a PHEV in the United States by 2010, and Ford is close behind. Several smaller Chinese auto companies have also announced plans to produce plug-in hybrids as part of their already large electric vehicle product array.

These plug-in hybrids will typically have an onboard charger that plugs into a standard electricity outlet and can be automatically recharged in four to six hours, using about that same amount of electricity as an electric dishwasher drains. In the United States, tens of millions of plug-in hybrids could be charged in this manner each night using low-cost off-peak power without requiring new electricity generation or delivery capacity. A typical PHEV represents a potential electricity supply source of about two kilowatts, meaning that a thousand such cars could provide two megawatts of power to a congested work area during peak-load periods. Using today's U.S. power supply system, a plug-in hybrid will, on average, generate just a third of the greenhouse gases produced by an equivalent gasoline-powered vehicle. This differential will continue to improve as older power plants are ultimately replaced by cleaner technology enabled by a smart power system.

The primary factor determining the cost and performance of the plug-in hybrid car is its electric storage battery technology. The lighter and more compact the battery, the more efficient and practical the vehicle; and the more energy the battery can store, the longer the driving range. The lithium-ion battery used in cell phones and other portable devices is the lightest and most powerful storage technology available. For a given amount of energy storage, the lithium-ion battery weighs one-fourth as much as today's lead-acid batteries and provides four to eight times the power. To put this in perspective, a 250-pound state-of-the-art lithium-ion battery would give a plug-in hybrid sedan a range of at least 50 miles without the use of gasoline backup power.

Unlike the lead-acid battery, lithium-ion batteries also have the potential for very long life. For example, the lithium-ion battery has demonstrated more than 3,000 deep-discharge cycles. In other words, the battery was drained of power and recharged to full capacity 3,000 times. This corresponds to the number of cycles a plug-in hybrid vehicle battery is expected to deliver over the vehicle's 10- to 15-year life. By comparison, a lead-acid battery can only survive about 10 percent as many discharge cycles.

Several battery producers are working closely with automakers to develop a mass production lithium-ion battery system for these advanced hybrid cars; this will thus engineer the biggest shift in car technology since the advent of the internal combustion engine. The cost-effective tipping point for the lithium-ion battery system is at about 100,000 battery packs annually. With roughly 16 million new cars sold in the United States every year, that tipping point should be easily reached by 2010 based just on General Motor's initial plug-in hybrid car production. An additional advantage is that the materials in these advanced batteries can be much more cost-effectively recycled with significantly less impact on the environment.

Is there really a market for the plug-in hybrid? In a 2001 study, the Electric Power Research Institute found that 30 to 50 percent of consumers surveyed would choose a plug-in hybrid even if it were priced up to 25 percent higher than a $19,000 conventionally powered car. What's more, 63 percent of respondents preferred the convenience of plugging in a car at home to going to the gas station. At the time of the survey, the U.S. national average price for gasoline was about $1.65 a gallon.

With today's five-dollar-gasoline and increased environmental consciousness, the market for these energy-efficient plug-in hybrids has certainly escalated even further. The market expectation is that the production of PHEVs will move into high gear by 2015 when the battery costs have been brought way down and the grid has the capability for two-way interconnection.

Portability was the "killer app" of the cell phone; therefore, it is not unreasonable to expect that portability of stored electricity could be a killer app for PHEVs. Indeed, plug-in hybrids are one more important smart microgrid opportunity that helps put consumers in control of their energy destiny.

COMPANIES AND INSTITUTIONS TO WATCH

A123 Systems (www.A123systems.com). Founded in 2001 and headquartered in Watertown, Massachusetts, A123 Systems develops and manufactures state-of-the-art lithium-ion batteries for a variety of applications including plug-in hybrid vehicles. Its high-power battery technology is based on nanoscale materials that are inexpensive, nontoxic, and extremely stable in electrochemical systems. A123 Systems' innovative manufacturing model operates a combination of facilities in China, Korea, Taiwan, and the United States.

AGM Batteries Ltd. (www.agmbatteries.com) is a joint-venture company, located in Scotland, manufacturing lithium-ion cells. Its joint-venture partners include AEA Technology, Japan Storage Battery Co., and Mitsubishi Materials Corp. In 2002, AEA Technology was awarded a multi-million-pound contract to supply batteries and chargers to the United Kingdom's new Bowman battlefield communication system based upon AGM's world-leading cell.

Andover Controls (www.andovercontrols.com) is now part of Schneider Electric, a world leader in automation and electricity management, and its subsidiary, TAC, a fast-growing building automation company using open, standards-based technology to integrate lighting, heating and cooling, access control, security monitoring, ventilation, and fire and smoke control. Schneider has 112,000 employees worldwide.

American Society of Heating, Refrigerating and Air-Conditioning Engineers (ASHRAE) (www.ashrae.org). Headquartered in Atlanta, Georgia, ASHRAE advances the arts and sciences of heating, ventilation, air conditioning and refrigeration to serve humanity and promote a sustainable world. Membership is open to any person associated with the field including indoor air quality, building design and operation, and environmental control for food processing and industry. Society committees include standards development, and advisories on technical matters and research needs.

Austin Energy (www.austinenergy.com) is the nation's 10th largest community-owned electric utility, serving 388,000 customers within the city of Austin, Texas, and surrounding counties. The utility has provided more than $1.5 billion profits to the community since 1976. The company generates its own power from coal, nuclear, natural gas, and renewable energy sources. Total generation capacity is just over 2,600 MW. The utility is a leader in energy efficiency, smart-grid development, and plug-in hybrid vehicles, and it claims to own the nation's first and largest green building program.

BYD Company Limited (BYDIT) (www.bydit.com), founded in 1995, is now listed on the Hong Kong exchange. The company has become the world's second largest producer of rechargeable batteries, including lithium-ion, nickel-cadmium, and nickel-metal-hybrid batteries. BYD's two major markets are IT components and automobiles. Its seven production facilities are located in China.

Center for Building Performance and Diagnostics (CBPD) (www.CBPD.edu) at the Carnegie Mellon University investigates the impact of advanced technology on the physical, environmental, and social settings in buildings. The center's goals include development of an innovative demonstration laboratory—the "Intelligent Work Place"—and evaluation of international developments in new, high-performance building design. It is the first technical center in the United States to focus on the building industry.

EnergyConnect Inc. (www.energyconnectinc.com). A wholly owned subsidiary of Microfield Group, Inc. EnergyConnect provides demand response technologies that enable and pay consumers to contribute to a smarter, more efficient and sustainable power grid. In so doing, it transforms energy consumers into active electricity market participants. the EnergyConnect web-based platform makes it east to trun many small decisions and transactions into major benefits for both consumers and utilities.

GAIA (www.gaia-akku-online.com)., located in Nordausen, Germany, is producing lithium-ion polymer systems, in which the liquid electrolyte has been replaced with a solid. The result is a flat, lightweight battery that is completely dry and can be flexibly shaped. Batteries as thin as four millimeters can be produced, with high energy density and output, making them ideal for high-volume markets, including autos.

General Motors (www.gm.com). General Motors was founded in 1908 and is headquartered in Detroit, Michigan. Until 2007 General Motors was the world's largest automaker and it remains the fifth largest company in the Fortune Global 500. General Motors manufactures cars and trucks in 35 countries and sells them under 12 brand names. General Motors employs some 280,000 people around the word and its 2007 revenues were $181 billion with total assets of $149 billion. It plans to introduce the Chevrolet Volt Plug-In hybrid vehicle in late 2010 as a 2011 model.

Honeywell Automation and Control Solutions (ACS) (www.honeywell.com), a part of Honeywell International, is a diversified technology and manufacturing company employing more than 100,000 people in 95 countries. ACS is an $11 billion strategic business group applying sensing and control expertise to diverse markets. ACS technology is at work in 100 million homes and 5 million buildings worldwide, as well as in transportation. The future will increasingly involve sensing devices connected and communicating wirelessly, increasing, amounts of data for processing.

J&F Labs (www.jandflabs.com) introduces the CORIS line of energy-saving plug-in modules. These devices plug into ordinary wall outlets (either 110 V or 220 V), turning power on or off to the device plugged into it. Users control groups of CORIS plug-in modules through a Web browser, establishing the desired schedules, temperatures, or price ranges for outlet operation.

Johnson Controls (www.johnsoncontrols.com) has expanded its traditional line of automotive products to include battery controls for hybrid electric vehicles, along with systems engineering and service expertise. It is the world's largest provider of lead-acid batteries. The company's PowerWatch technology is designed to communicate battery status to the vehicle and interacts with the vehicle to optimize battery performance, charging, and life. It is listed on the NYSE as JCI.

Lithium Technology Corp. (LTC) (www.lithiumtech.com). LTC designs, engineers, and builds a variety of lithium-battery energy storage systems for diverse industrial applications. In 1997 LTC began focusing on unique large-footprint stacked cell and circuit control systems. LTC has two principal centers of operations in Plymouth, Michigan and Nordhausen, Germany.

PJM Interconnection (www.pjm.com), headquartered in Valley Forge, Pennsylvania, is a federally regulated, regional transmission organization (RTO) that coordinates the movement of wholesale electricity in all or parts of Delaware, Illinois, Indiana, Kentucky, Maryland, Michigan, New Jersey, North Carolina, Ohio, Pennsylvania, Tennessee, Virginia, West Virginia, and the District of Columbia. Acting neutrally and independently, PJM operates the world's largest competitive wholesale electricity market and ensures the reliability of the largest centrally dispatched grid in the world. PJM's more than 450 members include power generators, transmission owners, electricity distributors, power marketers, and large consumers.

Power Cost Monitor (www.powercostmonitor.com) is a residential power meter monitoring device that tracks the energy consumed in the home. By attaching an optical pickup device on the electricity meter, it will transmit energy use back to the in-home display unit. The device is available for purchase on the Internet and can be installed by the homeowner.

Siemens Building Technology Division (SBTD) (www.building technologies.siemens.com). Headquartered in Switzerland, SBTD operates in 51 countries with manufacturing facilities in Europe, the United States, and Asia. SBTD offers an infrastructure technology portfolio designed for comfort and energy efficiency, security, and safety in buildings and public places. These capabilities are also expanding into the residential market through home automation systems.

Toyota Motor Corp. (www.toyota.co.jp/en) is headquartered in Japan and is currently the world's largest and most profitable automaker. Toyota is now the sixth largest company in the Fortune Global 500, and it has manufacturing or assembly plants in 23 countries, employing some 300,000 people. Toyota was founded in 1937, and its management philosophy is reflected in the terms *lean manufacturing* and *just-in-time production*. Toyota has also been the world leader in hybrid electric vehicle sales.

UQM Technologies (www.uqm.com) is a developer of energy-efficient, power-dense electric motors, generators, and power electronic controllers. A major emphasis is developing power systems for the emerging field of battery electric, hybrid electric, and fuel-cell vehicles. Located in Frederick, Colorado, the company showed sales of $6.7 million in 2007. It is listed on the American Stock Exchange as UQM.

U.S. Green Building Council (USGBC) (www.usgbc.org). The USGBC is a nonprofit organization committed to expanding sustainable building practices. Its 12,000 members include building owners, real estate developers, facility designers and managers, and government agencies. The USGBC's open, consensus-based LEED Green Building Rating System encourages and accelerates global adoption of sustainable green building practices. LEED projects are in progress in 41 countries including Canada, Brazil, Mexico, and India, in addition to the United States.

Viconics Inc. (www.viconics.com). Headquartered in Montreal, Viconics has been developing micro-controller-based HVAC temperature control solutions since the early 1990s. Viconics Inc. has developed a line of preprogrammed, communicating thermostats designed to control packaged heating and cooling equipment such as fan coils, rooftop units, and heat pumps, in addition to other modulating zoning equipment.

Watt Stopper/Legrand (www.wattstopper.com). Watt Stopper/Legrand manufactures energy-efficient lighting controls that are designed to put a stop to energy waste. They have a best-fit lighting control solution for commercial, institutional, industrial, and residential applications. Their comprehensive product offering of code-compliant lighting controls include occupancy and vacancy sensors, daylighting controls, panels, fixture controls, and Miro® wireless RF lighting controls.

Yamatake (www.yamatakeusa.com), established in 1906, is a leading manufacturer in the field of measuring and control technology for building and industrial automation. The product line of Yamatake Sensing and Control Ltd includes photoelectric sensors, proximity sensors, laser sensors, and fiber optic cables, as well as a complete line of process and power controls.

7

Rewiring Siegel Hall for Perfect Power

The Illinois Institute of Technology's smart-microgrid demonstration project in Chicago is one of the first applications of the principles behind the Galvin Electricity Initiative. This new system will ultimately feed Perfect Power to Siegel Hall, which is the epicenter of a larger system for all of IIT and ultimately the entire city of Chicago. It also establishes a replicable "cutting-edge" capability to enhance the efficiency and dependability of the nation's electricity grid, and to ensure an affordable and ultrareliable supply of electricity to all Americans in the 21st century.

W hat better place to test the merits of Perfect Power than a leading engineering school on a blackout-vulnerable campus? Nestled within the leafy Bronzeville neighborhood on Chicago's South Side, just minutes from downtown, is the 120-acre main campus of the Illinois Institute of Technology. Founded in 1890 with a million-dollar gift from Philip Armour, Sr., and originally named after the illustrious meat packer, the school's development parallels that of the American electrical system. After all, it was in 1892 when Samuel Insull left the fledgling General Electric Corp., took over as president of Chicago Edison (the local electric utility), and began to transform this very city, region, and the entire power industry with electric interurban streetcar lines, railways, a host of utility services, and a firm that evolved into today's Commonwealth Edison. Insull's companies employed Armour Institute graduates in disciplines that ranged from engineering to architecture, and business.

The Illinois Institute of Technology (ITT) is a private Ph.D.-granting university, with a multinational enrollment of some 6,000 students from more than 90 countries. The students can choose from 24 majors in five distinct academic divisions. More than 70 percent of the undergraduates live on campus, most in buildings that are today the signature of the Institute.

From 1938 until 1959, the fabled German architect Ludwig Mies van der Rohe headed IIT's architecture department and practiced his craft on campus, creating buildings of austere and minimalist designs. But because the buildings and its architecture are considered historic, they can't be significantly changed. Consequently, the overall look of IIT is fixed in the 1940s. The university's electrical infrastructure is of a similar era. For instance, the wires connecting the institute's buildings are buried underground, which once put the school way ahead of its time. Most of them, however, are made of lead insulated with a wrapping of paper. Two on-campus substations reduce the voltage and distribute the power supplied by Commonwealth Edison. However, the on-campus south substation was built about 60 years ago and hasn't been upgraded since; its north substation counterpart was renovated in 2001, but with obsolete electromechanical relay switches that cannot interact with intelligent, automated controls.

Indeed, the IIT campus is long overdue for a comprehensive infrastructure renovation. But like any renovation, replacing ancient electricity wiring, plumbing, leaking windows, and installing insulation is a serious challenge. This upgrade must be cost-effective without literally dismantling the structure. In the case of the IIT campus, the smart-microgrid architecture actually saves considerable money relative to the more conventional renovation approach and retains the physical status quo.

This opportunity is underscored by the fact that the school is hit by an average of three campuswide blackouts per year. Some of the problems rest with Commonwealth Edison's infrastructure issues, and the severe climate conditions that descend upon the Midwest. Other campuswide failures are an internal matter, since the school isn't wired to isolate single points of a problem. A tripped switch or blown wire that should conceivably black out only a few buildings can roll darkness through dozens, including Siegel Hall, the headquarters for ITT's Electrical and Computer Engineering Department, which is by far the largest department at the institute and one of its most prestigious.

In this peculiar circumstance, Department Chair and Bodine Professor Mohammad Shahidehpour—one of the world's leading experts on large-scale power systems and their optimization—recognizes that using the school as a Galvin Electricity Initiative prototype microgrid project is a teaching opportunity of a lifetime. The campus will essentially be rewired to create a Perfect Power microgrid with smart control switches, high-quality controls, and distributed backup power that automatically respond to power interruptions. "The project is an incredibly unique opportunity for IIT students to learn from and even help revolutionize the way we use power in the United States," he observes, "and an electrical system that's in dire need of transformation." Moreover, the school's internal politics and pressures of where, when, and how to best spend money makes the proposition a trial run for much larger, real-world interactions.

KEEPING THE LIGHT ON HIGHER EDUCATION

Stopping outages at the school will save hundreds of thousands of dollars at a time. John Kelly, the vice president of technology solutions for an Oakbrook Terrace, Illinois, firm Endurant Energy, that helps clients develop reliable and less-expensive energy systems, is working on the IIT Perfect Power demonstration project. He figures that a two-hour blackout costs the university $100,000 to $250,000. That's the cost of sending maintenance staffers out to manually restore power to buildings, lost faculty and staff productivity, damaged equipment, and the compromise and even total loss of critical academic experiments. And there also are hidden costs to power outages, from spoiled food to lost sales in cafeterias, reduced motor life from disrupted equipment, and even injuries during such events.

Working with Commonwealth Edison, the Juran Center for Leadership in Quality, Endurant Energy, and the S&C Electric Company, a venerable Chicago firm that for more than a century has manufactured electric power switching and protection equipment, the school intends to install intelligent switches into all of its buildings over a five-year period. In phases, it will also install fast-start turbines to provide automatic backup power to keep the school running should the feed from Commonwealth Edison's larger, off-campus Fisk substation go down.

The basics of this smart-microgrid project do not exactly involve rocket science (except for the intelligent controller capability, which provides a distributed "living" system for monitoring weather, real-time prices, and system conditions, learning and then reconfiguring the system for optimal performance). And in truth, IIT is not the first place in which a similar approach to routing power in a way that promotes reliability has been installed. The University of California's Santa Barbara campus replaced its dicey electrical system with a modular infrastructure and automated controls early in this decade. So too did a high-tech industrial park in Danville, Virginia. What's different at IIT is the application of quality principles and the ultimate quest for Perfect Power. It's also the beginning of a changing relationship with a regulated utility that could clearly benefit from the support of semi-independent microgrids within its overall system, the likes of which IIT intends to become.

At the moment, ComEd's Fisk substation feeds all of IIT's electricity through three separate circuits. The campus distribution system includes multiple building feeder cables, building transformers, and transformer supply breakers. Most of the school's buildings have some redundancy in supply feeds, but many have none. What's more, all of the switches on campus are manual, which means that when the power goes out, someone has to find the problem and manually restore power. Indeed, this is all too typical of today's power supply systems.

Oddly enough, IIT has an 8 megawatt cogeneration plant on campus. Built at a cost of $11 million, it was meant to generate hot water, steam, and electricity that would go a long way toward energy self-sufficiency for the university, while easing the peak neighborhood loads for Commonwealth Edison, which for a time struggled to bring enough power to light the night games of the Chicago White Sox. Alas, when ComEd negotiated a very favorable power contract with the school the cogeneration plant was no longer cost-effective without Perfect Power modifications. "About the only thing it does now," says Professor Shahidehpour, "is produce hot water. And besides it has never had demand-response control capabilities, which would have enabled it to reinforce the utility's system during peak demands for power."

The first Perfect Power pilot building at IIT will be the one that houses Shahidehpour's office and the Electrical Engineering Department, the Mies-designed Siegel Hall, which was completed in 1957. Supplied by two feeds from the north substation, the building has a transformer that steps down the power to 240 volts, which is then distributed through two panels on each of the structure's three floors. The electricity powers lights, computers, fans, and several rooftop and window air conditioners. Siegel Hall will be one of the first buildings to get automated switches and will, eventually, have direct current circuits, electricity storage, and solar panels on its roof. The ultimate Perfect Power design for Siegel Hall is shown in Figure 7–1. For the interim, it will be made "solar ready."

The IIT Perfect Power Microgrid will also help the campus meet its sustainability goals by reducing CO_2 emissions some 4,000 tons per year. If other schools, hospitals and communities across the State of Illinois follow the IIT lead in implementing Perfect Power microgrids they could provide at least 10,000 MW

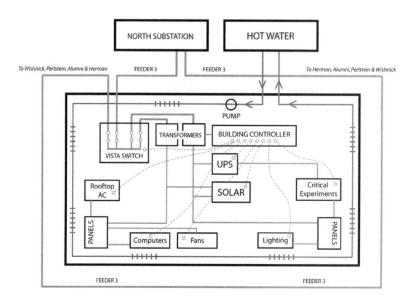

Figure 7–1 Perfect Power Design for Siegel Hall at the Illinois Institute of Technology

of clean, local generating capacity and reduce CO_2 emissions by more than four million tons per year while saving the citizens of Illinois considerable money in the process. A complementary first step is the ecofriendly "Smart Home: Green+Wired" demonstration house sponsored by the Chicago Museum of Science and Industry. This 2,500-square-foot house, built in 2008, incorporates the latest in smart energy efficiency and saves $1,250 a year in energy costs relative to a typical Chicago house of similar size.

INTELLIGENT SWITCHING

The most ingenious element to providing reliable power for the entire campus is the routing of its feeds, a scheme that's been drawn out by IIT graduate, Brianna Swenson who until recently was an S&C design engineer. A Minnesota native who attended the school on a varsity swimming scholarship, Swenson earned her undergraduate degree in electrical engineering in 2004 and a master's the following year. Swenson lives and breathes power systems. "More people," she states emphatically, "ought to know about electricity and what it means to their quality of life."

In any event, the manual switches and breakers in Siegel Hall and then the rest of the school's buildings will be replaced by an S&C switch and breaker system called *Vista*, which can respond to computerized signals and shift power at signs of trouble without interrupting power to users. And to make the total microgrid system more reliable, most buildings will receive power from a power loop, which will automatically isolate faults and reroute power flows to reach their destination from either direction. Previously, the electricity had to be restored manually and only a limited number of buildings had a redundant feed. The redundancy and automation is what creates a "high reliability distribution" concept, as pictured in Figure 7–2.

"Any time you had an isolated problem it would take out everything down the line," says Swenson. "With the feeder loop the problem is instantly isolated and everything keeps running." Eventually, the power from the ComEd grid will be supplemented—and backed up—by fast-start diesel-fired generators, natural gas–fired generators, solar power, and batteries

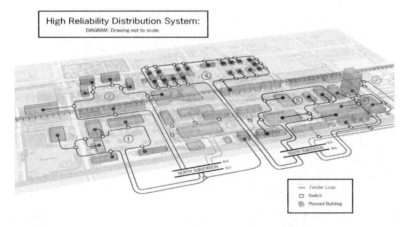

Figure 7–2   Perfect Power at the Illinois Institute of Technology

(which is also known as an *uninterruptible power supply*). The batteries can instantaneously carry critical buildings for several minutes, or until the generators can ramp up to carry the entire campus load. It is this distributed power capability that enables the IIT campus to operate as a self-sufficient microgrid whenever required to do so.

If Professor Shahidehpour is the promoter of Perfect Power on campus, Joe Buri, former facilities vice president, has been the person responsible for getting it built. With all campus buildings as well as its energy infrastructure under his purview, Buri has a practical view of the smart-microgrid project and is just as enthusiastic about its benefits. He saw the realities of new campus buildings and the renegotiation of the university's bulk power contract as opportunities to begin the migration to Perfect Power. "We are building two new residence halls by 2010 and we will build and power them the right way to help meet our campus sustainability goals," said Buri. "Also by integrating dynamic, time-of-use pricing into our contract with Constellation New-Energy, we will save a lot of money in the process."

Fortunately IIT is in a utility region that offers the option of buying electricity in real time. Instead of paying a premium to the utility or a third-party electricity provider to supply fixed-price electricity, IIT can leverage the Perfect Power system to enter the real-time electricity markets. Moreover, by avoiding peak power prices, which frequently exceed 25 cents per kilowatt hour, the Perfect Power system can cap the school's electricity costs at 8 to 10 cents per kilowatt hour. When the work is completed and the intelligent management system is installed, IIT will be its own smart microgrid, capable of producing its power when overall system demand upon ComEd is high or electricity supply is short, which also significantly raises the price of electricity.

With that new-found electricity price response capability, IIT can precisely follow those peak times when the price of

ComEd's power exceeds the cost of generating it on campus, which is currently estimated at 1,000 to 1,500 hours per year. Had IIT been able to use such a system in 2005 and 2006, it would have saved approximately $1 million a year on the costs of its electricity. The estimated cost of the total Perfect Power system is $12.8 million. However, IIT won't have to build a new east campus substation, which would have cost $5 million, and it already would have been forced to spend $2 million just to upgrade basic equipment. The remaining $5 million investment will be paid back by those annual $1 million savings from eliminating peak power purchases, annual outage cost savings of at least $500,000, and then $1 million a year or more in additional research funding made possible by Siegel Hall's Perfect Power supply. It is worth noting that each million dollars of this energy cost savings is equivalent to a $20 million endowment check written to IIT.

The IIT Perfect Power prototype microgrid design has also been awarded a $7 million Department of Energy grid modernization investment. This highly competitive DOE award was made in recognition of the IIT Perfect Power design's replicable "cutting-edge" capability to enhance the efficiency and dependability of the nation's electricity grid and to ensure an affordable and ultrareliable supply of electricity for all Americans.

Commonwealth Edison and its parent company, Exelon — one of the nation's largest utilities, which generates and delivers electricity to more than five million customers in Illinois and Pennsylvania — and its CEO, John Rowe, have been instrumental in making this prototype smart-microgrid project possible, and are also watching its progress with considerable self-interest. In a perfect world, ComEd would have an additional substation supplying IIT. However, building a new substation and distribution equipment would cost the utility an estimated $8 million. The university's eventual Perfect Power microgrid system will obviate the need for that investment.

ENHANCING THE UTILITY'S UTILITY

As at IIT, ComEd's investment decisions are practical and directed, and dabbling in alternative energy projects simply isn't part of the culture, nor is it allowed by regulators. After several major power failures in the late 1990s that affected downtown Chicago, regulators brought the hammer down on Commonwealth Edison. Letting suburbs go dark is one thing; trapping executives in elevators will get you in deep trouble with one of the world's best-known mayors — Richard M. Daley of Chicago. Consequently, keeping the lights on in Chicago's Loop is the priority. And that's not always easy in an area where an aging infrastructure strained by thunderstorms, ice storms, bitter cold, or sweltering heat can wreck havoc on the community. Observe is what the utility primarily does in the areas of technology, says James Crane, Exelon's Energy Delivery Group's research and development manager. "The truth is that I'm a department of one, although I have relationships with companies large and small, the government agencies and research institutes that are looking into all of these areas. It's just that we're very limited in terms of available people and what we can and can't do."

"We're really good at crisis management," adds Crane. "If we get 100-mile-per-hour winds and have 750,000 customers out of power, we can mobilize and get most customers reconnected quite quickly. But we don't have the people nor can we afford to invest in new technologies. I work with lots of universities, government agencies, and research groups, and we're interested in what's developed. But if you look at power in New York, which sells for 22 cents per kilowatt hour, and here where it's just 10.5 cents per hour, we're one of the least expensive suppliers. We also have regulators on site and in our offices every day, and thus have very little flexibility to develop automated distribution systems."

ComEd also faces a talent shortage. Reorganizations, severance packages, the natural attrition of Baby Boomer retirements and a dearth of electrical engineering students focusing on the electric power supply system is building into a perfect storm of a personnel shortage. A test bed at a place such as IIT, where the conventional electricity infrastructure can link to a system of the future, can prove that smart microgrids are capable of taking pressure off utilities during peak periods of power demand. As a result, less money will be invested in assets that provide power only a small percentage of the time.

IIT's campus smart microgrid will bring its electrical system into this century, and Professor Shahidehpour hopes the demonstration project will inspire more electrical engineering students to embrace careers in power technology and management. In turn, Commonwealth Edison might find that IIT is an ideal place from which to recruit its next generation of talent. It's a resource loop that could begin to serve Chicago again as well as it did in the 1890s—a small step from the utility's perspective, but a giant leap forward for its customers.

As a result, the IIT Perfect Power microgrid project has inspired a much broader consumer-focused initiative to create a smart, 21st-century electricity grid throughout Illinois and open the state's retail electricity market to entrepreneurial competition benefiting all citizens. To this end, the Illinois Collaborative on Electric Grid Modernization has been established by the Chicago-based Center for Neighborhood Technology and the Galvin Electricity Initiative to complete a comprehensive statewide stakeholder educational and smart grid policy development process in 2008.

Key supporters and honorary chairs of this initiative are Chicago's Mayor Daley, a tireless advocate of innovation to achieve a more efficient and environmentally sustainable city and state, and Dennis Hastert, former Republican Speaker of the U.S. House of Representatives. Other active supporters include the Building Owners and Managers Association of Chicago, the Midwest branch of the Natural Resources Defense Council (NRDC), the Illinois Citizens Utility Board for consumers, and legislators on both sides of the political aisle in the Illinois General Assembly.

UNIVERSITIES AS SMART
ELECTRICITY EDUCATORS

The leadership value of transforming university campuses into smart microgrids that demonstrate the value of Perfect Power service to the broader community is spreading across the country. Harvard University, for example, has been operating its own internal, interconnected energy supply system for 80 years. This system supplies 50 megawatts of peak electricity supply to some 70 university buildings. Consistent with this extensive energy service experience, and the state of Massachusetts' goal to build as little additional centralized electricity supply capacity as possible, Harvard's new 340-acre Allston Science Complex development is designed to be at the cutting edge of clean, smart-microgrid implementation.

Harvard's Energy Model for the Future and Green Campus Initiative requires a 50 percent campuswide greenhouse gas emission reduction. In order to meet this requirement, the campus will be served by a set of interconnected, smart, combined heat and power microgrids comprehensively providing each building with electricity, processed steam, chilled water, heating, cooling, and ventilation. In addition, each new building must, at a minimum, meet the LEED (leadership in energy and environmental design) gold performance standard. This smart-microgrid energy network will also use on-campus power generation to supplement the bulk utility power supply. This capability will enable Harvard to optimally meet its energy load requirements with absolute reliability while taking advantage of time-of-use bulk electricity pricing. The campus smart-microgrid network is being designed to readily assimilate continuous improvements in technology on an open-access, plug-and-play basis, including the use of geothermal energy.

This innovative Perfect Power commitment is being made because it provides the lowest-cost strategic energy solution for the Harvard University community. However, in contrast to IIT, Harvard does not yet enjoy the active encouragement and support of its electric utility supplier in navigating the path to Perfect Power. Fortunately, the state of Massachusetts has stepped in to help the university and others overcome this constraint to progress.

State legislation now requires each electricity distribution utility to establish a "smart grid" program using the electricity distribution system initially augmented with advanced smart meters and time-of-use pricing. The objective is to reduce electricity usage by at least 5 percent for each customer who participates in the program. Harvard will certainly be at the head of the list. Massachusetts Governor Deval Patrick has further reinforced the importance of educating the grid in order to achieve his goal of an "energy neutral" development environment in the state.

INSTITUTIONS AND COMPANIES TO WATCH

Building Owners & Managers Association (BOMA) of Chicago (www.boma-chicago.org), founded in 1903, represents the interests of the office industry in Chicago, including owner/operators of 270 private, institutional, and government buildings, and 150 companies that provide services to commercial office buildings. The 8,000 companies of BOMA/Chicago represent 81 percent of the rentable building space in the downtown Chicago area.

Center for Neighborhood Technology (CNT) (www.cnt.org). Since 1978, the nonprofit Chicago-based CNT has worked to show urban communities locally and all across the country how to develop more sustainability. With smarts, creativity, and innovation, and before the term "sustainable development" was even widely used, CNT has been demonstrating its unique brand of sustainable development: development that is good for the economy and the environment; that makes better use of existing resources and community assets; and that improves the health of natural systems and the wealth of people—today and in the future.

Commonwealth Edison Co. (ComEd) (www.exeloncorp.com). ComEd is the retail electric utility serving 3.6 million customers in Chicago and northern Illinois. It maintains 78,000 miles of power lines as part of this service responsibility. ComEd is a subsidiary of the Exelon Corporation, the largest U.S. utility holding company. ComEd's annual revenues, from sales of over 71 million megawatt hours of electricity, total some six billion dollars.

Constellation NewEnergy (www.newenergy.com) was founded in 1995 as NewEnergy Ventures at the advent of open markets for electricity. It was purchased in 1999 by AES, and then in 2002 by the Constellation Energy Group headquartered in Baltimore, Maryland. It was merged with Constellation's gas supply and transportation business in 2004. Today, the company is the leading supplier of competitive energy to North America's businesses. It has annual revenues of $8 billion, and meets peak load of more than 15,000 MW.

Endurant Energy LLC (www.endurantenergy.com). Headquartered in Oakbrook Terrace outside Chicago, Endurant is a leader in the emerging clean energy industry. It plans and implements innovative and alternative energy solutions, and develops and owns new distributed energy assets for commercial office buildings. Endurant currently manages a portfolio of sustainable power generation assets in Illinois, New York, and California.

Harvard University (www.harvard.edu). Founded in 1636, Harvard is the oldest institution of higher learning in the United States. The university grew from 9 students with a single master to an enrollment today of more than 18,000 degree candidates in 10 principal academic units. The faculty includes 2,000 positions on the campus, plus 7,000 faculty appointments in affiliated teaching hospitals. The university has produced 7 U.S. presidents and more than 40 Nobel laureates. Harvard's endowment is valued at close to $30 billion.

Illinois Citizen's Utility Board (CUB) (www.citizensutility board.org) was created in 1983 by the Illinois General Assembly as a nonprofit, nonpartisan organization to represent the interests of residential utility customers in the state of Illinois. The statute directs CUB to intervene in the rate-making proceedings before the Illinois Commerce Commission (ICC) and in the courts and before other public bodies. CUB claims to have saved Illinois consumers more than $10 billion.

Illinois Institute of Technology (IIT) (www.iit.edu) opened in 1893 as the Armour Institute, offering professional courses in engineering, chemistry, architecture, and library science for students of all backgrounds. IIT was created in 1940 by the merger of the technical Armour Institute and the liberal arts program of the Lewis Institute. A law school and business school were added in 1969. Today, IIT is a private, Ph.D.-granting institution with four campuses in the Chicago area. The main, 120-acre campus was designed by Ludwig Mies van der Rohe, one of the 20th century's most influential architects.

Juran Center for Leadership in Management (http://carlson school.umn.edu). The Juran Center is part of the University of Minnesota's Carlson School of Management. The center emerged from Dr. Joseph M. Juran's vision for a century of quality. Its mission is to discover and disseminate knowledge to help leaders develop a permanent quality advantage and contribute to the health, welfare, and prosperity of all people. The Juran Center has been a leader in developing and disseminating quality leadership and management principles such as Six Sigma.

Natural Resources Defense Council (NRDC) (www.nrdc.org), founded in 1970, NRDC has become one of the nation's most effective environmental action organizations, with 1.2 million members. It is currently focused on a number of global issues, including climate change, oil dependence, nuclear weaponry, energy efficiency, health and pollution, biodiversity, disappearing wildlands, and ocean sustainability.

S&C Electric Company (www.sandc.com). S&C Electric is a global provider of equipment and services for electric power systems. Founded in 1911, the Chicago-based company designs and manufactures switching and protection products for electric power transmission and distribution. In addition, S&C offers a wide range of engineering, laboratory, and testing services for electric utilities and commercial power systems.

8

The Blank Canvas
of Mesa del Sol

*The futuristic new community of Mesa del Sol in Albuquerque,
New Mexico, is a bright beacon for Perfect Power. Mesa del Sol
will provide a near perfect opportunity to apply uncompromised
principles of quality to smart microgrids as the basis for achieving
a sustainable energy future. To build this ambitious 37,000-home,
12,900-acre new planned city, the developer, the utility, the city,
and the state are united in convincing the New Mexico regulators
to enable a Perfect Power mecca serving the best interests of
every citizen in the state.*

Wedged between Interstate 25 and Kirtland Air Force
Base, with New Mexico's dusty-hued Sandia Moun-
tains to the northeast and the city of Albuquerque due
north, is an expanse of more than 12,900 largely empty acres.
It's a sparsely vegetated mesa of dirt, rock, and sand, but Mesa
del Sol is splendidly located, especially for a visionary energy
project. It rests but a few minutes drive from the city's uptown
and downtown, the University of New Mexico, the Albuquerque
International Sunport—which is what locals call the main civilian airport around here—and Sandia, one of the nation's major
national energy laboratories. Los Alamos, another national
energy lab and the birthplace of the atomic bomb, is only two
hours drive away. In addition to nuclear power, both of these
Department of Energy institutions are leaders in smart grid and

renewable energy technology developments. The Santa Fe Institute, a think tank of global proportions, is also nearby. Of the 750,000 people living in this metropolitan region, there's clearly a demographically disproportionate concentration of Ph.D.s, thought leaders, and energy technology developers. Capping this leadership concentration are New Mexico's two U.S. senators who are the Senate energy leaders for the Democratic and Republican parties, respectively.

As state and local officials like to boast, New Mexico is also blessed with 308 days of annual sunshine. With a high desert climate that offers four distinct seasons, Albuquerque is neither as hot as Phoenix nor as cold as Denver. In recorded history, the area has been unscathed by earthquakes, tornadoes, hurricanes, floods, and fires, yet another set of civic bragging rights.

This last large, truly empty and available piece of the Albuquerque real estate pie is slated to be developed into one of the largest, master-planned communities in the United States. Held in trust by the state for the University of New Mexico, Mesa del Sol is within Albuquerque's city limits. Forest City Covington LLC, a partnership of Forest City Enterprises, a $10 billion publicly traded company headquartered in Cleveland, Ohio, which has been developing properties since 1921, and Covington Capital are developing Mesa del Sol as the ultimate "sustainable" community.

According to Albert Ratner, cochairman of the Board of Forest City Enterprises, and Barry Lang, principal of Covington Capital, the project was "conceived as an antidote to the urban dysfunctions of longer commutes, sprawl, and the increasing hassles of everyday life in large cities." The first goal is maximum efficiency in the use of natural resources, including both water and energy. A second goal is to attract the smart, cutting-edge businesses and leaders who will create a 21st-century economy in these communities. Consistent with these goals, Albert Ratner has invited Bob Galvin to apply his Perfect Power and urban congestion control principles to Mesa del Sol.

New Mexico's state-wide quality initiative actually began in 1992 when Senators Bingaman and Domenici and then

Governor Bruce King vowed to make New Mexico a "Quality State," as inspired by the Malcolm Baldridge National Quality Award won by Motorola in 1988. The goal is to make all of New Mexico "Committed to a State of Excellence." As part of this commitment the city of Albuquerque is focused on being a national urban leader for sustainable community development. It requires that all new buildings in the city be carbon-neutral, to eliminate any increase in CO_2 emissions.

The development goals for Mesa del Sol are therefore keenly supported by Albuquerque Mayor Martin Chavez and the environmentally minded New Mexico Governor Bill Richardson, the former U.S. Secretary of Energy. Mesa del Sol provides an ideal blank canvas for comprehensively achieving the Galvin Electricity Initiative's goal of Perfect Power and for transforming the outmoded designs, policies, and regulations that, unknown to many conservationists, severely limit the development of truly sustainable communities. There are no legacy infrastructures or outmoded technologies to impede the path to perfection. In short, Mesa del Sol represents an unprecedented and unique opportunity to provide a comprehensive, sustainable urban development template for the future. Such a template is critically important given the fact that globally, cities consume 75 percent of the world's energy and produce 80 percent of its greenhouse gas emissions.

The land itself is still fairly open, save for a manufacturing plant that was built by Advent Solar, which develops photovoltaic technologies and manufactures solar cells and panels, and the Albuquerque Studios, which boasts several of the largest sound stages in the world and is a state-of-the-art film production facility. Despite the still mostly empty space, there's a surfeit of detailed maps, artistic renderings, and schematics for an urban center, a town center, village centers, and plots for homes, parks, and schools. See www.mesadelsolnm.com.

With an ultimate goal of 100,000 residents, 37,500 homes, 18 million square feet of commercial space, and jobs for about 50,000 people, Mesa del Sol is an ambitious and long-range project. It is moving forward aggressively with new home construction beginning this year in spite of the recent subprime real estate mortgage crisis. In addition to Advent Solar and Albuquerque Studios, more than 2,750 jobs have been brought to Mesa del Sol by Schott AG, a leader in glass, optics, and solar technology, and Fidelity Investments, a leader in financial services. Public Service Company of New Mexico, or PNM, the local utility, is also collaborating to make Mesa del Sol a living laboratory for the development of a community-scale Perfect Power microgrid system.

PNM is one of the nation's more progressive utilities, applying Six Sigma quality principles to all new distribution system designs. This exceptional utility quality commitment is a result of PNM's earlier efforts to successfully resolve persisting power quality issues plaguing one of Honeywell's most important computer chip manufacturing facilities located in New Mexico. The Six Sigma quality process identified a cost-effective solution that lowered costs while dramatically improving power system performance. PNM also allows its customers to interconnect customer-owned distributed power generation systems to the PNM distribution system.

The Mesa del Sol build-out will continue over the next 30 years but the path to Perfect Power starts this year and is intended to meet the needs of its first industrial tenants and residential tracts. Indeed, Mike Daly, the president of Forest City Covington, and the business leader responsible for the Mesa del Sol development, has reiterated the importance of Perfect Power to the development's success. "As I continue to evaluate the needs of the tenants and homeowners that we are seeking to attract to Mesa del Sol, our competitive edge depends on providing top-quality energy services." Prior to coming here, Daly worked for Forest City Enterprises on developing assisted-living facilities in New York and New Jersey, and commercial buildings in New York City for Forest City Ratner. "I was proud of that work and gratified, but when I looked at what we could do here in building a sustainable community that was affordable, had a great school system, and incorporated all of the quality of life and environmental benefits, I realized that this could be the company's best project ever."

The resulting Perfect Power system goals Daly has established include: digital quality electricity service throughout; an energy system that produces minimal carbon emissions; the ability to proactively mitigate higher-peak power prices; and the placement of all electrical infrastructure underground to enhance reliability while eliminating esthetic penalties. A complementary dimension of Mike Daly's leadership is his commitment to ultimately include a large (100 MW) solar thermal power generator in the Mesa del Sol development that will serve greater Albuquerque. But this clean energy system can only be sustainable with the appropriate regulatory and market incentives in place.

ELECTRICAL HEALING

Meeting these priorities will make Mesa del Sol the embodiment of Perfect Power. It will be able to monitor the precise amount of electricity that's needed by Mesa del Sol at any point in time. Its Perfect Power system design concept was developed by Endurant Energy in conjunction with PNM, the Electric Power Research Institute, Forest City Covington, and a number of builders using the latest technology. The goal is to use the automated Vista switches made by S&C Electric so that any distribution faults can be isolated and automatically served by rerouted power, eliminating the need for manual fixes.

With energy efficiency and solar power built into homes and offices, and distributed power generators plus battery power storage as a backup, this smart-microgrid design can not only provide stable voltage, but enable Mesa del Sol to shave its demand for power by about 15 percent during peak periods. In addition to the cost savings to residents, this would eliminate the need for Public Service of New Mexico to build an outer transmission loop for Mesa del Sol and reduce the need for required substations from seven to four, along with the commensurate infrastructure connecting those facilities. It also reduces PNM's current need for over 200 megawatts of additional generating capacity to meet peak demand growth in the Albuquerque metropolitan area and to maintain an adequate power reserve margin.

In fact, just eliminating the three substations, 12 circuits, 80 switches, and 600 transformers would save PNM—and ultimately its customers—more than $30 million. The savings on the outer transmission loop alone would be about $10 million. And while some of the energy efficiency investments have up-front costs, the funding could be incorporated into an on-bill financing program over 10 to 20 years independent of any ownership changes. This financing would be more than paid back by the savings on electricity.

Alas, although PNM supports the project, the utility also believes that New Mexico's current electricity regulations would require them to construct the more expensive conventional capacity anyway. That's because current regulatory rules deny PNM and Forest City Covington a share of the economic savings that such energy efficiencies and renewable power sources woven into a microgrid will provide. Lacking such an iron-clad guarantee, PNM would not be able to recover the microgrid implementation costs through electricity rates, even though the result would be much less expensive to the state's citizens. This unfortunate limitation is exacerbated by the fact that New Mexico has also yet to offer consumers time-of-use electricity pricing that would spur investment in Perfect Power features that reduce peak power demand. As a result, PNM lacks the incentive to implement a demand response program, including the system-wide installation of smart meters.

The first chicken has just met the first egg.

The conundrum is not beyond solution, but it is a prime example of the counterproductive, "way we have always done it" regulations and laws that have thwarted the development of smart microgrids. Both utilities and regulators are creatures of habit, especially when it comes to the incredibly arcane world of "rate cases." This is the process of establishing what the utilities can charge for a kilowatt hour of electricity based on how much they've invested to guarantee power to all existing and potential future consumers in their service area, albeit without regard to modern standards of efficiency or quality. No matter what state engages in these occasional cases, it's invariably a contentious affair involving attorneys, consumer activists, and enough bureaucratic documentation to fill Madison Square Garden—little of which actually gets read by the regulators.

There is, however, a hopeful breaking point with this formidable tradition, and it's the increasing demand for environmentally neutral energy. As states require utilities to increase the percentage of electricity that comes from wind, solar, and other alternative sources, and in turn, lower the volume of carbon dioxide produced from fossil fuels, the barriers to more efficient and reliable smart grids start to crack. Recognizing the fundamental importance of smart microgrids in both improving energy efficiency and in more rapidly facilitating the use of clean, renewable energy, PNM, Mesa del Sol, and the Galvin Electricity Initiative are collaborating to put the facts and benefits of Perfect Power before the New Mexico Public Regulation Commission (PRC). In addition to the traditional utility rate case process, these facts and benefits can also be presented in response to the PRC's new Integrated Resource Planning (IRP) docket.

The IRP docket now requires utilities to analyze the cost impact of CO_2 emissions at costs ranging from \$8 to \$40 per metric ton of emissions. Following the passage of this new requirement, PRC Commissioner Jason Marks stated that "these new resource planning rules, including the new carbon costs, give the PRC a powerful tool to divert future development away from the coal-fired electricity generation plants that are huge sources of greenhouse gas emissions." The IRP docket thus provides an important opportunity to change the regulatory policies that now impede Perfect Power implementation at Mesa del Sol and elsewhere in New Mexico. Another way to look at the IRP process is that for the first time it provides a forum enabling both utilities and entrepreneurial electricity providers to respond to the same price signals and incentives. In order to attract investment to clean alternative energy sources such as efficiency and renewable energy, the PRC must ensure confidence in full cost recovery plus a fair return on investment. In effect, this is the same business deal they now offer utilities for coal-fired power generation.

Meanwhile, the plans surrounding Mesa del Sol involve huge energy efficiencies no matter how the system is ultimately configured. Because of its commitment to achieving a sustainable community, PNM intends to include smart meters and demand response as part of this advanced technology package. What's more, Mesa del Sol's sustainability master plan specifically calls for a large number of parks and open spaces; paths for walking and cycling between homes and employment centers; alternative clean energy; and advanced grid management. Housing units will range from 900 square feet to 1,000 square feet, with costs ranging from about $160,000 to some $700,000—an eclectic range that would house a diverse community.

IN A LAND WITH A CRITICAL MASS OF BRAINPOWER

As noted in the Mesa del Sol plan for its Perfect Power microgrid development, Mesa del Sol provides a sublime place in which to concentrate knowledge from the Sandia and Los Alamos labs, the Electric Power Research Institute, as well as academics from the University of New Mexico and the Gas Technology Institute. Using this knowledge base, each development phase will be able to confidently deploy the latest in innovative equipment. In keeping with this leadership commitment, Mesa del Sol will also require builders to achieve at least a 15 percent improvement over the latest International Building Code efficiency standards. The first 250 homes built in Mesa del Sol, set to complete construction in 2009, will therefore contain the most efficient lighting available, high-performance windows, ultraefficient heating and cooling systems, and Energy Star appliances. Moreover, houses and offices here will also be "solar-ready." That is, each will have a solar photovoltaic breaker, electrical wiring, and roof connections. This type of preparation by the construction industry is unprecedented in the United States.

The increased construction cost of a 2,500-square-foot sustainably built home in Mesa del Sol with a fully installed solar photovoltaic power system is about $20,000. However, the combination of state sustainable-building tax incentives and federal tax credits reduces this cost differential to $8,000. What's more, PNM is currently offering homeowners a 13-cent-per-kilowatt-hour credit for all electricity they create from solar power. This reflects the cost savings advantage to PNM resulting from the reduced need to build generating capacity while also meeting the state's new renewable portfolio requirements. The net result is a mortgage payment that is increased by about $55 per month, but an average utility bill that is reduced by $140. This means a net monthly cash increase of $85 in the homeowner's pocket. A better home with a positive cash flow.

Efficiency is one thing, and reliability is another. Despite New Mexico's lack of natural disasters, power reliability and quality is certainly an issue. Ever since his appointment in May of 2007 by Governor Richardson as New Mexico's cabinet secretary of economic development, Fred Mondragon has been getting an earful from businesses in a new industrial park near the city of Santa Teresa, along the Mexican border and not far from El Paso, Texas. Although he's spent 15 years in public administration and another 15 as the chief executive officer and administrator of a prestigious hospital, Mondragon explains that, "Never in my life have I learned so much in such a short period about peak demand prices for electricity, and what happens when there are even minor service interruptions."

Mondragon is committed to assuring that better wisdom will prevail at Mesa del Sol. "This is a real chance to do creative things, especially given the location," he notes. "There's even room for a solar thermal and solar panel array between Kirtland Air Force Base and Mesa del Sol. And by introducing all of the green practices in building construction and in the layout of the buildings, it has the chance to be something really special." Needless to say, Mondragon has joined Albuquerque Mayor Chavez and New Mexico Governor Richardson in pledging their support and guidance for changing the regulatory policies that now constrain a Perfect Power infrastructure at Mesa del Sol and elsewhere in the state. They also emphasize the importance of communicating the value of smart microgrids to the rural communities and Indian reservations of New Mexico. Political support from outside Albuquerque will be essential to gaining state approval for these essential policy changes.

The importance of this support is already urgently crucial to Mesa del Sol, where a company that wants to build a thin-filmed solar manufacturing plant demands absolute power reliability as a precondition for locating in the community. "But, based on the Endurant design, that will require an additional Perfect Power investment of about $10 million at the beginning of the project," says Forest City Covington's Mike Daly. "It's not that much money over the life of the entire construction of Mesa del Sol, but it's a big investment now. What we need to do is aggregate enough customers and companies so that we can make the commitment within the context of our Perfect Power priorities." The new state IRP docket should provide the forum for making that commitment much easier.

"The quality and cleanliness of power ought to be rewarded and put into the rate base for utilities," offers Daly. "It would better serve the interests of society if utilities could finance a tenant's energy-efficiency–related investment. We should be building modern infrastructure before the capacity is needed, but that's apparently not the way utilities operate, since they aren't motivated to make projections." These are the kinds of regulatory policy changes on which Mesa del Sol, PNM, and the Galvin Electricity Initiative will test the commitment of the city and state leadership.

A MODEL—AND ROLE MODEL

The future is now for the developers and backers of Mesa del Sol. They are convinced that if they build it, residents and businesses will come, especially for a well-thought-out community that meets the needs of the present without compromising the ability of future generations to meet their own needs. As a piece of Mesa del Sol promotional literature states, "A sustainable community brings people out of their homes and cars, encouraging them to be active, healthy and connected to their environment and each other." Maybe they won't even notice the presence of Perfect Power. But as it evolves into something that saves and never fails, that's exactly the point. What will be noticed is the ability of the community and its citizens to play an active role in the provision and utilization of their energy needs. This is certain to increase their quality of life and provide an important competitive advantage.

Other communities and utilities are also taking their first steps on this perfect service quality path. For example, Xcel Energy has gained much notoriety this year with the announcement that it intends to make Boulder, Colorado, the nation's first fully integrated smart-grid city, beginning in August 2008. Boulder is home to the University of Colorado and several federal institutions, including the National Institute of Standards and Technology (NIST), which is already involved in smart-grid efforts for the federal government. "Smart Grid City is the first step toward building the grid of the future," said Dick Kelly, Xcel Energy CEO. "In Boulder, we will collaborate with others to integrate all aspects of our smart-grid vision and evaluate the benefits." To realize this smart-grid vision, Xcel has established a smart-grid consortium including Accenture, Current Group, Schweitzer Engineering Laboratories, and Ventyx. The planned smart-grid innovations include: transformation of the existing metering infrastructure to provide real-time, two-way communications throughout Boulder's distribution microgrid; installation of all necessary programmable systems to fully automate home energy use; and integration of the infrastructure needed to support distributed generation including photovoltaic solar panels, wind turbines, and plug-in hybrid vehicles.

What isn't yet clear is whether the citizens of Boulder will have access to the electricity price and use information they need to make informed decisions themselves or whether they must continue to depend on the utility to decide for them. In either case, this initial $100 million effort, including government funding, is intended to form the basis for a larger smart-grid deployment throughout Xcel's eight-state service territory.

Another notable and more established example is that of Kansas City Power & Light (KCP&L) under the leadership of Michael Chesser, the CEO of its parent corporation, Great Plains Energy Inc. Its comprehensive energy plan includes distribution automation, demand response, and energy efficiency as integral portions of the company's overall IRP implementation strategy. KCP&L is also utilizing select distribution circuits in its system to develop and demonstrate new smart distribution automation technologies, including network protectors, substation reclosing relays, and dynamic voltage controls. All of these projects are being done jointly with a variety of technology providers, including S&C Electric, Telemetric, CellNet, and Cooper.

KCP&L is also a utility leader in creating smart microgrids within its distribution system that enable entrepreneurs to save money and add value for both the utility and its customers. These smart technology development and deployment initiatives are reflective of the new utility/entrepreneurial collaboration model that is essential to successfully travel the path to Perfect Power. Indeed, the business model for 21st-century electricity service must be built on the emergence of thousands of innovative entrepreneurial doers and investors.

INSTITUTIONS AND COMPANIES TO WATCH

Accenture (www.accenture.com) is a global management consulting, technology services, and outsourcing company with annual revenues of $20 billion. The company has built an alliance network of more than 150 market leaders and innovators, ranging from HP to Microsoft; it helps clients enter new markets, improve performance, and deliver products and services more efficiently. Accenture has offices in 150 cities around the world.

Advent Solar, Inc. (www.adventsolar.com). Founded in 2002 in Albuquerque, New Mexico, Advent is a manufacturer of advanced solar cells and modules that operates under the principles of lean manufacturing. A spin-off from Sandia National Laboratories, the company employs the emitter-wrap-through cell design using ultrathin silicon wafers. By using thinner silicon, the company is less susceptible to the availability and cost of its raw materials. Back contact cells eliminate grid obscuration and reduce assembly costs.

Cellnet + Hunt (www.cellnethunt.com). Cellnet + Hunt is a leading provider of advanced metering and smart-grid communications solutions to utilities worldwide. It operates the largest single advanced metering infrastructure in the United States, serving more than 11 million utility customers. As part of a broader energy solution network, Cellnet + Hunt will soon become Landis + Gyr as a single global brand.

Constellation NewEnergy (www.newenergy.com) was founded in 1995 as New Energy Ventures at the advent of open markets for electricity. It was purchased in 1999 by AES, and then in 2002 by the Constellation Energy Group headquartered in Baltimore, Maryland. It was merged with Constellation's gas supply and transportation business in 2004. Today, the company claims to be the number-one supplier of electricity to North American businesses. It has annual revenues of $8 billion, and it meets peak loads of more than 15,000 megawatts.

Cooper Industries (www.cooperindustries.com). Headquartered in Houston, Texas, Cooper has become a worldwide manufacturer of electrical products that distribute and control electricity, provide circuit protection, illuminate facilities, support electronic and telecommunications components, and offer fire and security detection. With over $5 billion in annual electrical product revenues, Cooper has nearly 100 manufacturing locations around the world, and sourcing centers in China, Mexico, India, and Eastern Europe.

Covington Capital (www.covingtoncapital.com). With offices in California and Ohio, Covington Capital is an entrepreneurial real estate firm that develops and invests in industrial, commercial, and residential projects, as well as raw land, throughout the United States. Covington specializes in projects that require extensive public sector interface or partnership, as well as those requiring creative financing solutions.

Current Group (www.currentgroup.com) was founded in 2000 as a privately held organization based in Germantown, Maryland, to provide integrated smart-grid solutions. Their services combine sensing technology, two-way communications, 24/7 monitoring, and enterprise analysis software to provide location-specific, real-time data for utilities and customers. The company also offers high-performance broadband services and home energy management services. Investors include EnerTech Capital, Google, Goldman Sachs, and Liberty Associated Partners.

Fidelity Investments (www.fidelity.com) is a privately held, diversified financial services company. Founded in 1949, it now serves more than 23 million investors through individual and institutional accounts. It manages more than 400 different funds and is the largest U.S. mutual fund company with $1.6 trillion of assets under management. Fidelity also manages more than $280 billion of international assets. In addition to mutual funds, the company provides brokerage, retirement, estate planning, and wealth management services.

Forest City Enterprises, Inc. (www.forestcity.net) is a $10 billion publicly traded real estate company engaged in the ownership, development, and management of real estate throughout the United States. Based in Cleveland, Ohio, it operates under three strategic business units: Commercial, Residential, and Land Development. Forest City has adopted the principles of sustainability in every property and project, balancing environmental resources, economic objectives, and social systems—the triple bottom line of people, planet, and profit. Forest City considers this long-term view as key to its competitive advantages.

Honeywell International (HON) (www.honeywell.com) is a major American multinational conglomerate headquartered in Morristown, New Jersey. The current Honeywell International Inc. is the result of a merger with Allied Signal in 1999. Its 2007 revenues of $34.5 billion came from the production and sale of a variety of consumer products, energy management capabilities, engineering services, and aerospace systems for a wide range of customers worldwide. HON is known for its aggressive implementation of Six Sigma–plus quality manufacturing methodologies.

Los Alamos National Laboratory (www.lanl.gov). Los Alamos was established in 1943 as a test laboratory supporting development of the atomic bomb. Today it is operated by Los Alamos National Security LLC as part of the Department of Energy's (DOE) national laboratory structure. In addition to its core national security mission, Los Alamos plays a leading role in environmental and materials sciences. Its recent efforts have included breakthroughs in nanotechnology and high-performance computing.

The National Institute of Standards and Technology (NIST) (www.nist.gov) is a nonregulatory federal agency within the U.S. Department of Commerce whose mission is to promote U.S. innovation and competitiveness by advancing measurement science, standards, and technology. NIST laboratories, located in Gaithersburg, Maryland, and Boulder, Colorado, conduct research on a wide variety of physical and engineering sciences. Their facilities include the Center for Nanoscale Science and Technology, the IT Laboratory, and Chemical Science and Technology Laboratory.

New Mexico Economic Development Department (www. edd.state.nm) assists companies in New Mexico with education, information, and hands-on instruction on how to use tax incentives, job-training reimbursements, and other programs to save money, hire new employees, and increase their business. The Job Training Incentive Program awarded $3 million to local businesses in 2006. Other EDD assistance is available for low-cost ISO 9000 certification, exports, and trade, and setting up business incubators.

New Mexico Public Regulation Commission (NMPRC) (www.nmprc.state.nm.us) regulates the privately owned electric utilities, as well as telecommunications, motor carriers, and insurance industries in the state of New Mexico. Its purpose is to ensure fair and reasonable rates as well as reasonable and adequate services to the public as stipulated by law. The five Commissioners represent five geographical districts of the state, and they operate from offices in Santa Fe.

Powercast, LLC (www.powercastco.com) was founded as a private company in 2003 in Ligonier, Pennsylvania. The company has developed unique transmitter and receiver modules that can send electric power wirelessly, via radio waves, to energize low-power devices. The company expects these modules to be imbedded into consumer products so that they can be charged or powered directly without wires. Powercast is currently testing modules for use by original equipment manufacturers. Its first products are expected to be for sale in 2008.

Public Service Company of New Mexico (PNM) (www.pnm. com). PNM is the largest utility in New Mexico, providing electricity and national gas service across the state. It also sells power on the wholesale market in the western United States. It is organized under the holding company structure of PNM Resources Inc. PNM sells some 8 million megawatt hours of electricity to its own customers each year and provides an additional 12 million megawatt hours for resale.

Sandia National Laboratories (www.sandia.gov). Sandia was established in 1949 and is now part of the DOE national laboratory structure. Sandia Corporation, a Lockheed Martin Company, manages Sandia for the DOE National Nuclear Security Administration. Sandia's mission is to meet national needs in five areas: nuclear weapons, energy and infrastructure assurance, nonproliferation, defense systems and assessments, and homeland security.

Santa Fe Institute (www.santafe.edu). The Santa Fe Institute is an independent, not-for-profit, research and education center founded in 1984. It performs multidisciplinary collaborations in the physical, biological, computational, and social sciences. These efforts bring together scientists and researchers from universities, government agencies, research institutes, and private industry. The institute's goal is to understand the complex adaptive systems critical to addressing key environmental, technological, biological, economic, and political challenges facing the United States and the world.

Schott AG (www.schott.com), founded in 1884 in Jena, Germany, is a leading international manufacturer of high-quality industrial glass products, such as fiber optics and components used in solar flat-panel displays. After WWII, the company moved to Mainz, Germany. In 2008, Schott announced plans to build a factory in Albuquerque, New Mexico, to build receivers for concentrated solar thermal power plants, and 64 MW of solar photovoltaic (PV) modules. The company is already making 15 MW of PV in Massachusetts. Its plans are to produce 450 MW of crystalline PV annually, along with 100 MW of thin-film PV wafers.

Schweitzer Engineering Laboratories (SEL) (www.selinc.com), headquartered in Pullman, Washington, introduced the world's first microprocessor-based protective relay in 1984 that revolutionized the power protection industry. Products and services include communications security, transmission and distribution protection, and transformer, bus, breaker, and capacitor protection. The company also produces revenue-metering systems. SEL now provides technical support to customers in 121 countries, and it manages 36 regional technical service centers in the United States.

Telemetric (www.telemetric.net). Headquartered in Boise, Idaho, Telemetric is a leader in wireless communication and infrastructure solutions for the utility industry. These solutions deliver secure, reliable communications over the existing cellular infrastructure to enhance system reliability, reduce costs, and help utilities make the most of their electricity distribution assets.

Ventyx (www.ventyx.com) is a business solutions provider to the energy, utility, and communications industries. The company holds a large market share in asset management software and services with more than 400,000 users in 40 countries. It also holds positions in mobile workforce management systems and worldwide energy analytics. The company claims that 48 of the top 50 power generators in North America use a Ventyx solution, and that 27 percent of transmission line mileage relies upon a Ventyx solution.

WildCharge (www.wildcharge.com), a privately held company located in Scottsdale, Arizona, was founded in 2005. The company has developed the first wire-free charging pad, with a flat, thin conductive surface useful for charging cell phones or other mobile electronic devices. Devices placed on the pad will instantaneously receive power, with charging speeds comparable to wall sockets. *Time* magazine selected WildCharge's technology as one of the best inventions of 2007. WildCharge has an R&D facility near Boulder, Colorado.

Xcel Energy (www.xcelenergy.com) is a diversified energy company, headquartered in Minneapolis, Minnesota, with 3.3 million electricity customers and 1.8 million natural gas customers in eight western and midwestern states. The company has revenues of $9 billion and owns nearly 35,000 miles of natural gas pipelines, nearly 8000 MW of coal-fired generation, 5000 MW of gas-fired generation, and nearly 2000 MW of nuclear generation.

9

Changing the Rules of the Game, Honorably

In order to create a new system that takes advantage of Perfect Power microgrids, the constraining rules of today's electricity game must be changed. In most jurisdictions around the nation, only utility companies may run power lines across or under a street, which essentially renders microgrids illegal. The policy initiatives of the Galvin Electricity Initiative call for cutting through the Federal, state, and local red tape; breaking the monopoly power of the state electric utilities with effective deregulation; and requiring utilities to perform according to modern standards of efficiency and reliability.

The California Public Employees' Retirement System, more commonly known as CalPERS, provides pension fund, healthcare, and other retirement services to roughly 1.5 million California public employees. It controls more than $250 billion worth of stocks, bonds, real estate, and other assets. On matters of corporate social responsibility, corporate governance, and even mainstream politics, CalPERS has considerable influence. However, when CalPERS wanted to install a natural gas–powered turbine to produce heat and cooling for two 15-story buildings it owned in La Jolla, California, CalPERS ran smack against the law. At issue was whether the two buildings, which were right across the street from each other, could share their heat and power. Indeed, in most jurisdictions around the United States, it's illegal for a private party, even CalPERS, to string a power line across a public street, or put a pipeline under it. The only entity with the ability to do this is the local electric utility. Overcoming the prerogative of a regulated public utility can turn the strongest institution into the proverbial 98-pound weakling.

These rules may have made sense in the 1890s, when they were written. But today, the prohibition against running private power lines under or across streets is one of *the* major barriers to the cost-effective development of smart microgrids and a Perfect Power system.

CalPERs did manage to get around these outdated regulations. It turned out that because CalPERS owned the one-block, brick-covered street, Executive Square Drive, it could create an energy-saving microgrid. "It's really one of the first true microgrids that we've been able to build," says Kevin Best, whose firm, RealEnergy, conceived of, designed, and managed the project. "And it's the only one I know of that operates on distributed power and runs under what would otherwise be a public street. But it's these types of regulations and prohibitions that seem to thwart many promising ways to generate and share power over small grids, and which in turn could take stress off of the bulk power grid."

Hundreds of other entrepreneurial energy development companies with billions in capital have found similar barriers to supplying the market. Under current regulations, utilities own the commercial and multi-family building distribution system and meters, and can use this monopoly to effectively block the private sector from investing in advanced technologies that save energy and money.

The biggest impediment to the smart grid transformation is neither technical nor economic, but regulatory barriers left over from an earlier era. In all other regulated industries, these kinds of barriers have long been eliminated, and with rapidly positive results. For example, it was only 30 years ago when AT&T still reigned as the monopoly provider of telecommunications services throughout the United States. Consumers didn't even own their telephones, but "rented" them from AT&T. In fact, it was illegal to plug a non-AT&T phone into the AT&T network.

Thanks to courts and regulators who decided to change the rules to benefit the nation and its consumers, telecommunications underwent a transformation. The subsequent open networks and markets have since spawned an incredible wave of innovation, private investment, and economic development benefiting all consumers, suppliers, and the prosperity of our nation alike. Moreover, so many of the products and services we take for granted—from wireless e-mail to pod-casts—were not even imagined when those regulations first fell. In many ways, the smart grid is the energy equivalent of the Information Superhighway. Few could have predicted the profound impact that e-mail, e-commerce, and wireless communications have made. Similarly, the benefits of the smart grid will grow as it enables more and more innovation.

THE BUSINESS CASE FOR PROFOUND CHANGE

Government intervention in energy markets has produced an array of public failures. By hindering the deployment of smart, clean technologies, this intervention has been at cross-purposes with efforts to improve efficiency and reduce emissions.

"Probably the most important thing that could happen to the electrical system is if public service commissions and the regulatory staffs of the utility companies would sit down with their bosses and agree to put the social benefits of upgrading the infrastructure into their business case," suggests Steve Pullins, president of the Knoxville, Tennessee–based Horizon Energy Group and a long-time leader of the Modern Grid Initiative. "But time after time these forces come together and get locked into the same old process of a rate case. So once again there are no incentives for change or innovation."

Pullins' biggest criticism is the fundamental inefficiency of the electric utility industry. "What you end up with is a utility that builds a tremendous amount of generation capacity at the expense of the consumers, and then runs those assets at 100 percent for maybe three hours a day," Pullins continues. "Then it runs at 80 percent capacity for five hours and finally at only 20 percent capacity for 16 hours. If I did that in any other business I'd be a lousy manager, but it's how utilities operate. We chase the peak; it's our tradition to build and get paid for that peak and because we're a monopoly, we think it's OK. It is not OK. A smart grid that eliminates that expensive peak is a doable alterative, even if it takes 15 to 30 years."

If utilities and state regulators don't initiate energy conservation, Pullins believes that the federal government ought to take a leading role in developing the new electricity infrastructure. "But the industry doesn't expect the Department of Energy (DOE), or any other federal agency, to really step up to the plate and take leadership. The history of this country is to wait for an overt crisis, and we're not quite there yet. Moreover, If you look at the DOE's $24 billion budget, and see that they're investing only $125 million on infrastructure, you get some perspective on their intentions."

In contrast to the United States, the European Union (EU) has mandated a binding "20–20–20" strategy with the concurrence of each member country. This mandate requires each country to achieve at least a 20 percent increase in energy efficiency, a 20 percent energy share for renewables, and a 20 percent reduction in greenhouse gas emission by 2020. It is leading to a variety of investment initiatives for smart, ultra-reliable microgrid implementation with electricity producers and consumers alike.

For now, the United States must live with the fact that its electrical supply is regulated primarily at the state level. This means 50 different, and often conflicting, sets of rules that apply to an even more diverse industry, made up of 1,200 state-regulated utilities plus some 2,000 municipal utilities with their own local regulations. Federal regulatory oversight is effectively limited to the interstate transmission of electricity and to a few federal utilities such as the Tennessee Valley Authority and Bonneville Power Administration. As a result, state utility regulations governing utility monopolies that are intended to protect consumers from predatory suppliers in fact lead to a counterproductive result. This result encourages utilities to maximize sales while erecting barriers to consumer decisions on how much electricity to use when demand is high, and thus more expensive, and how and when to shift activities when the demand and cost is lower.

MOVING THE UTILITY COMPANY CHEESE

Society can't count on regulated utilities to make the necessary changes in a vacuum. They are merely participants in a game, pure and simple, and behave and perform according to the regulated rules of that game where winning is measured by the utility's returns to its stockholders. Jeff Sterba, the president and CEO of Public Service New Mexico and the chairman of the Edison Electric Institute, stated the fundamental regulatory change issue very well at the April 2007 GridWeek Conference in Washington, D.C.: "A lot of people think of utilities as rats, that we just charge customers whatever price we need, and that we're not interested in helping customers," he said. "Well, as a good friend and colleague of mine, John Rowe (the president and CEO of Exelon, the largest utility in the country) once said, "Okay, so everyone thinks we're rats. Show us the cheese, and we'll do the right thing."

So if the utility industry and the state and federal regulators are either unable or unwilling to start showing that cheese, who can? In July of 2007, the U.S. Conference of Mayors, a group representing all major cities in the United States, passed a resolution that endorsed the technologies and policies that support smart-grid concepts, including the digital automation of the entire electrical supply system. It was a start, and one of the first times that elected city officials have taken a leadership position on an issue where state legislators and regulators have not. Cities recognize that in many ways they have the most to gain from a smart grid and the most to lose in its absence. The ability to attract and maintain their corporate economic base, and therefore their urban viability, is increasingly dependent on the quality and cost of electricity service they provide.

"And there are a lot of potential players who can help start the change," insists Steve Hauser, vice president of strategy for the Washington, D.C., firm GridPoint and also the president of the GridWise Alliance, which advocates modernization of the nation's electrical system. "At the federal level you have the Interstate Commerce Commission that is supposed to create appliance standards and create protections for consumers. You have the Department of Energy and the Environmental Protection Agency, both of which should have an interest in this topic. There's the Senate and the House of Representatives, which actually develop legislation that addresses the grid, its weaknesses and what can be done to change it." In fact, the 2007 Energy Security and Independence Act, signed by President Bush last December, has an entire section devoted to smart-grid encouragement and incentives. But the tone of the legislation remains quite passive to avoid interfering with the "rights" of each state. It's no wonder that the result is a new, much larger generation of "sad sockets"! (See Figure 9–1.)

Ah, but there's more. "Although there are 50 state regulatory commissions who haven't done much as yet, you also have 50 state governors and 50 state legislatures who have influence over those regulators," adds Hauser. "Large electrical consumers also have a voice, as do the growing power of consumer advocates. Right now those activists are focused on climate change and greenhouse gasses and haven't yet put the benefits of the smart grid into their argument, but they will. And then when you get past the mayors you're dealing with local building codes, which again are a force for changing how we use electricity."

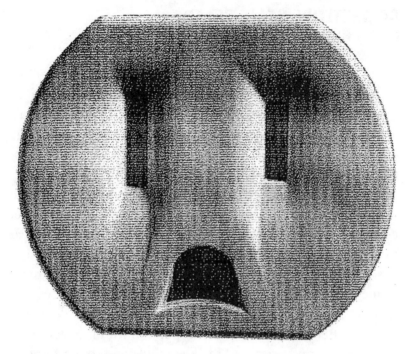

Figure 9–1   You'd Be Sad, Too, If You Were Leaving Your Customers in the Dark

STEP BY STEP BY STEP

The Galvin Electricity Initiative recommends a set of coordinated policy initiatives to tackle this maze of unproductive municipal, state, and federal regulations. We are specifically calling for a four-dimensional combination of state and federal policies that opens the door to real competition and raises the reliability and efficiency bars for electricity service quality to a much higher level:

1. The creation of competitive state retail electricity markets
2. Performance-based state utility regulation
3. Mandatory, strict power distribution reliability standards
4. Comprehensive federal electricity efficiency standards

COMPETITIVE STATE RETAIL ELECTRICITY MARKETS

Retail electricity markets must integrate consumers as active partners in balancing the electricity supply/demand equation. This depends on providing dynamic, time-of-use price signals to consumers plus open access to entrepreneurial technology and service innovations. This will also provide electricity suppliers with the business incentives to operate most efficiently and to achieve perfect service reliability. Unfortunately, the so-called deregulation of electricity markets at the state level continues to hold retail consumers captive to their local monopoly utility, while the range of electricity service offerings has actually declined. As summed up well by Leonard Hyman, former head of the Utility Research Group and first vice president at Merrill Lynch, restructuring started out as deregulation, an attempt to introduce competition into the electricity sector before *rigor mortis* set in. The movement soon morphed into an income redistribution scheme, with consumers least likely to end up on the receiving end." It is therefore particularly disingenuous for regulation to oppose time-of-use pricing and retail competition with the red-herring argument that it might penalize the poor.

Today, we simply have a remodeled regulatory structure in which utilities are still encouraged to consider regulators as their real customers, and true retail competition remains effectively prohibited in nearly every state. By comparison, in a robust free market, the forces of competition drive prices to a level that equates the marginal cost of supply to the marginal consumer value. This leads to long-term cost reductions relative to fixed regulatory rates. Dynamic pricing also promotes more equitable distribution of these costs based again on consumer value.

The Alliance for Retail Choice, which brings together many of the nation's leading retail energy suppliers, has developed a methodology and baseline assessment of retail market progress in each state. Based on this assessment, it has also developed a set of specific regulatory policy recommendations to break the current barriers to retail market progress. State regulators could, for example, require that new developments pay for and own the site electricity distribution and metering infrastructure. This approach would lower costs to consumers and unleash private investment into new clean technologies and smart energy management systems. When the building owners also own the electricity infrastructure they can recoup the investment cost within a significantly reduced net monthly ~~~~~~~~ h more satisfied tenant.

~~~~~~~~ to respond to dynamic price signals ~~~~~ ntial part of the solution to the fragility ~~~~ ne nation's bulk power system. Indeed, a ~~~~ ision of the 2005 Federal Energy Policy ~~~~ , dysfunctional, average electricity pricing ~~~~ onal policy specifically encourages states and their utilities to offer consumers both the option of real-time pricing and the smart metering equipment to make it universally possible. Without a federal mandate, however, most utilities and state regulators have been reluctant to support the transition of consumers from passive protected users to proactive informed users, as has occurred in other regulated industries such as transportation and telecommunications. This "one size, one source fits all" regulatory culture and rate structure is equally obsolete in today's electrical world. Retail competition is an essential milestone on the path to the benefits of Perfect Power.

PERFORMANCE-BASED STATE UTILITY REGULATION

Traditionally, electricity rates have rigidly linked a utility's financial health to the amount of electricity it sells. Today, regulatory changes are needed to "decouple" utility cost recovery and compensation from simply the amount of electricity sold, and instead focus on establishing a dynamic partnership between utilities and their customers by setting utility rates that are based on utility performance. That is, utilities earn revenues for achieving the efficiency, reliability, and environment quality goals established by consumer choice and behavior. In addition to decoupling utility electricity sales from profits, performance-based rate making offers positive financial incentives for utilities to actually reduce bulk electricity sales and make improvements to achieve a smart-grid system. The result would be increased efficiency, reduced CO_2 emissions, and a policy structure that puts demand reduction "negawatts" on an equal incentive basis with supply megawatts in the electricity marketplace.

This will, of course, also place greater responsibilities on each state regulatory commission to benchmark utility performance, set standards, and reward performance accordingly. Certainly, the knowledge and mechanisms to wisely apply these regulatory leadership principles are widely available, but it means somewhat more effort on the part of the regulators and their staffs. However, until this transformation in regulatory practice is thoroughly implemented, the nation's power system is likely to retain its incentive to maintain the past, rather than to create a much higher value future for consumers.

MANDATORY, STRICT POWER DISTRIBUTION RELIABILITY STANDARDS

Such standards are critically needed to support the digital economy and provide greater infrastructure security. Today's electric reliability standards generally ignore power outages of less than three to five minutes, literally a costly eternity in an instantaneous digital world. The Federal Energy Regulatory Commission (FERC) has the ultimate authority to establish these strict standards within the context of interstate electricity commerce. However, the bulk of reliability issues reside in the state-regulated, local power distribution systems which are outside of FERC jurisdiction. Moreover, distribution reliability is measured and reported as an average across all the distribution systems in each state. As a result, many consumers, particularly in residential areas, tend to receive much lower electricity service reliability than the reported state average.

Most state regulatory commissions also use the excuse that they can't justify spending system-wide rate-payer money to fix local reliability deficiencies. As a result, many communities have offered to take over responsibility for their local power distribution system and to invest millions of dollars to improve its reliability. Unfortunately, these same regulatory commissions typically deny the request as contrary to the public interest or put an exorbitant price on the transfer. Cities nationwide are caught up in this same Catch 22 situation, with no way out.

The political authority of each state has thus far also restricted FERC from actively intervening to close this glaring reliability gap of immense national security and competitiveness proportions. As a result, U.S. consumers and businesses suffer much lower electricity service reliability than their counterparts in many European and Asian countries as shown earlier in figure 2–4. The electricity sector needs to establish and adhere to up-to-date total system reliability standards that strive for perfection and realistically reflect today's consumer needs and expectations.

COMPREHENSIVE FEDERAL ELECTRICITY EFFICIENCY STANDARDS

Federal standards are needed that reward investment in a smart electricity enterprise. The need to use energy more efficiently grows in importance as the prices of oil, natural gas, coal, and even uranium are reaching historic highs. Certainly, a variety of more energy-efficient technological innovations are already available to support such standards. At the same time, regulators need to financially incentivize utilities in the face of declining unit sales through performance-based "rate decoupling" measures that reward efficiency and reliability improvements, rather than simply the number of kilowatt hours sold.

While the Department of Energy's appliance efficiency standards are currently generating a 1 percent per year improvement in electricity efficiency, this rate of improvement could be significantly increased, mainly through dynamic communications and control systems that enable the real-time exchange of data between the power supply system and each consumer's appliances and devices, or what Steve Hauser calls "the loads." "The real magic comes when any kind of motor, fan, heat pump, refrigerator, or lighting system senses that demand is high and automatically throttles back 5 percent, 10 percent, or whatever is needed to keep the demand from spiking to a peak," Hauser explains. Also, as discussed in Chapter 6, federal energy-efficiency standards should address the rampant deficiencies in both commercial and residential building codes. The result could ultimately transform buildings from being the largest consumers of energy into efficient, net energy providers.

The loads are not only sensing increasing demand but a rising price in the electricity. So, a "demand-response capability," enabled by smart appliances and intelligent metering at a home or office building, and intelligence master control systems for microgrids, is an important part of the solution to the fragility of the nation's bulk power grid. "With intelligence built in, these could also respond to signals regarding pollution, which is yet another regulatory lever that could be pulled to initiate a change," adds Hauser. "However, this also assumes that the world of codes, standards, and economic issues around rates can be resolved. None can be done easily today."

Indeed, electric power systems in the United States employ over 150 different communication standards, and the building construction industry employs an additional 28 such standards. None are mutually compatible, and, as a result, the power system and the consumers' buildings and appliances are unable to communicate with each other. A universal electricity language has been proposed by both the International Electrotechnical Commission and the Electric Power Research Institute. And yet, getting widespread adoption from manufacturers in developing nations—where most appliances are assembled—is for now an elusive quest. This resistance is a throwback to the logic of electricity appliance manufacturers a century ago, who thought the key to market control was each "owning" their own proprietary electricity socket and plug design. These manufacturers soon learned the hard way that their collection of sad sockets only served to limit the market potential for everyone.

FORGING A NO-FAULT DIVORCE

What is it that will force these four dimensions of smart-grid enabling policy change, so long resisted, to happen now? The simple answer is economic and political self-interest on the part of lawmakers, regulators, and utilities alike. Electricity rate increases have been largely avoided for decades because raising prices to consumers is seen as a political third rail which regulators endeavor to avoid, literally at all costs. Today, however, nearly every utility and regulatory commission is finding it impossible to maintain this extended rate freeze in the face of rapidly rising energy costs and infrastructure renewal needs. As a result, they must find a new value proposition that justifies the inevitable rate increases to consumers (voters) and their state and local governments. Giving consumers these tools to better control their electricity service cost while fundamentally improving their quality of service will be a necessary quid pro quo. An informed public that understands the fundamental value of a modern power system, and the exorbitant price they are paying for an antiquated one, is also essential to this long-overdue policy transformation. Figure 9–2 shows the dramatic cost/benefit advantages of the smart grid.

At the federal level, tax policy also has important implications for electricity system innovation. Smart-grid technologies face significant economic disincentives created by tax laws that prevent utilities from fully and promptly recovering their investments in new technologies. Tax rules require capital costs to be depreciated over many years, whereas energy and other operating costs

Target Sector Costs	10-Year Investment Level (dollars)	Source of Benefits	Potential Benefits/ year (in billions of dollars, by 2015)
Residential	$7–10	"Smarting up" of customer premises (smart homes, intelligent buildings)	$6–8
Commercial	$13–20	Enabling of demand response and AMI deployment	$5–8
TOTAL	**$20–30**	Investments in smart-grid technologies	$2–3
		DG, smart-grid-interactive storage technologies and microgrids	$1–2
		TOTAL/year	**$14–21**

Figure 9–2   Smart-Grid Costs versus Benefits

can be fully deducted from taxable income. The result serves to preclude innovation and results in over-consumption of energy and over-production of CO_2. Tax rules should be changed to accelerate depreciation on smart meters and other smart-grid technology, expediting their installation. This policy change should also permit recovering the remaining book value of the retired obsolete equipment that has been replaced, again rewarding honorable utilities that play by the new rules. The tax structure should also be changed to put demand-side investments in smart, efficient buildings and retail service innovation on an equal footing with supply-side investments.

None of these policy "cheese" recommendations would in any way bring harm to the utilities. In fact, their participation in this grand service transformation is critical. However, realizing the difficulties involved and time required to change these entrenched policies and regulations, the Galvin Electricity Initiative is emphasizing immediate decentralization of the electricity distribution network with more local control. As described earlier, this can be achieved by allowing entrepreneurial companies, commercial electricity consumers, and even residential communities to form alliances and create smart microgrids that incorporate independent distributed power generation and storage capabilities.

It is already happening and the delightful term for it is "grid divorce." According to Steve Pullins, about 185,000 small businesses and communities have already divorced themselves from the conventional power grid. Because they aren't linked to the utility, they don't have to ask for permission to produce the power they use. Following this path to Perfect Power, however, is a Draconian alternative which would not be necessary if the policy changes we advocate were in force.

Today the legal right to build and operate a microgrid hinges primarily on one issue—is the microgrid defined as, or perceived to be, a public utility? If so, it stands little chance of being permitted to operate, particularly within the service territory of another public utility, which is often the case. Further, the administrative and financial burden of being designated as a public utility is likely to be prohibitive. Consequently, yet another rule change within the context of a competitive retail electricity market policy is needed if smart grids are to flourish.

The thing is, a widespread divorce from the conventional grid certainly isn't in the best interests of the nation. Smart microgrids create the greatest benefits when they are interconnected with the local utility electricity distribution system and fully utilize the resources of the nation's bulk power system to the best advantage of consumers, entrepreneurs, and utilities alike. It means allowing someone other than the regulated utility to install and operate power lines that cross streets. This is the essential core architecture of the Perfect Power electricity system. Together, this interconnected web of grids, both large and small, raises and refines the reliability, efficiency, and quality of the bulk power supplied by the utility distribution system to 21st-century standards.

Ultimately, unrestricted interoperability requires the seamless, end-to-end connectivity of hardware and software from the consumers' appliances all the way back through the grid to the power source. As industries as diverse as telecommunications and banking illustrate, interoperability is a necessary basis for the innovation that creates new value for consumers. Indeed, this comprehensive grid interoperability fully opens the path to universal Perfect Power service.

At one time, America's electricity supply system was a state-of-the-art wonder of the world. It helped bring a level of prosperity unmatched by any other nation. But our system must be put back on the path to perfection in order to meet the significantly higher 21st-century standards of reliability, security, efficiency, cost of service, and environmental impact. The primary barrier to this essential progress is an outmoded state policy regulatory structure that seeks to preserve the past rather than incent the innovative future.

Coal and natural gas prices have more than doubled over the past year, and the cost of a new centralized power plant has more than doubled since 2000. The resulting business-as-usual double and triple-digit utility rate increase proposals that pose an economic "train wreck" for cities and states provide both the opportunity and necessity to make these long-overdue policy changes. Each citizen must answer the challenge and demand that the rules of the game be changed, honorably, and promptly.

INSTITUTIONS AND COMPANIES TO WATCH

Alliance for Retail Choice (ARC) (www.allianceforretail choice.com). The ARC brings together many of the nation's leading retail energy suppliers. It advocates continued development of retail energy markets that provide customers the opportunity to choose the products and services most consistent with their needs. The ARC provides a focused voice for competitive energy retailers and their customers in selected public policy forums on the federal and state level.

California Public Employees Retirement System (CalPERS) (www.calpers.ca.gov). Headquartered in Sacramento, California,

CalPERS manages retirement and health plans for more than 1.4 million beneficiaries from more than 2,500 California government agencies and school districts. CalPERS was created in 1931 by an amendment to the California State Constitution. The need to prudently manage risk and retirement provides the context for CalPERS asset allocation and liability management.

Edison Electric Institute (EEI) (www.eei.org) is the trade association of the investor-owned electric utilities who represent 70 percent of electricity sold in the United States. Organized in 1933, EEI represents the interests of its members in the legislative and regulatory arenas. It provides advocacy, authoritative analysis, and critical industry data to its members, Congress, government agencies, the financial community and opinion-leader audiences.

Exelon–Commonwealth Edison Co. (ComEd) (www.exelon corp.com). ComEd is the retail electric utility serving 3.6 million customers in Chicago and northern Illinois. It maintains 78,000 miles of power lines as part of this service responsibility. ComEd is a subsidiary of the Exelon Corporation, the largest utility holding company in the United States. ComEd's annual revenues, from sales of over 71 million megawatt hours of electricity, total some six billion dollars.

Federal Energy Regulatory Commission (FERC) (www.ferc. gov). FERC is the independent U.S. government agency that regulates the interstate transmission of electricity, natural gas, and oil. FERC is also responsible for ensuring the reliability of the nation's high-voltage interstate transmission system. FERC's responsibilities do not include regulation of retail electricity to consumers or approval for electric generation, transmission, or distribution facilities. These are within the purview of state public utility commissions.

GridPoint Inc. (www.gridpoint.com), founded in 2003 and based in Washington, D.C., is a leading clean technology company and a pioneer of an innovative smart-grid platform that aligns the interests of electric utilities, consumers, and the environment. This platform is based on an intelligent network of clean distributed resources that controls load, stores energy, and produces power. GridPoint has recently raised over $100 million in new capital, including a large investment by Goldman Sachs Group, the Altira Group, and New Enterprise Associates.

GridWise Alliance (www.gridwise.org), founded in 2003, is a consortium of public and private stakeholders aligned around a vision of transforming the U.S. electric power system into one that is more intelligent, efficient, resilient, and secure. Alliance members include electric utilities, IT companies, equipment vendors, and new technology providers. GridWise Alliance provides a forum where members can meet, exchange ideas, and work cooperatively on a common set of issues, with the goal of moving our industrial-age electric grid into the information age.

GridWise Architecture Council (www.gridwiseac.org). The GridWise™ Architecture Council assembles a focused team of experts to articulate the guiding principles that constitute the architecture of an intelligent, transactive, energy system and see that GridWise evolutionary directions remain true to these principles. GridWise Architecture takes into account the entire horizontal and vertical ranges of business sectors concerned with this future energy system, as well as other standards bodies and consortia.

Horizon Energy Group LLC (www.horizonenergygroup.com). Headquartered in Maryville, Tennessee, the Horizon Energy Group provides energy services to help clients develop modern, smart power systems. In addition to advanced distributed and renewable power systems, it provides advanced system control methodologies and asset intelligence. Horizon Energy activities include operations and projects in Latvia, the Middle East, and Japan, as well as the United States.

International Electrotechnical Commission (IEC) (www. iec.ch) is the leading global standards organization that prepares and publishes international standards for all electrical, electronic, and related technologies. These serve as a basis for national standardization and as references for drafting international contracts. The IEC's objective is to meet the requirements of the global marketplace efficiently and to improve the quality of the products covered by its standards.

Modern Grid Initiative (www.moderngrid@netl.doe.gov) was created by the DOE's Office of Electricity Delivery and Energy Reliability and the National Technology Laboratory as a coordinated national program to accelerate the modernization of the U.S. electric power delivery system. It builds upon a national technology strategy that includes Grid 2030 and the National Electric Delivery Technologies Roadmap.

RealEnergy, LLC (www.realenergy.com), based in Yountville, California, has developed, built, owned, and operated more small, clean, and green on-site power plants than any other independent power producer or distributed energy developer in North America. It has developed 43 discrete facilities with electric grid interconnections, and it is focused on investing in clean, renewable power plants.

10
Consumers at the Controls

Consumers want more detailed information about the energy they use so they can better control when and how they turn on their lights, heat, and air-conditioning. In response, a new industry is taking shape that is scrambling to make homes and commercial buildings "intelligent." This emerging intelligent energy industry includes four basic market sectors: residential retrofit, new homes, commercial office buildings, and smart microgrids. We estimate U.S. investments alone of about $30 billion over the next decade in smart home energy controls and commercial building intelligence. The return on this investment will be at least $10 billion per year, plus even larger environmental, productivity, and societal benefits.

Three converging trends are transforming traditional assumptions about the behavior of electricity consumers and also the very value proposition of the electric utility industry itself. These are technological advances, rising customer service expectations, and climate change as a broad public concern. These trends are now fueling each other like warm ocean water feeds energy to a hurricane. Just as engaged consumers are already using computers, cell phones, VCRs, the Internet, Tivos, and iPods to control their information needs, similar forces are beginning to pull the utility industry toward a more interactive, consumer-participation network that is based on new communications technology and real-time information flows.

We have entered an era where the electric utility industry and its behaviors are out of step with reality. While the bravery and character of linemen and emergency workers remains unquestioned, this is an industry that still employs thousands of people to manually read meters each month, when the technology has existed for years to do it remotely. It's a business built on gross commodity measures in an era when instant, highly precise responses to differentiated consumer demands drive decisions in most every other type of market.

However, this status quo will rapidly change as the United States and the rest of the world confront rising electricity prices and dramatic advances in wireless communication. Consequently, it's easy to envision a time in the near future when virtually all electricity-using devices in homes and businesses will incorporate real-time transmitting sensors, individual Internet protocol addresses, and two-way communication capabilities that can automatically and instantaneously manage all power load demands and changes for the consumer. Individual appliances and devices in the home will be able to directly engage the marketplace as agents serving their residential owners. "Your thermostat and your water heater are day-trading for you," says Ron Ambrosio at IBM's Watson Research Center.

This new-found intelligence is attracting an array of value-added new services enabling consumers to individually and collectively "plug in" to the power business, while conveniently controlling their electricity choices and costs. Using a growing menu of automated energy management devices, and renewable energy sources with efficient battery storage, consumers will become active partners with utilities in the electricity enterprise, which is quite a reversal of fortunes.

Businesses are eager to leverage existing capabilities to meet this demand for greater control. This includes security companies with electronic systems that are capable of controlling home energy use with only a few additions. Telecommunications companies such as Comcast, SBC, and Verizon already can provide phone, Internet, and television service and certainly have the bandwidth to market and maintain home energy management networks. These companies also could face competition from large retailers—think Wal-Mart, Lowes, or Best Buy—which could package equipment, control devices, and a subscription service that could pay for itself through lower utility bills.

This emerging business opportunity was made clear in a survey and report by IBM Global Business Services, a division of Big Blue that develops fact-based strategic insights on critical issues faced by senior executives. The study "Plugging in the Consumer: Innovating Utility Business Models for the Future," predicts a steady progression toward what it called a "participatory network," in which consumers proactively manage energy use. The essence of this progression is outlined in Figure 10–1.

"The next five years will be pivotal for the utility industry," said IBM's Michael Valocchi, in a press release about the November 2007 report. "Consumer needs and roles are expanding, and many are no longer content to be passive recipients of a limited array of services." Consumers, suggests Valocchi, want more choices about the type of energy they buy, more control over its cost, and greater consideration of the power generation's environmental impact. As a result, he noted, "Utility companies need to revisit long-held beliefs about how to best serve customers." If not, those consumers, now well accustomed to shopping online, will be facing new choices on how to serve themselves.

After surveying 1,900 consumers from six countries— Germany, Australia, the United States, Japan, the United Kingdom, and the Netherlands—and nearly 100 utility company executives from 26 countries in Europe, North America, and the Asia-Pacific region, IBM not surprisingly found that at least half of the respondents would welcome opportunities for self-generation of power, Perfect Power reliability, and selling excess power back to a utility. Likewise, more than half of the executives believed that the new technologies and businesses competing in this space would start moving a significant number of

Figure 10–1 Rapid Increases in Media Capabilities Shape Consumer Expectations

	Television Consumer	Electricity Consumer
Passive	• Passive receipt of content • Limited sources of content generation • Major media companies exclusively control content • Provider-customer relationship one-to-many, driven by demographics and geography	• Passive receipt of power • Limited sources of power generation • Incumbent utilties exclusively control power generators • Provider-customer relationship one-to-many, driven by demographics and geography
Active	• Consumer interest drives new and more targeted choices in content • More interest in and leverage of information on quality indicators for content (e.g., TV program rating systems) • Broader choice of providers drives more active role in provider selection • Consumer does not control content, but has stronger influence via choices • Introduction of time-shifting technologies enables more active selection and management of content at individual level	• Consumer interest drives new and more targeted choices in power supply • More interest in and leverage of information on quality indicators for content (e.g., green energy standards) • Broader choice of providers drives more active role in provider selection • Consumer does not control generation, but has stronger influence via choices • Introduction of residential time-of-use programs and green power options enables more active selection and management of generation deployment at individual level
Participatory	• Interactivity and involvement with content and service providers increases • Consumers active in producing content and influencing content distribution • Rapid creation of new content types as technology change causes explosion in capabilities • Dynamic, value-based pricing of content • Provider-customer relationship dynamic is increasingly customized to specific entertainment and information interests, with consumer analytics a key driver	• Interactivity and involvement with generation and service providers increases • Consumers active in generating power and influencing generation planning decisions • Rapid creation of new power supply options as technology change causes explosion in capabilities • Dynamic, value-based pricing of power (e.g., time-of-use) • Provider-customer relationship dynamic is increasingly customized to specific energy management goals, with consumer analytics a key driver

Source: "The end of television as we know it," IBM Institute for Business Value, January 2006; IBM Institute for Business Value analysis commercial and residential consumers to self-generation within a decade. And, of course, such developments in turn feed the development of smart microgrids and grid networks.

Advanced metering breaks the "iron curtain" now blocking consumer access to the time-of-use pricing information they need to efficiently and cost-effectively control their electricity use. Pennsylvania has already achieved a 50 percent penetration rate and leads the nation in that respect, although most of the citizens have yet to be given access to dynamic, time-of-use electricity pricing which should be the default rate option for all consumers everywhere. Pennsylvania, and several other states, have determined that a miniscule system benefit charge of about $0.0005 per kilowatt hour would be sufficient to pay for smart meters for everyone. The resulting cost would average about 45 cents per month for residential consumers and $3 per month for commercial consumers. This is typically less than 10 percent of the monthly savings that would correspondingly accrue to those consumers.

Smart metering capabilities are getting a further large boost in California where an always-on smart electricity metering gateway system that automatically adjusts appliance electricity use when the price becomes critical was part of a three-year, $20 million experiment by the three large California investor-owned utilities. The result was a remarkable 43 percent peak load reduction. Accordingly, the California Public Utilities Commission (PUC) has mandated rapid installation of advanced metering infrastructure by the three California utilities—Pacific Gas and Electric (PG&E), Southern California Edison (SCE), and San Diego Electric and Gas—as a means of cutting into the rapid growth of peak electricity demand.

PG&E will be investing $1.8 billion to install roughly 10 million smarter electric and gas meters in more than 6 million households and small businesses by 2011. PG&E estimates that 89 percent of this advanced metering infrastructure (AMI) cost can be recovered just through the operational benefits to the utility. SCE is investing a similar amount in AMI to cover their markets in southern California. The size of the California markets will help drive down costs and increase the functionality of the next generation of meters. Shifting power demand off peak is the primary goal of the PUC, but clearly other capabilities should be built in to enable the power system to become a network for services.

The smarter meters being installed in California may enable utilities to fire their meter readers and remotely connect and disconnect service, but do not necessarily provide universal real-time pricing information to their millions of retail customers. If the growth of the Internet tells us anything, it's that it is always cheaper in the long run to be technologically prepared and to bring consumers up to full speed now, rather than keeping them in the dark waiting for the inevitable upgrade. Jackalyne Pfannenstiel, chair of the California Energy Commission, has very appropriately stated that utility load-management efforts have "underfocused" on the need to get real-time electricity usage and rate information to consumers. "There's a lot of both technology and technique that would be possible right now, but I would argue that most customers, and not just residential customers, don't have any idea of the things they could be doing [to save energy and money]."

Utilities just don't seem quite ready to put the customer in charge. For example, PG&E is also asking its customers to enroll in a "smart air conditioning" program, called, naturally, SmartAC. PG&E intends to pay customers $25 for each air conditioner that's either fitted with a new smart switch or thermostat, and which can be automatically controlled by the utility during heat-waves, reducing demand and hopefully preventing brownouts and blackouts. Using radio signals, PG&E would command the air conditioners to cycle down and allow room temperatures to increase by up to 4 degrees. Customers who get the thermostat are also able to control their heat and air conditioning through an Internet Web site. Moreover, if consumers decide that they're being baked alive during an August afternoon, they are also able to temporarily get out of the program—if they call PG&E. While SmartAC is well intended as a means of reducing peak power demands, it's again structured in a manner that leaves the utility—not the consumer—in control.

In contrast, several consumer-focused entrepreneurial business models are already established and others are rapidly emerging. These include intelligent turnkey building automation systems that integrate Web-enabled energy management capabilities; turnkey system integrators that custom design and install decentralized generation, storage, and uninterruptible Perfect Power solutions; corporate service providers that provide a transparent accounting of all demand and response savings and credits; and Perfect Power retailers that shed load, shift load, store power, produce power, and exchange power with the utility grid, within contractual guidelines.

Corporations actively offering or developing these types of consumer electricity control capabilities include such well-known firms as Cisco, Dell, HP, Intel, Microsoft, and Motorola. To accelerate the rollout of their solutions, these information technology companies are cooperating with consumer electronics firms like Mitsubishi, Panasonic, Samsung, Sharp, and Sony.

The automated home control product part of the industry is most notably represented by the Homeplug Alliance, which includes such big brand names as Linksys, GE Security, Comart, and Radio Shack. Another fast-growing approach to home control involves wireless home networks using either Z-Wave or ZigBee, both of which are low-speed and low-bandwidth radio frequency–based routing protocols. The Z-Wave Alliance includes Cisco, Intel, Intermatic, Logitech, and Panasonic. The ZigBee Alliance lists Motorola, Cisco, Texas Instruments, and Eatan as some of its participants. A third protocol is being offered by Insteon, which is a proprietary data transmission approach developed by SmartLab that can work with both the programmable logic controller and radio frequency configurations. Comp USA, Digital Living, and Home Automated Living are among those using this data transmission protocol.

As utilities and regulators come to grips with the reality of rapidly rising electricity costs, it seems clear that consumers will eventually want to combine information about the price of electricity at given points in time with patterns of power use. This is what's meant by demand response (DR). As DR programs multiply, this will create demand for more Web-based electricity services and new regulatory rate structures that move away from average pricing to time-of-use pricing. Utilities can obtain the capacity they need at a fraction of the cost from existing customers and entrepreneurs by making long-term DR contracts available. These "non-wires" capacity solutions also enable consumers to see the value of combining energy management with other family scheduling and "protection" routines such as security, medical monitoring, homeowners' insurance, and maintenance services. At the same time, utilities and regulators will be encouraged by consumers to employ smart metering infrastructure which operate as DR-enabling backbones.

The American economy may be in at least temporary decline, but the DR market is poised to take off. At present the U.S. demand response business segment earns annual revenues of about $4 billion. Investors smell opportunity here and companies are maneuvering to get their slice, either as national players or as sophisticated niche players. As different strategies prove their value over the next several years, the best practices will establish the business landscape together with a lot of investment, hiring, and acquisition. Indeed, DR is a common thread among the four discreet sectors of entrepreneurial Perfect Power deployment: residential retrofit, new homes, commercial office buildings, and smart microgrids.

RESIDENTIAL RETROFITS

The residential retrofit market features Web-based and networked home control systems that are becoming cheaper, increasingly versatile, multifunctional, and consumer-simple. These systems

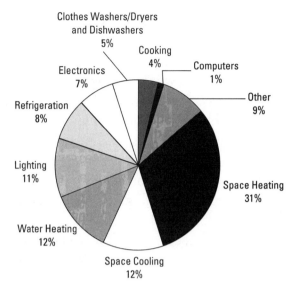

Figure 10–2 Energy Use in the U.S. Residential Sector

can manage entertainment, security, lighting, heating, cooling, and every aspect of home energy use, as displayed in Figure 10–2. They are remotely controllable from everywhere, including a household personal computer, a handheld remote, or a cell phone. Once programmed by the consumer, the appliances and devices in a home operate automatically to optimally meet the consumer's requirements.

More than 100 vendors are now active in the home automation and digitized control field. Many of these were noted above. And as with most technologies, what starts out as an expensive luxury will be replicated on a much broader and simplified scale, which ultimately converts the convenience into a necessity. Indeed, more than two-thirds of U.S. households are Internet-connected and most have the capability for in-house networking. The vast majority of these households also have broadband capabilities including either a digital subscriber line (DSL) or cable. Not only does broadband capability provide fast connections, but the routers required to connect to the Internet can also serve as network hubs for all applications including electricity use management.

Most routers are now wireless, which enables easy networking of electricity control functions without costly and cumbersome wiring installation requirements. The initial electricity management focus will be on lighting control applications using products like those developed by Intermatic (HomeSettings) and Motorola (HomeGenie). Such entry-level applications are already available in retail outlets like Best Buy, Circuit City, Home Depot, Lowe's, Radio Shack, and Sears. Moreover, a range of comprehensive midmarket, home energy management systems is becoming available at a cost of about $500. These will yield a nominal two-year payback for a typical home with an annual electricity bill of $1,200, if the home has the necessary access to time-of-use electricity pricing.

Faced with such competition, and regulatory and legislative pressures, utilities will almost certainly begin to market their own Web-enabled energy control systems—once the regulatory logjam is broken and new incentives are in place. In so doing, utilities will be able to provide DR default options for consumers who do not want to self-manage or sign up with third-party DR service providers. It will also be in the self-interest of utilities and regulators to disseminate consumer energy use data and grid utilization information so that third-party providers can offer joint programs with the utility to extend the DR response into a wider array of value-added services. Indeed, the National Energy Security and Independence Act which became federal law in December 2007, directs states and regulators to make electricity prices and use information available to all consumers at all times. However, it remains to be seen how positively and promptly the states respond to this federal directive.

NEW HOMES

Already nearly half of all new U.S. home buyers are opting for home-automation capabilities. That proportion is expected to continue to grow, reaching more than 10 million new homes by 2015. Many of these new homes will be part of planned developments and community-based initiatives such as Mesa del Sol in New Mexico. Such large developments are able to exercise considerable leverage with utilities in negotiating power distribution improvements including smart meters. What's more, the builders will be able to brand these residential developments as "high-tech and high-reliability" communities with full slates of Perfect Power capabilities rolled in at the lowest cost to the new home buyer. As these developments take hold, in-home appliances with automatic demand-response capabilities will also be increasingly sold with their own electricity supply contracts as a competitive advantage in an era of rising electricity costs. Perfect Power communities have the added benefit of becoming an economic magnet for high-tech businesses and research facilities, adding to the local tax base.

COMMERCIAL OFFICE BUILDINGS

The Galvin Electricity Initiative envisions that by 2015, essentially all the managers of commercial office buildings will have a Web-enabled electricity account–monitoring capability. This will be set up either with their own local utility or with their electricity retail provider—such as Suez Energy and the Baltimore-based Constellation New Energy, which help businesses in North America purchase and manage electricity as a strategic asset—or through an outsourcing contract with one of the growing number of third-party demand-response managers, such as Comverge, EnerNOC, and ConsumerPowerline.

In parallel, the "big four" building system control providers— Johnson Controls, Honeywell, Invensys, and Siemens—are beginning to aggressively market Web-enabled energy control solutions for both new and retrofit buildings. The opportunity is immense, since the U.S. commercial building market consists of some 5 million buildings representing 75 billion square feet of floor space, and consuming 35 percent of the nation's electricity each year. Today, about one-third of all U.S. buildings larger than 100,000 square feet have energy management systems.

Over the last several years, open architectures have also been developed to allow full Web-enabled building power management systems. These have been joined with new smarter and more powerful Web-enhanced sensors in plug-and-play wireless sensor networks. One company that sees a huge value in this information technology and building automation system convergence is California's Cisco Systems, which recently launched its Cisco Connected Real Estate (CCRE) initiative.

Increased building intelligence will be applicable to existing as well as new buildings. Furthermore, retrofit improvements can generally occur without any local utility involvement. So, for the first time, commercial electricity management will be an open playing field where building managers, owners, and tenants alike will be able to truly discover and easily manage their energy needs as they decide. This completely changes the game. More stakeholders will have a seat at the energy design table; new constituencies will have to be recognized; new business propositions will emerge; and the marketing of energy will change. This will be the end of the blind energy lease charge which restricts tenants from knowing their actual energy use, the "one size fits all" building management approach, and the energy service deficiency excuses that building owners can throw at tenants. These benefits make a convincing economic case. The cost of "smarting-up" a building is in the range of $3 to $6 per square foot. However, this investment will typically yield energy savings, worker productivity improvements, and additional service revenues totaling at least $4 per square foot each year.

These benefits also have society-wide economic and environmental implications. The ability of smart buildings to precisely trigger on-demand responses could reduce the commercial sector's peak electricity demand by 10 to 15 percent, equivalent of 33–50 thousand megawatts of conservation. Many new providers are emerging to service this large commercial market— including the likes of EnerNOC, EnergyConnect, and Infotility, which are typically operating under initiatives sponsored by the local utility or the local independent transmission system operator, entities that would rather avoid building new generation facilities and transmission infrastructures. These new providers install, service, and generally retain ownership of the hardware and pay their clients for the energy savings. In return, they are paid by the utility on a long-term contractual basis for the peak electricity reserve their services provide. A notable example is the extensive array of commercial and public buildings in Pennsylvania being serviced by EnergyConnect under contract with PJM Interconnection, the regional independent grid operator. The result reduces PJM's peak power load by more than 150 megawatts.

SMART MICROGRIDS

The fourth and most comprehensive Perfect Power deployment scenario is through smart microgrids, incorporating and servicing an array of commercial buildings and residences. As discussed earlier, such microgrids in the size range of 1 to 10 megawatts provide maximum benefits to both consumers and suppliers from exploiting economies of scale and precision. The economies include lower power infrastructure costs, load diversity, and the sharing of thermal loads. However, these microgrids will often require the right to exchange power from one building to another, which will require changes in government policies and regulations.

Hundreds of clean energy development companies with billions of dollars in capital are combing the United States looking for opportunities to install solar and other cleaner energy systems on commercial and multi-family residential buildings. The commercial building market alone has sufficient roof space for up to 1,000 MW of solar photovoltaic systems. However, these entrepreneurs face an insurmountable barrier in utility regulations. Even in cases where the building owns the electricity distribution system, regulations prohibit the building owner from reselling clean electricity to the tenants. In effect, the utility has a micro-monopoly within each building to sell electricity to each tenant or resident, preventing the building owner from pursuing clean, efficient energy options.

Beyond policy changes, microgrids will increasingly be facilitated by utility and private sector investments in smart, advanced metering infrastructure. This AMI technology creates the conditions necessary for consumers and utilities to manage electricity demand together in a real-time environment. The AMI technology base is advancing rapidly through the efforts of over 30 commercial players, including major global corporations such as General Electric and Siemens. Worldwide, more than 50-million advanced meters have already been deployed. Italy has been an international pioneer in this area, with the installation of roughly 30 million meters to date. By the end of 2008, a similar number of these smart meters are expected to be in place in the United States with the number increasing to at least 65 million by 2015—or about 60 percent of all buildings and households.

Work by the Galvin Initiative suggests that there is the potential in the United States for at least 2,500 smart microgrid sites. These are just in the largest 35 to 40 U.S. urban or suburban service areas with above-average electricity rates. This total represents some 12,500 commercial buildings with a floor space approaching 1.75 billion square feet. By 2010, the Galvin Initiative envisions at least a dozen entrepreneurial developers—including such firms as the Illinois-based Endurant Energy LLC—installing about 25 smart microgrids per year, a rate that will rapidly double to at least 50 microgrid projects annually.

In sum, we estimate investments of about $30 billion over the next decade in smart home energy controls and commercial building intelligence, which by 2015 can be expected to return consumer benefits of at least $10 billion per year. And those are the kinds of numbers that no consumer, utility, or regulator can afford to ignore.

COMPANIES AND INSTITUTIONS TO WATCH

Automated Logic, Inc. (www.automatedlogic.com), located in Atlanta, Georgia, designs, develops, and manufactures hardware and software for building automation systems. Products are used for monitoring and controlling critical building functions such as heating, air-conditioning, and lighting. Founded in 1977, ALC customers include Marriot, JC Penny, Lockheed Martin, Target, Cisco, and United Parcel Service.

Carrier (www.corp.carrier.com), located in Farmington, Connecticut, has been a world leader in air-conditioning, heating, and refrigeration since 1902, when Willis Carrier invented the basics of modern air-conditioning. Carrier is now a subsidiary of United Technologies Corp. The company has $13 billion in sales, and it has installed its products in the Sistine Chapel, Mount Vernon, and the Great Hall of the People in Beijing.

Cellnet (www.cellnet.com), located in Atlanta, Georgia, operates the single largest advanced metering infrastructure network in the United States, which includes more than 11 million electric, gas, and water endpoints for utilities. Cellnet offers a wireless data communications network for automated meter reading, distribution automation, and supervisory control and data acquisition systems.

Cimetrics (www.cimetrics.com), headquartered in Boston, Massachusetts, has been a pioneer in open system communication for building automation for more than 12 years. Cimetrics BACnet software protocol stacks provide the underlying communication technology for a majority of the building automation systems manufacturers in the world.

Cisco Connected Real Estate (CCRE) (www.cisco.com). CCRE harnesses the power of the Internet to create a single, open standard, multiservice Internet protocol platform over which building automation systems can be connected and innovative tenant services can be offered. The result is intended to create new revenues for building owners while providing a more productive and secure workplace, and giving tenants greater control over their environment. These CCRE capabilities are available worldwide through Cisco's more than 200 offices in 60 countries.

Comverge Inc. (www.comverge.com). Based on over 25 years of industry experience, Comverge provides demand-response solutions to over 500 U.S. utility clients and 4.5 million consumer electrical devices involving 495 megawatts of contracted capacity. Its "pay-for-performance" programs provide capacity that can increase electricity reliability, reduce emissions, and defer utility capital infrastructure needs.

Constellation New Energy (www.NewEnergy.com) was formed in 1995 as New Energy Ventures, and it is now the largest competitive electricity supplier in North America. Constellation New Energy sells more than 15,000 megawatts of peak load electricity and nearly 300 billion cubic feet of natural gas, producing annual revenues of more than $8 billion. Its corporate goals include bringing the power of choice in energy to consumers across North America and to being a top national supplier of renewable energy.

Consumer Powerline (CPNL) (www.consumerpowerline.com) is a full-service, energy-asset management company and a leading provider of demand-response solutions in the United States, with more than 750 megawatts under management. CPNL operates in the New York, New England, California, Mid-Atlantic, and Texas markets, working with the owners of commercial, residential, and institutional buildings. The company shares with the customer the incremental savings or revenues it generates. Current customers include the owners of 75 million square feet of commercial real estate and 110,000 residential units.

Control4 (www.control4.com). With Control4, homeowners can consolidate the many different systems in their home into one, and automate them to be more energy efficient. Control4 gives you control of your lighting, temperature, security, multi-room music and home theater, all from a single, easy-to-use remote. Conserving energy has never been easier.

Delta Controls (www.deltacontrols.com), located in Surrey, British Columbia, Canada, offers a fully integrated building automated control system, including native BACnet HVAC access and lighting control. Delta Control solutions extend to energy management, Web connectivity, HVAC temperature controls, building security and safety, lighting, and open protocols and enterprise integration.

Ember (www.ember.com). Ember develops wireless sensor and control network technologies that help make our living and working environments smarter and energy efficient. Ember's ZigBee-based semiconductors and software enable communication between devices embedded in a variety of building and home automation products. Ember is headquartered in Boston and has a semiconductor development center in Cambridge, England and distributors worldwide.

Endurant Energy LLC (www.endurantenergy.com), located in suburban Chicago, is a leader in the field of clean energy, providing services and tools to assist utilities, facility owners, land developers, and government agencies in integrating new energy technologies, managing energy commodity price risks, improving energy reliability, and reducing environmental impacts.

EnergyConnect, Inc. (www.energyconnectinc.com), located in Portland, Oregon, is a leading provider of energy automation services for diverse markets, including utilities, industrial customers, independent system operators, and regional transmission organizations. Its objective is to reduce electricity consumption at times of peak usage using price signals, standby generators, and energy storage devices. The company is a wholly owned subsidiary of the Microfield Group, Inc.

EnerNOC Inc. (www.enernoc.com). Headquartered in Boston, EnerNOC provides demand-response and energy management solutions to commercial, institutional, and industrial clients as well as to utilities and grid operators. EnerNOC's Megawatt Network is intended to achieve the same effect as a peaking power plant, but at a significantly lower cost and with no incremental carbon emissions. In October 2006, EnerNOC became the first carbon-neutral company in the energy management industry.

HomePlug Powerline Alliance (www.homeplug.org) is one of the key networking alliances for high-speed powerline carriers. Thirteen companies formed the Alliance in 2000 to leverage the existing power system as a communication network. They issued the HomePlug 1.0 specification in 2001. Their board of directors includes representatives from Comcast, Intel, Cisco, Motorola, Radio Shack, Samsung, and Texas Instruments.

Honeywell Automation and Control Solutions (ACS) (www.honeywell.com), a part of Honeywell International, is a diversified technology and manufacturing company employing more than 100,000 people in 95 countries. ACS is an $11 billion strategic business group applying sensing and control expertise to diverse markets. ACS technology is at work in 100 million homes and 5 million buildings worldwide, as well as in transportation. The future will increasingly involve sensing devices connected and communicating wirelessly increasing amounts of data for processing.

IBM Global Business Services (www.ibm.com/services/us/ gbs/bus). IBM Global Business Services is the world's largest consulting service organization. It is a division of the International Business Machine Corporation and provides business consulting services worldwide in sales marketing, acquisitions, business strategy, supply chain, logistics, and procurement. IBM Global Business Services has consultants positioned in virtually every country and culture. One recent, publicly available report is entitled, "Expanding the Innovation

Horizon," available online at http://www-935.ibm.com/services/us/gbs/bus/html/bcs_index.html.

Infotility, Inc. (www.infotility.com). Formed in 2000, Infotility provides intelligent agent software enabling electricity utilities to increase the reliability, efficiency, and utilization of their grid assets. Infotility's interest-based, distributed, Gridagents software is specifically applicable to smart-grid networks for integrating and managing renewable and distributed energy resources, microgrids, intelligent load controls, and future grid assets such as plug-in hybrid cars.

Intermatics (www.intermatic.com), located in Spring Grove, Illinois, manufactures and services wireless home automation products for lighting and energy efficiency. Products include home automation brands like HomeSettings, InTouch, and Timeswitch, "the little gray box with the yellow dial"; Malibu landscape lighting; surge protection devices; and spa and pool controls.

Invensys (www.invensys.com) is a global leader in industrial, commercial, and residential automation controls, headquartered in the United Kingdom and listed on the London Stock Exchange. It provides control devices for products in residential homes and commercial buildings, including thermostats, HVAC and water heating, as well as appliances for cooking, refrigeration, laundry, and dishwashing. Invensys also installs and manages energy meters for retailers, banks, utilities, and manufacturing facilities.

Johnson Controls (www.johnsoncontrols.com) has expanded its traditional line of automotive products to include battery controls for hybrid-electric vehicles, along with systems engineering and service expertise. It is the world's largest provider of lead-acid batteries. The company's PowerWatch technology is designed to communicate battery status to the vehicle and interact with the vehicle to optimize battery performance, charging, and life.

Lanis+Gyr (www.landisgyr.net), together with Ampy, Cellnet+ Hunt, and Enermet, provides advanced metering solutions to energy utilities around the world. The company was acquired by the Bayard Group Pty Ltd in 2004 in an effort to build a global metering business. Landis+Gyr just released its latest version of the most widely used advanced meter management system in Europe, and it is targeting business in the Middle East.

Linksys, (www.linksys.com) a division of Cisco, is a leader in home networking, and has shipped more than 70 million wireless devices. It has led in the development of Wireless-N, a new networking standard that raises the bar on the levels of convenience, range, and speed of wireless devices. With Wireless-N, devices work at greater distances and allow seamless streaming of video and multimedia.

Lutron (www.lutron.com) was founded in 1961 with the introduction of the world's first solid-state electronic device to dim lights in the home. Lutron, headquartered in Coopersburg, Pennsylvania, is today a leading manufacturer of lighting controls worldwide for homes, offices, and mixed-use space. Company growth has averaged 20 percent a year. Their new interactive Web site allows visitors to play with interactive dimmers and assess the energy savings involved.

OPC Foundation (www.opcfoundation.org). The OPC Foundation is dedicated to ensuring interoperability in automation by creating and maintaining open specifications that standardize the communication of acquired process data, alarm and event records, historical data, and batch data to multi-vendor enterprise systems and between production devices.

Optimal Technologies (www.otii.com) develops solutions to help electric utilities, businesses, and consumers optimize their energy usage. Optimal's United States base office is in Raleigh, North Carolina, and international headquarters is in Bridgetown, Barbados. The company's mission is to enable a more efficient, reliable, and environmentally responsible electric power grid from generation to appliances, and to develop the technologies necessary to achieve this mission.

Siemens Building Technology Division (SBTD) (www.building technologies.siemens.com). Headquartered in Switzerland, SBTD operates in 51 countries with manufacturing facilities in Europe, the United States, and Asia. SBTD offers an infrastructure technology portfolio designed for comfort and energy efficiency, security, and safety in buildings and public places. These capabilities are also expanding into the residential market through home automation systems.

Suez Energy North America (http://www.suezenergyna.com) is a diversified energy company based in Houston, managing positions within the energy value chain in the United Sates, Mexico, and Canada, including electricity generation and cogeneration, natural gas and liquefied natural gas, renewable resources, asset-based trading and origination, and retail energy sales, and related services to commercial and industrial customers.

ZigBee Alliance (www.zigbee.org). The ZigBee Alliance was formed in 2002 as an association of companies working together to enable reliable, cost-effective, wireless networks monitoring and control products based on an open global standard. The alliance is composed of some 240 promoters and participants, and it provides worldwide support to users of the ZigBee Compliant Platform. The goal of the ZigBee Alliance is to provide consumers with wireless intelligence built into the widest possible array of everyday devices.

Z-Wave Alliance (www.zensys.com). The Z-Wave Alliance was formed in 2005 by more than 160 independent manufacturers who have agreed to build wireless home control products based on the Zensys Z-Wave open standard. Z-Wave allows users to create a wireless, two-way, mesh network within a home for single point control of all compatible devices. The Z-Wave Alliance was established to address key market obstacles including incompatible technologies, unfocused and ineffective standardization attempts, and uncompetitive prices.

11

Creating a Green-Collar Revolution: New Companies and New Jobs

The individuals and companies, large and small, that are part of the smart-grid movement, are on the cusp of creating whole new categories of jobs. From retrofitting and maintaining homes and buildings for active energy efficiency to financing such conversions—with combined monthly payments being less than today's utility bill alone—this evolution suggests a new role for trade schools and unions, along with stimulating and rewarding employment for 21st-century electricians and electronic technicians.

In northern California, tucked between U.S. Highway 101 and the west end of San Francisco International's runway 1R, is a collection of rather nondescript buildings and tanks. To a casual observer, they would appear to be part and parcel of the airport. In truth, the facility is a wastewater treatment plant that belongs to Millbrae, a community of about 20,000 people, nearly all of whom live on the opposite side of the freeway. Flanked by the constant rumble of traffic and the crescendo of departing airliners, it is the unlikely site of a minor technological miracle. The architect of this peek into the future is Dick York, a white-bearded, bespectacled, suspender-wearing 60-year-old veteran of the distinctly unglamorous profession of sewage control. In the two years before his recent retirement, York took an old facility in a dirty business to the leading edge of environmentalism and electricity innovation.

York's plant was reputedly the first in the United States to receive and process inedible restaurant grease, and, through a self-funded and purposely crafted system, to convert that waste into methane and then electricity, which in turn is used to meet at least 80 percent or more of the total facility's electrical needs. Working with Chevron Energy Solutions, York oversaw the installation of a new 250-kilowatt microturbine generator, part of $5.5 million investment that will be paid for by reduced maintenance expenses and disposal fees paid by grease haulers working on behalf of the local restaurants. And it didn't cost the residents of Millbrae a penny. Cranked up late in 2006 and running on the 3,000 gallons of grease that's collected daily from traps outside the city's finest eateries and fast-food restaurants, the new generator also produces heat that's fed to the plant's digester tanks, conditions that cause the microorganisms working inside to thrive. At the end of the day, Millbrae residents get better wastewater processing, a convenient disposal system for its restauranteurs, and a model clean-energy facility.

Restaurants in the United States generate about 4.2 billion pounds of grease annually, much of which is buried in landfills where it decomposes and eventually will release methane, one of the most potent greenhouse gases, into the atmosphere. The system developed by York and Chevron Energy Solutions is now being replicated and expanded in Rialto, a suburb of Los Angeles with about 100,000 residents. That's where a 900-kilowatt fuel-cell power plant will generate electricity without combustion from the methane produced from kitchen grease and wastewater sludge. While cutting greenhouse gas emissions equivalent to taking more than 1,000 cars off of the road each year, it will also cut the city's energy costs by an estimated $800,000 per year.

York's $5.5 million project, he suggests, was both a serendipitous development and a demonstrative proof point for the city's eventual partner. "At first, Chevron Energy Solutions said we were too small of a project for their business model, but when we added in the collection of grease as a food source for the bacteria in the digester, and proposed generating electricity at no costs to our ratepayers, they penciled it in and agreed to manage the investment. Since then I've made presentations at a number of colleges and wastewater forums and while there are always a few naysayers, the idea of treating waste as an energy resource is getting new attention from entrepreneurs and cities alike. Although you could convert the grease into biodiesel for motor vehicles, electricity is my preferred energy path because of the versatility and cleanliness of electricity in the home, business, and factory."

ALTERNATIVE ELECTRICITY GENERATION

Indeed, while often articulated as alternative energy developments, an increasingly large part of this innovation activity is going into the production, distribution, and control of electricity from novel, clean sources. It's a sector that includes forward-thinking individuals such as York; massive and venerable corporations such as Chevron; relatively young burgeoning giants like Google; and small but potentially influential firms such as the Yountville, California–based RealEnergy. Many are looking to make electricity from diverse new photovoltaic materials, including nanotechnology, while others are counting upon innovative wind turbine designs and locations, including some offshore, and their turbine design cousins placed under the sea to capture tidal and wave movements. Still others, including RealEnergy and its CEO Kevin Best, see electrical power in the manure from cattle and dairy farms, which through a conversion process similar to that used in Millbrae, turns an environmental liability into valuable electricity.

Another such example is found at Central Vermont Public Service, an investor-owned utility that serves more than 158,000 customers in 152 counties. CVPS has harnessed the power of four dairy farms in that state—each with more than 500 cows—by putting the manure in digesters, which create methane that's burned in generators to make electricity. Consumers who sign up for "Cow Power" pay a 4-cent-per-kilowatt-hour premium, which helps subsidize the program. The environmental benefits of reducing the methane released to the atmosphere and eliminating the manure-borne pathogens that are killed in the digesters yields great social benefits as well as reliable power. Indeed, CVPS has the highest JD Power customer service satisfaction ratings in the East, and its bills—despite the extra payment for Cow Power participants—are among the lowest in New England.

With electricity production costs of most solar power systems now running about 25 cents per kilowatt hour, this source of electricity still has a long way to go before economically competing with coal, which in some cases generates electricity at one-tenth the cost. The retail price for electricity averages 11 cents per kilowatt hour in the United States, but it is nearly double that in certain areas of California and around New York. The ultimate aspiration for solar, wind power, and most any other form of alternative power generation is the concept of "grid parity," or producing electricity for the same price or less than do utilities from coal-fired and nuclear power plants. Bringing out innovation in places large and small, this trend is also creating jobs, the number of which is still fairly speculative, but significant in the opinion of numerous experts.

One of the most important contributors to achieving grid parity for renewable energy is the smart, electronically controlled grid. The use of renewable solar and wind energy in today's obsolete, electromechanically controlled transmission and distribution networks requires large quantities of conventional backup power and/or storage. This is necessary to compensate for the natural supply variability of these clean energy sources, but it significantly raises their cost and reduces their environmental value. In contrast, a modern smart grid can maintain absolute supply/demand balance with far less backup power and storage.

In effect, silicon is the backup that closes the power gap in a smart, green grid. As discussed throughout this book, the most effective approach from an environmental, energy supply and economic perspective alike will be Perfect Power microgrids that incorporate distributed solar photovoltaics and, in effect, make every rooftop a clean, quiet and safe 21st-century powerplant.

Renewable energy research and investment is being further stimulated by the growing expectation that a price will soon be placed on carbon emissions. According to the famed venture capitalist John Doerr of Kleiner Perkins, investors poured $1.8 billion into California's green technology companies in 2007, up 45 percent from the previous year. What's more, Doerr believes that California's new global warming law alone will lead to businesses employing an estimated 83,000 people in high-quality jobs, and generating $4 billion in new annual revenue. With the right market dynamics, he contends, "green technology could be as big tomorrow as the Internet is today."

The quest for grid parity was behind Google's November 2007 announcement, when it vowed to spend "hundreds of millions of dollars" to produce competitive solar panel–derived electricity. Indeed, the name of the project is: "Renewable Energy Cheaper Than Coal, or RECC." Google will spend at least $20 million to get started in 2008, with plans to hire 30 new employees. Google drew fulsome and arguably outsized praise for its proclamation, but such is the faith that its powerful brand currently engenders.

Google, however, is hardly alone in this quest. Consider the San Jose, California–based SunPower Corp., which manufactures and installs solar photovoltaic panels in homes and businesses, and has major customers including FedEx, Microsoft, Target, Johnson & Johnson, Lowe's, and Wal-Mart. With more than 1,500 employees, most of whom are located in the Philippines, the firm has forecasted its 2008 revenues at nearly $1.3 billion, with earnings of more than $150 million. What's more, it is projecting 2009 revenues 40 to 50 percent higher than for 2008. Perhaps the leading solar company in the United States, the firm is financially backed by legendary Silicon Valley entrepreneur T.J. Rodgers, the CEO of Cypress Semiconductor. An integrated firm that makes its own cells, panels, and the systems that are installed in homes and office buildings, SunPower is facing a plethora of competition. It is banking on the concept of distributed power; that is, placing the solar photovoltaic panels that generate electricity pretty much at the location where they are used, especially roof-tops in what will be net zero-energy buildings.

Other firms, however, are basing their business model on the idea of a remote, centralized solar-thermal "farm," essentially a field of mirrors located in a sunny location that focuses the sun's rays on tubes of water that make steam that in turn drive an electricity-generating turbine, not unlike a conventional plant that burns coal. Spain, one of the world leaders in solar thermal, is now installing a 100-megawatt plant near Seville. The advantage of solar thermal is its inherent capability for energy storage, which pushes its capacity factor—the percentage of time available to generate power—to around 70 percent. As a 21st-century sustainable community prototype, Mesa del Sol, for example, intends to incorporate both the distributed and centralized solar business models to best advantage.

The firm getting the most attention for solar thermal is Ausra Inc., which has a pilot in its testing and commissioning phase in Australia. In late 2007, the firm announced an agreement with Pacific Gas & Electric, the huge northern California utility firm, to build a 177-megawatt plant in central California's San Luis Obispo County, which is expected to come online in 2010. The plant will ostensibly use no fuel, little water, take up only one square mile of land, and would release no air or water emissions. Located in Palo Alto, California, this one facility alone will create 350 skilled jobs during construction and leave behind 100 permanent jobs once the facility is completed. Ausra also claims that its fairly simple technology can produce electricity for 10 cents a kilowatt hour and perhaps even less. While this is an arguable proposition, it is one that hasn't deterred investors from banking on the firm.

Still other companies are looking at new ways to generate solar power without mirrors or the conventional silicon solar panel, the latter of which are energy-intensive to manufacture. In fact, a conventional panel requires about three years of productive use before it generates as much power as it took to make it. Consequently, one of the potential "killer applications" in solar is the so-called thin-film panel, in which a coating of copper, indium, gallium, and selenium is essentially painted or printed onto a polymer film. One of the leaders in this area is another Palo Alto–based firm, NanoSolar. Its CEO, Martin Roscheisen, believes that a manufacturing plant that his company intends to build in Silicon Valley will have an advantage in both the costs it takes to make the thin-filmed panels and in their diverse applications.

NanoSolar's thin-film panels, contends Roscheisen, will be 80 to 90 percent cheaper to produce than a conventional panel. Although the materials in the thin-film sheets don't produce electricity any more efficiently than regular panels—at best, most solar panels convert only about 20 percent of the sun's energy that strikes them into electricity—it can be incorporated into many more places. The idea is that the thin film can improve its economics by doing dual duty by eventually being incorporated into roofing tiles, windows, and even walls.

RETROFITTING SMART BUILDINGS AND LINKING THEM INTO MICROGRIDS

Materials such as thin-film panels will eventually comprise a large piece of the smart buildings and homes that interact with intelligent grids both large and small. But even on the small scale of an individual home or office building, interconnectivity which enables every electric device and appliance to communicate with its power supply is essential to reliability and efficiency—just as it is to aggregations of commercial buildings and the energy management provided by firms such as Energy Connect, Comverge, and EnerNOC. One of the more promising smart-grid companies is the Washington, D.C.–based GridPoint which focuses on homes and small buildings and has an intelligent platform that will eventually allow these consumers and their appliances to automatically interact with utilities.

Founded in 2003 and run by CEO Peter Corsell, a young entrepreneur who once worked in the State Department and as a CIA analyst specializing in U.S.-Cuban relations, GridPoint offers computerized energy control systems for households, but most notably a battery storage device for backup that's about the size of a small refrigerator. Called the GridPoint Connect Series, this plug-and-play appliance can automatically provide clean and silent electricity during blackouts and brownouts, but more importantly can power critical loads in a household or building during times of peak power. What's more, the Connect—which is essentially a large battery that functions like a generator—can be charged by solar power or wind power during the day, or it can be recharged from the grid during periods of low demand at night. It is also designed to be integrated with a plug-in hybrid electric vehicle. The company has been backed by about $90 million of venture-capital funding, including $48 million poured into the company by Goldman Sachs in October of 2007.

Most of the action in the small building and household arena is currently the purview of small firms and entrepreneurs. Consider northern California's Scott Sullivan, a 38-year-old University of California–Santa Cruz economics major who is the founder, chairman, and CEO of SoundVision, a firm that works primarily with relatively wealthy early adopters. Although the company's original business model was based on the installation of home entertainment systems, its subsequent development exemplifies the type of company that will ultimately install a full and holistic range of energy savings and control devices in both new and retrofitted homes. Founded as a side business in 1998, Sullivan's firm now employs 22 people and does roughly $4.5 million in annual business.

Along with home entertainment systems, Sullivan says that many of his clients want complete lighting control, all of which is connected to occupant detectors that turn off the lights if no movement is sensed within 10 or 20 minutes. "The lighting and automatic window shades also are tied into a security system, so that if an intruder comes in, lights start flashing and the shades go up and down," he explains. "For some clients we build in battery backups to take over in case of power failure. Since we work with architects, designers, lighting professions, and builders on high-end homes—which usually have big-screen televisions with instant-on features—I wouldn't consider us an energy-saving company, even though our equipment reduces *the potential* use of electricity." But when Sullivan's company is done with a completely wired home, the potential for a house that could, ultimately, interact with a microgrid or a utility is already in place.

The interaction between a home and a microgrid or utility is the final hurdle of an electrical revolution, suggests Lawrence Silverman, a 60-year-old entrepreneur who attended MIT and ended up in the nascent field of digital lighting controls primarily for entertainment centers, restaurants, and high-end hotels. In the late 1970s, Silverman partnered with *Billboard Magazine* to create a video music network in a format that was later adopted by MTV. Today he's the director of Broadband Energy Networks, a Pennsylvania-based firm that packages networked information, energy, and automation services. Silverman is also a member of the Gridwise Architecture Council and spends much of his time advocating a change in how consumers interface with utilities. From the work he's done with businesses, Silverman knows that the Internet enables a power user to control lights, heat, security, and a number of other functions. "But now that information seems kind of intangible, useful to the individual but fenced off from communication with a networked grid of thousands of users," he observes. "A smart control meter has to interact in both directions if it's to have value to the system. Once we have smart meters that can sidestep utility industry regulations—or get governments to change those regulations—this sector of the business, retrofitting homes and buildings with energy saving equipment, will finally take off."

While companies such as Silverman's and Sullivan's are today fairly small, it's not much of a stretch to envision thousands of similar operations serving communities across the nation, if not also in other parts of the world. Similar to plumbing companies, building contractors, and other service sectors, retrofitting homes and buildings to efficiently control electricity could create businesses that more than rival the increasingly common home computer service business.

It's only natural that the financial industry would follow these developments, as there is money to be made from funding energy-saving systems. Lower utility payments will theoretically lower utility bills, and yet yield the lender a profit. In fact, the New Resource Bank in San Francisco was established primarily to serve resource-efficient businesses and nonprofits. A full-service bank that takes in its share of ordinary deposits, the bank uses that money to make loans to organic farmers, sustainable home and office construction, and solar installations. Formed in late 2006, the bank already has nearly $60 million in assets.

Venture-capital funding for clean technology in 2007 also jumped some 70 percent over 2006 levels to $3 billion, even though venture-capital spending overall rose less than 20 percent. These financial commitments signal a bright future for the emerging clean technology industry.

Yet another important element of the private sector financing industry is now positioned to help finance the reinvention of the electricity system. The Internal Revenue Service (IRS) has recently ruled that electricity transmission and distribution networks are real estate assets that can be transferred into a real estate investment trust (REIT). The rents from leasing these assets to an operator will also only be subject to one level of taxation.

As traditional regulated sources of utility funding remain unwilling and/or unable to fund the cost of system modernization, REIT financing becomes an offer that cannot be long refused.

GREEN AT WORK

If one considers all of the dimensions of reinventing the electricity system and developing alternative means of generating power, the realm of "green-collar jobs" is wide, deep, and very encompassing. Figure 11–1 indicates the range of industries that are already engaged in the rapidly growing array of smart, green grid business opportunities. Indeed, it includes not only those who design and manufacture solar panels, but electricians who retrofit old buildings and install gear in new construction. It includes the employees of banks and investment houses that fund electricity-making ventures, headhunters who place alternative energy executives in new ventures, and journalists who cover this field for news outlets and feature publications and Web sites. The professors and staff at the Illinois Institute of Technology, for example, who are educating the next generation

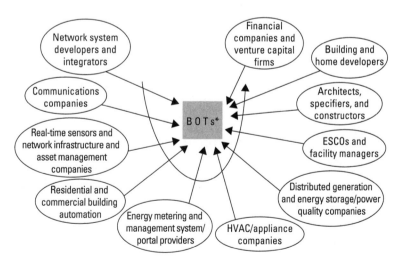

Figure 11–1   Many New Entrants and Types of Players in the Green Economy
*BOTs = business opportunity templates.

of power engineers, could also be said to be part of the green-collar revolution.

As *Fortune* magazine reported in late 2007, the total market capitalization of solar companies worldwide, which was a mere $1 billion in 2004, had just three years later hit $71 billion and is still climbing. In spite of this progress, *The Wall Street Journal* pointed out in a March 2008 article about this new sector of employment, that the U.S. Bureau of Labor Statistics currently doesn't break out "green collar" work as part of an industry or occupation. And yet the *Journal* contends that emerald-hued businesses are an economic bright spot for a nation that has lost nearly a quarter of its manufacturing jobs, roughly 3.5 million in this decade alone.

According to Peter Beadle, the president of Greenjobs.com, a Fairfield, California–based firm that matches employers and job applicants, the solar field alone may employ more than two million people by 2020. "That number was based on a prediction several years ago by a European photovoltaic association, which saw its first forecast exceeded by two or three times what they'd originally projected," explains Beadle, who launched Greenjobs.com in 2004, pretty much on faith, hope, and prayer. "Now the assumption is that the multiplier effect—the indirect jobs generated by solar work—are 1.5 to 3 times the number of direct positions. The growth potential is certainly there."

A former executive with British Petroleum and who in his last job served as president of BP Solar Inc., Peter Beadle started his Greenjobs Web site with zero circulation and very few job listings. Although the growth has been gradual, he now gets more than 100,000 hits per month, has 10,000 job seekers registered and has about 1,000 dues-paying companies listed on a site that in some ways must compete with the largely free Craig's List. There are other competitors, but the Scotland-born Beadle feels that he's providing a more substantive service than most others, screening applicants when asked and offering a networking forum to bridge the gap between "aspiring talent and potential employers," he adds. "And I find it encouraging that employers are actually paying for the service, which suggests we're on to something substantial."

Another rapidly growing dimension of the green, renewable energy business is wind power. According to the American Wind Energy Association, the U.S. wind-power industry grew by 45 percent in 2007, boosting its entire generating capacity by a third. The trade group figured that at the start of 2008, there were nearly 20,000 jobs in the wind energy sector, double the number from the previous year. Worldwide, $65 billion were invested in renewable power systems in 2007 compared to just $30 billion three years ago. Figure 11–2 displays the wide array of renewable energy technologies and their relative development status. Only a small fraction of these technologies have reached commercial readiness.

Renewable energy is beginning to cross the divide toward filling a significant role in world energy markets. High energy prices, climate change, and energy security are converging to drive clean renewable energy. As discussed earlier, the magnitude of this role is ultimately dependent on the wide-scale implementation of smart microgrids as the essential vehicle needed to practically tie renewables into existing electricity supply systems. Cambridge Energy Research Associates (CERA), for example, forecasts that renewable power could produce

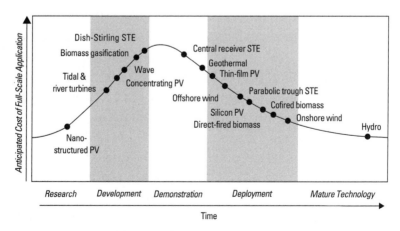

Figure 11–2 Renewable Technology Development

as much as 16 percent of the world's electricity by 2030. Key considerations include cost, scale, reliability, and compatibility. In the absence of the necessary technology, policy, and economic advancements this total could shrink to 7 percent. According to CERA, in order to reach the higher mark, clean power should see $7 trillion of worldwide investment by 2030.

While there is apparently a plethora of new jobs coming online—and what might be especially good news for U.S. workers is that many of these can never be sent offshore—there is a potential impediment to developing Perfect Power and getting the most from the green energy revolution. It's an impending dearth of electrical power engineers and other skilled members of a rapidly aging workforce. By 2010, one in three workers in the United States will be 50 or older, a trend that's similar in other developed countries. More pertinent to this discussion is the fact, reports the U.S. Bureau of Labor Statistics, that the demand for civil engineers, electrical engineers, mechanical engineers, boilermakers, and linemen will outstrip the current supply by an average of more than 20 percent. By 2012 there will be roughly 10,000 more power industry jobs available than trained personnel to fill them.

Although China and India are graduating electrical power engineers at a much greater rate, North America, and Europe are facing huge gaps. The Institute of Electrical and Electronic Engineers reports that there are more than 350,000 electrical engineers now working in the United States, along with some 23,000 registered power engineers. Those numbers are part of a report from the office of Washington State Senator Maria Cantwell, which points out that each year, "There are only about 500 undergraduate degrees awarded in the area of power engineering—compared to nearly 2,000 in the 1980s."

This is not merely a brain drain, but an intelligence drought that has spanned at least two generations mirroring the concurrent drought in electric power investment and innovation. It will certainly affect utilities which, like the oil industry, are facing a wave of retiring technical professionals. And it could limit the ability of small entrepreneurial companies to deliver promising new services. The lack of skilled manpower may also severely affect the nuclear power community, should climate change concerns revive an industry that produces great quantities of electricity with no greenhouse gas emissions. More than a third of the nation's 20,000 nuclear energy workforce will be eligible for retirement within five years.

The situation is, however, a tremendous opportunity for a lifetime of gainful and rewarding employment. Matching the supply to the demand will require forward thinking. As *The Wall Street Journal* has pointed out, Washington State had jumped into a leadership position in this area by founding a Center of Excellence for Energy Technology at Centralia College, expressly for students looking to work in the energy industry. Along with two community colleges, the school is attempting to develop power industry and renewable energy workers such as mechanics and boilermakers, who according to the Center's director can find entry-level work paying $33,000 to $62,000 annually, after only two years of school.

If they've not yet noticed, officials at trade schools and electrical unions now have at their disposal a powerful recruiting pitch. The reinvention of the electrical system is certain to produce millions of well-paying jobs that can't be sent off overseas and are not only economically valuable in that they save energy, but command respect for their environmental benefits as well. What's more, the design, construction, and maintenance of microgrids and smart electrical control systems generate the kind of rewarding work that can last for entire careers.

Indeed, perhaps with a rising awareness about the wondrous versatility of electricity, youths considering career paths will see a bright future in what was once a stagnant profession. After all, Perfect Power is at the nexus of environmental concerns, the demands for digital age power, and the development of a better quality of life around the world.

INSTITUTIONS AND COMPANIES TO WATCH

American Wind Energy Association (AWEA) (www.awea.org). The AWEA, located in Washington, D.C., is a national trade association representing wind power project developers, equipment suppliers, services providers, parts manufacturers, utilities, researchers, and others involved in the wind industry. In addition, AWEA represents hundreds of wind energy advocates from around the world promoting wind power growth through advocacy, communication, and education.

AGM Batteries Ltd. (www.agmbatteries.com) is a joint-venture company, located in Scotland, manufacturing lithium-ion cells. Its joint-venture partners included AEA Technology, Japan Storage Battery Co., and Mitsubishi Materials Corp. In 2002, AEA Technology was awarded a multimillion-pound contract to supply batteries and chargers to the United Kingdom new Bowman battlefield communication system based upon AGM's world-leading cell.

Ausra Inc. (www.ausra.com), based in Palo Alto, California, develops and deploys utility-scale solar thermal power technology to serve global electricity needs in a dependable, market-competitive, environmentally responsible manner.

Ballard (www.ballard.com), located in Burnaby, British Columbia, is a global leader in the design, development, and manufacture of hydrogen fuel cells for cogeneration, backup power, and transportation. It is partnered with the automotive industry through AFCC, owned by Daimler AG, Ford Motor Co., and Ballard. In the cogeneration area, it is involved in a joint venture with Ebara Ballard Corp. in Japan. Revenues for 2007 reached $65 million.

Broadband Energy Networks, Inc. (www.broadbandenergy networks.com), based in Upper Darby, Pennsylvania, develops information-based solutions that improve the efficiency, comfort, and safety of businesses, buildings, and homes. It is a leading supplier of networked automation products and services that control the use of critical operating resources—electricity, gas, water, heating and cooling, information, communications, and secure access.

BYD Company Limited (www.bydit.com), founded in 1995 is now listed on the Hong Kong exchange. The company has become the world's second largest producer of rechargeable batteries, including lithium-ion, nickel-cadmium, and nickel-metal-hybrid batteries. BYD's two major markets are IT components and automobiles. Its seven production facilities are located in China.

Cambridge Energy Research Associates (CERA) (www.cera.com) is a leading advisor to international energy companies, governments, financial institutions, and technology providers. Its services help decision makers anticipate the energy future and formulate timely, successful plans in the face of rapid change and uncertainty. CERA's expertise covers all major energy sectors, and its team of experts is headed by Dr. Daniel Yergin, chairman, who is the Pulitzer Prize–winning author of *The Prize: The Epic Quest for Oil, Money and Power.*

Capstone Turbine Corp. (www.microturbine.com), founded in 1988, is a leading producer of low-emission microturbine systems. Its products are compact, turbine generators suitable for applications ranging from remote locations to city centers, delivering high-quality power from a variety of fuels. In 2007, Capstone shipped its 4,000th unit, and reached $21 million in sales. Capstone, headquartered in Chatsworth, California, is now listed on the NASDAQ exchange as CPST.

Central Vermont Public Services Company (www.cvps.com), based in Rutland, Vermont, is the largest electric company in that state. Organized in 1929 by the consolidation of eight electric companies, it can trace its roots to more than 100 companies, one dating back to 1858. It serves over 158,000 customers in 152 communities.

Chevron Energy Solutions (www.chevronenergy.com), based in San Francisco, California, partners with institutions and businesses to improve facilities, increase efficiency, reduce energy consumption and costs, and ensure reliable high-quality energy for critical digital era operations.

Elliot Energy Systems (www.elliotmicroturbines.com), located in Stuart, Florida, is a leading manufacturer of microturbines for use in distributed electricity generation and combined heat and power applications. Their 100-kW turbine is designed for industrial and commercial applications and represents over 10 years of research, development, and testing. The optional remote monitoring system allows the turbine to be integrated with the building controls system.

GAIA (www.gaia-akku-online.com), located in Nordausen, Germany, is a company producing lithium-ion polymer systems, in which the liquid electrolyte has been replaced with a solid. The result is a flat, lightweight battery that is completely dry and can be flexibly shaped. Batteries as thin as four millimeters can be produced, with high energy density and output, making them ideal for high-volume markets, including autos.

Google Inc. (www.google.com/corporate) is based in Mountain View, California, and its mission is to organize the world's information and make it universally accessible and useful.

Greenjobs (www.greenjobs.com) is located in Fairfield, California. It was launched in 2004 to focus specifically on all aspects of employment in renewable energy worldwide. It is staffed and supported by people with a long experience in the field of renewable energy, and its goal is to become the leading provider of employment services and information in this field.

GridPoint Inc. (www.gridpoint.com), based in Washington, D.C., is a leading clean technology company and a pioneer of an innovative smart-grid platform that aligns the interests of electric utilities, consumers, and the environment. This platform is based on an intelligent network of distributed resources that controls load, stores energy, and produces power.

Nanosolar Inc. (www.nanosolar.com), based in San Jose, California, is a global leader in solar power innovation, setting standards for affordable green power with solar cell technology of distinctly superior cost efficiency, versatility, and availability. Leveraging recent science in nano-structured materials, it has developed a critical mass of engineering advances that profoundly change the cost efficiency and production scalability of solar electricity cells and panels.

New Resource Bank (www.newresourcebank.com), headquartered in San Francisco, California, was founded by entrepreneurs, and highly experienced bankers, who understand how excellent banking can empower businesses, organizations, and individuals to make greater impact on their efforts. The bank is dedicated to providing the best banking by offering the highly personalized services of a community bank along with the convenience and security of a large bank, and its shareholders have built leading Bay Area companies as well as leading green and sustainable businesses.

Oak Ridge National Laboratory (ORNL) (www.ornl.gov), ORNL is the department of energy's largest science and energy laboratory. ORNL was established in 1943 as part of the Manhattan Nuclear Project. Today, the laboratory supports the nation with peacetime science and technology services that include a variety of energy technologies and strategies. ORNL's overarching mission is to provide solutions to America's grand scientific challenges. ORNL's annual funding exceeds $1.2 billion, and it is managed by a partnership of Battelle and the University of Tennessee.

RealEnergy, LLC (wwwrealenergy.com), based in Yountville, California, has developed, built, owned, and operated more small, clean, and green on-site power plants than any other independent power producer or distributed energy developer in North America. It has developed 43 discrete facilities with electric grid interconnections, and it is focused on investing in clean, renewable power plants.

SolFocus (www.solfocus.com), located in Mountain View, California, and Spain, is intent upon developing innovative solar energy solutions competitive with fossil fuels. It currently has a portfolio of solar concentrating photovoltaic (CPV) systems, intelligent tracking systems for CPV, flat-panel PV systems, and solar thermal systems. Madrid-based SolFocus Europe was launched in 2007.

SoundVision (www.svsf.com), based in Novato, California, has installed thousands of home entertainment systems and, increasingly, lighting, energy, and security systems that can be controlled through numerous connections, at home or anywhere with Internet access.

SunPower Corporation (www.sunpowercorp.com), headquartered in San Jose, California, designs, manufactures, and delivers the highest efficiency solar electric technology worldwide, to residential, commercial, and utility-scale power plant customers. Its customers benefit from lower electric bills, meaningful financial returns, and maximum carbon emissions savings. The firm expects to compete with retail electric rates by reducing system cost by 50 percent by 2012.

Coda

Nearly two years have passed between the start of work on this book and its publication. During that period the price of crude oil has more than doubled on world markets, while motor gasoline, diesel, and jet fuel in the United States cost twice as much as in 2006. Public and congressional anger over soaring energy prices is superseded only by a gnawing fear that there just might not be sufficient supply to meet global demand, with populations clearly competing for limited resources. Concerns about carbon dioxide emissions and their role in a warming climate are greater than ever, even as the atmospheric levels of greenhouse gasses continue to rapidly rise, thanks to economic growth in China, India, and other newly prospering nations. The idea of "going green" dominates public discussions and media reports on new buildings and alternative forms of energy production. In fact, "going green" appears to be taking shape as a fundamental social ethic.

Meanwhile, in May 2008, Dianne Odell, a 61-year-old Tennessee woman, died when an electrical power outage shut down the iron lung on which she had relied for breath since polio struck her at the age of three. Dianne Odell's family members were unable to get a standby emergency generator started. A remarkable woman, who earned a high school diploma and wrote a children's book even while confined to the iron lung, Ms. Odell couldn't hold out until medical help arrived—or until the local utility restored service. If a clean, affordable electrical system that never fails is the ultimate energy end game for the 21st century, Odell's tragic demise is a cruel reminder that a great deal of work remains undone.

It may be that electricity is too obvious and ubiquitous to be viewed as something that can change the way we live for the better. Since it already revolutionized the world more than a century ago, what else is there for electricity to accomplish?

Well, plenty. In fact, we hope we've made the case that many additional possibilities are already within reach, and that countless advances as yet unimagined will unfold with the advent of Perfect Power. Despite all the focus on alternative and renewable forms of energy, we must consider how that energy is eventually delivered to and employed by the consumer.

Solar power, after all, is converted to electricity. So too is the energy contained in fluid currents of atmosphere, wind that causes mechanical blades to spin and that in turn generates … electricity. Nuclear plants produce prodigious quantities of energy, specifically in the heat that turns water into pressurized steam that drives turbines that make … electricity. Falling water held back by dams is turned into hydro*electric* power, as do waves and tidal flows when these future energy resources are harnessed. Coal, natural gas, and fuel oil are also burned for the heat that makes pressurized steam that drives turbines that make electricity. Even hydrogen-powered fuel cells—an element that's been touted as the future of clean energy—depends on electricity for its production and also ends up producing electricity that drives motors.

The ability of electricity to most efficiently convert all of the world's energy resources into the goods and services that mankind needs is the key to a globally sustainable energy future, and certainly in the case of the United States to national energy self-sufficiency. Indeed, the United States is endowed with more abundant, diverse, and readily available energy resources than any other country in the world. Given these realities, there is no justifiable reason for the United States to continue to put its citizens and others in harm's way because of short-sighted dependence on insecure and outrageously expensive imported energy.

Given the environmental costs of making electricity—and there are material, labor, aesthetic, social, and environmental costs associated with every form of energy production, be it conventional or alternative—it behooves society to squeeze the maximum use out of each and every watt or thermal unit. A watt of renewable energy that is wasted in a home or office is as morally repugnant, and practically ignorant, as a watt wasted from electricity generated from burning coal.

The same philosophical cant is behind the quest for reliability that's near perfection. Dianne Odell's iron lung might seem like an archaic piece of equipment, but a guaranteed, steady, and unwavering flow of electrons was not only vital to her life-sustaining machine, but especially so to the microprocessor-loaded devices of the Digital Era. That's why we believe that Perfect Power is so inclusively important, if only because it represents a holistic viewpoint on reinventing and gaining the most from a modernized electrical system.

Our consumer-focused, bottom-up, microgrid innovation strategy does indeed challenge the conventional wisdom that transformative change must occur through incremental, top-down mechanisms within the established highly centralized industry structure. In fact, change that profoundly disrupts the business and policy status-quo is, unfortunately, initially rejected literally at all costs by the incumbent industry. As a result, successful transformative commercial innovation, as demonstrated for example by the cell-phone and lap-top computer revolutions, is always led by outside entrepreneurial leadership organizations who are motivated by the new business opportunities that disruptive innovation enables.

In spite of the profound benefits, transformative change of this magnitude and scope poses a daunting challenge. It is well known that human culture tends to resist every significant change, but ultimately most changes "for the good" are eventually adopted, often to the significant benefit of those that resisted the most. This pattern of resistance and benefit is particularly true for an industry technically and politically entrenched as is the regulated monopoly electricity supply industry. Fortunately, today's younger generations who have grown up in the new digital, Internet world, better appreciate the critical importance of this transformation. They are now moving into positions of market dominance as well as providing business and policy leadership needed to make it happen.

The convictions surrounding the Perfect Power Initiative are sound and for the good of all. As a general rule, the "beyond our original imagination" benefits that derive from almost every new service, such as air travel, computers, cell phones, medical solutions, and so on, have eventually dazzled all of us. Perfect Power promises to surpass all of them, both as a growth business and as an affordably welcome service for everyone. We base this conclusion on our combined century of practical experience in successfully developing and applying limit-breaking innovations to achieve service excellence benefiting consumers, suppliers, and our nation. With a properly demanding and even contrary spirit, the looming crises of today can become the perfect services, lower costs, and heightened values of tomorrow.

Change is on the way. While most Perfect Power microgrids are still in the design stage, we are seeing hopeful signs of entrepreneurs who aggregate the energy potential of commercial buildings, creating "pseudo-microgrids," if you will, that reduce electrical consumption. We see more and more utilities willing to install smart meters, although the intelligence is typically limited to primarily serving the utility, not giving control to the consumer. We see mayors of many larger cities asking for changes in utility regulations and communities seeking a divorce from the mainline grids, even though the national system would be better off through careful integration.

Smart electricity that comes from the other side of the wall socket is indeed the energy end game, but only if it is used in appliances that don't waste the precious resource with unnecessary loads of lighting and power-leaking "instant-on" features that remain in far too many dumb appliances. Smart electricity is the energy end game, but only if building and homeowners adopt zero net energy opportunities that emphasize efficiency, stretching out the utility of solar panels and other shared distributed electricity-generating sources. Instead of depending on the one-way travel of electricity with aging equipment that's increasingly unreliable and needs replacement, we can transform the power system by installing an entirely new generation of innovative entrepreneurial hardware and software that is ready and waiting for us.

In closing, we have attempted to bring clarity to what are nuanced and often complicated issues. But the bottom line is simple: Consumers, communities, and utilities alike are being confronted with a "perfect storm" of converging cost, quality, and environmental issues that urgently require the smart, entrepreneurial transformation of our obsolete electricity infrastructure and its state-regulated monopoly, retail service business model.

This book is intended to be an urgent wake-up call to action by all concerned citizens. Positive change depends on informed and resolute voices being heard by the industry and political influentials who now prevent most citizens from controlling their energy, environmental, and economic destiny to best personal and societal advantage. We are entering an unprecedented window of opportunity for this positive transformation, but it will depend on all of us to make it happen.

We also offer a warning for the citizens of this new Century. In periods of profound change, the most dangerous response is to incrementalize your way into the future. **Electricity is, and will continue to be, the ultimate agent for progress.** Seize the opportunities that electricity presents as literally a matter of life and death importance.

With energy prices soaring a new president will take up the energy issue to stay in good graces of the voters. If the next president sincerely wants to make the United States energy self-sufficient and secure, and to fight climate change, the focus must be on first creating a smart power system that gives all Americans better, cleaner, and more efficient energy choices. Voters must demand these changes and challenge the candidates to remove the policy barriers to achieving a 21st-century Perfect Power system. Americans need to "recall" the grid. Our power system needs a recount—it is costly, dangerously antiquated, and dirty. Voters do indeed need to vote for change, to *perfect the grid!*

—The Authors

Glossary of Technical Terms

AC: *See* Alternating current.

ACE: *See* Area control error.

Adequacy: The ability of the electric system to supply the aggregate electrical demand and energy requirements of customers at all times, taking into account scheduled and reasonably expected unscheduled outages of system elements.

AGC: *See* Automatic generation control.

Alternating current: Alternating current; current that changes periodically (sinusoidally) with time.

Apparent Power: The product of voltage and current phasors. It comprises both active and reactive power, usually expressed in kilovoltamperes (kVA) or megavoltamperes (MVA).

Area control error (in megawatts): A negative value indicates a condition of undergeneration relative to system load and imports, and a positive value denotes overgeneration.

Automatic generation control: A computation based on measured frequency and computed economic dispatch. Generation equipment under AGC automatically responds to signals from an energy management system (EMS) computer in real time to adjust power output in response to a change in system frequency, tile-line loading, or to a prescribed relation between these quantities. Generator output is adjusted so as to maintain a target system frequency (usually 60 Hz) and any scheduled megawatt (MW) interchange with other areas.

Blackstart capability: The ability of a generating unit or station to go from a shutdown condition to an operating condition and start delivery power without assistance from the bulk electric system.

Bulk electric system: A term commonly applied to the portion of an electric utility system that encompasses the electrical generation resources and bulk transmission system.

Bulk transmission: A functional or voltage classification relating to the higher voltage portion of the transmission system, specifically, lines at or above a voltage level of 115 kV.

Bus: Shortened from the word *busbar*, meaning a node in an electrical network where one or more elements are connected together.

Capacitor bank: A capacitor is an electrical device that provides reactive power to the system and is often used to compensate for reactive load and help support system voltage. A bank is a collection of one or more capacitors at a single location.

Capacity: The rated continuous load-carrying ability, expressed in megawatts (MW) or megavolt-amperes (MVA) of generation, transmission, or other electrical equipment.

Cascading: The uncontrolled successive loss of system elements triggered by an incident. Cascading results in widespread service interruption, which cannot be restrained from sequentially spreading beyond an area predetermined by appropriate studies.

Circuit: A conductor or a system of conductors through which electric current flows.

Circuit breaker: A switching device connected to the end of a transmission line capable of opening or closing the circuit in response to a command, usually from a relay.

Control area: An electric power system or combination of electric power systems to which a common automatic control scheme is applied in order to (1) match, at all times, the power output of the generators within electric power systems and capacity and energy purchased from entities outside electric power systems, with the load in the electric power systems; (2) maintain, within the limits of good utility practice, scheduled interchange with other control areas; (3) maintain the frequency of the electric power systems within reasonable limits in accordance with good utility practice; and (4) provide sufficient generating capacity to maintain operative reserves in accordance with good utility practice.

Contingency: The unexpected failure or outage of a system component, such as a generator, transmission line, circuit breaker, switch, or other electrical element. A contingency also may include multiple components, which are related by situations leading to simultaneous component outages.

Control area operator: An individual or organization responsible for controlling generation to maintain interchange schedule with other control areas and contributing to the frequency regulation of the interconnection. The control area is an electric system that is bounded by interconnection metering and telemetry.

Current (electric):   The rate of flow of electrons in an electrical conductor measured in amperes.

Curtailability: The right of a transmission provider to interrupt all or part of a transmission service due to constraints that reduce the capability of the transmission network to provide that transmission service. Transmission service is to be curtailed only in cases where system reliability is threatened or emergency conditions exist.

Cyber-Security: The protection of computerized systems and electronic information from unauthorized access and attack. Cyber-security measures include firewalls, encryption, antivirus software, and intrusion detection/protection systems.

Cyber-security is vital to the protection of the nation's power supply infrastructure and is emphasized by the U.S. Department of Homeland Security.

Demand: The rate at which electric energy is delivered to consumers or by a system or part of a system, generally expressed in kilowatts or megawatts, at a given instant or averaged over a designed interval of time. *Also see* Load.

DC: *See* Direct current.

Direct current: Current that is steady and does not change sinusoidally with time. *Also see* Alternating current.

Dispatch operator: Control of an integrated electric system involving operations such as assignment of levels of output to specific generating stations and other sources of supply; control of transmission lines, substations, and equipment; operation of principal interties, and switching; and scheduling of energy transactions.

Distribution: For electricity, the function of distributing electric power using low-voltage lines to retail customers.

Distribution network: The portion of an electric system that is dedicated to delivering electric energy to an end user, at or below 69 kV. The distribution network consists primarily of low-voltage lines and transformers that "transport" electricity from the bulk power system to retail customers.

Disturbance: An unplanned event that produces an abnormal system condition.

Electrical energy: The generation or use of electric power by a device over a period of time, expressed in kilowatt hours (kWh), megawatt hours (MWh), or gigawatt hours (GWh).

Electric utility: Person, agency, authority, or other legal entity or instrumentality that owns or operates facilities for the generation, transmission, distribution, or sale of electric energy primarily for use by the public, and is defined as a utility under the statutes and rules by which it is regulated. An electric utility can be investor-owned, cooperatively owned, or government-owned (by a federal agency, crown corporation, state, provincial government, municipal government, or public power district).

Emergency: Any abnormal system condition that requires automatic or immediate manual action to prevent or limit loss of transmission facilities or generation supply that could adversely affect the reliability of the electric system.

Emergency voltage limits: The operating voltage range on the interconnected systems that is acceptable for the time and sufficient for system adjustments to be made following a facility outage or system disturbance.

Energy emergency: A condition when a system or power pool does not have adequate energy resources (including water for hydrounits) to supply its customers' expected energy requirements.

Energy management system (EMS):   An EMS is a computer control system used by electric utility dispatchers to monitor the real-time performance of various elements of an electric system and to control generation and transmission facilities.

Fault: A fault usually means a short circuit, but more generally it refers to some abnormal system condition. Faults are often random events.

Federal Energy Regulatory Commission (FERC):   An independent federal agency that, among other responsibilities, regulates the transmission and wholesale sales of electricity in interstate commerce.

Flashover: A plasma arc initiated by some event such as lightning. Its effect is a short circuit on the network.

Flowgate: A single or group of transmission elements intended to model megawatt (MW) flow impact relating to transmission limitations and transmission service usage.

Forced outage: The removal from service availability of a generating unit, transmission line, or other facility for emergency reasons or a condition in which the equipment is unavailable due to unanticipated failure.

Frequency: The number of complete alternations or cycles per second of an alternating current, measured in hertz (Hz). The standard frequency in the United States is 60 Hz. In some other countries the standard is 50 Hz.

Frequency deviation or error: A departure from scheduled frequency; the difference between actual system frequency and the scheduled system frequency.

Frequency regulation: The ability of a control area to assist the interconnected system in maintaining scheduled frequency. This assistance can include both turbine governor response and automatic generation control.

Frequency swings: Constant changes in frequency from its nominal or steady-state value.

Generation (electricity): The process of producing electrical energy from other forms of energy; also, the amount of electric energy produced, usually expressed in kilowatt hours (kWh) or megawatt hours (MWh).

Generator: Generally, an electromechanical device used to convert mechanical power to electric power.

Grid: An electrical transmission and/or distribution network.

Grid protection scheme: Protection equipment for an electric power system, consisting of circuit breakers, certain equipment for measuring electrical quantities (e.g., current and voltage sensors), and devices called *relays*. Each relay is designed to protect the piece of equipment it has been assigned from damage. The basic philosophy in protection system design is that any equipment that is threatened with damage by a sustained fault is to be automatically taken out of service.

Ground: A conducting connection between an electrical circuit or device and the earth. A ground may be intentional, as in the case of a safety ground, or accidental, which may result in high overcurrents.

Imbalance: A condition where the generation and interchange schedules do not match demand.

Impedance: The total effects of a circuit that oppose the flow of an alternating current consisting of inductance, capacitance, and resistance. It can be quantified in the units of ohms.

Independent system operator (ISO): An organization responsible for the reliable operation of the power grid under its purview and for providing open transmission access to all market participants on a nondiscriminatory basis. An ISO is usually not-for-profit and can advise utilities within its territory on transmission expansion and maintenance but does not have the responsibility to carry out the functions.

Information Sharing and Analysis Centers (ISACs): ISACs are designed by the private sector and serve as a mechanism for gathering, analyzing, appropriately sanitizing and disseminating private sector information. These centers could also gather, analyze, and disseminate information from government for further distribution to the private sector. ISACs also are expected to share important information about vulnerabilities, threats, intrusions, and anomalies, but do not interfere with direct information exchanges between companies and the government.

Interchange: Electric power or energy that flows across tie-lines from one entity to another, whether scheduled or inadvertent.

Interconnected system: A system consisting of two or more individual electric systems that normally operate in synchronism and have connecting tie-lines.

Interconnection: When capitalized, Interconnection refers to any one of the five major electric system networks in North

America: Eastern, Western, ERCOTT (Texas), Québec, and Alaska. When not capitalized, interconnection refers to the facilities that connect two systems or control areas. Additionally, an interconnection refers to the facilities that connect a nonutility generator to a control area or system.

Interface: The specific set of transmission elements between two areas or between two areas comprising one or more electrical systems.

Island: A portion of a power system or several power systems that is electrically separated from the interconnection due to the disconnection of transmission system elements.

ISO: *See* Independent system operator.

Kilovar (kVAr): Unit of electrical potential equal to 1,000 volts.

Kilovolt-amperes (kVA): Unit of apparent power equal to 1,000 volt amperes. Here, apparent power is in contrast to real power. On AC systems the voltage and current will not be in phase if reactive power is being transmitted.

Kilowatt hour (kWh): Unit of energy equaling 1,000 watt hours, or one kilowatt used over one hour. This is the normal quantity used for metering and billing electricity customers. The retail price for a kWh varies from approximately 4 cents to 15 cents. At 100 percent conversion efficiency, one kWh is equivalent to about 4 fluid ounces of gasoline, 3/16 pound of liquid petroleum, 3 cubic feet of natural gas, or $1/4$ pound of coal.

Line trip: Refers to the automatic opening of the conducting path provided by a transmission line by the circuit breakers. These openings or "trips" are to protect the transmission line during faulted conditions.

Load (electric): The amount of electric power delivered or required at any specific point or points on a system. The requirement originates at the energy-consuming equipment of the consumers. *Also see* Demand.

Load shedding: The process of deliberately removing (either manually or automatically) preselected customer demand from a power system in response to an abnormal condition, to maintain the integrity of the system and minimize overall customer outages.

Lockout: The state of a transmission line following breaker operations where the condition detected by the protective relaying was not eliminated by temporarily opening and reclosing the line, possibly several times. In this state, the circuit breakers cannot generally be reclosed without setting a lockout device.

Market participant: An entity participating in the energy marketplace by buying and selling transmission rights, energy, or ancillary services into, out of, or through an ISO-controlled grid.

Megawatt hour (MWh):   One million watt hours.

Metered value: A measured electrical quantity that may be observed through telemetering, supervisory control, and data acquisition (SCADA), or other means.

Metering: The methods of applying devices that measure and register the amount and direction of electrical quantities with respect to time.

NERC: *See* North American Electric Reliability Council.

Normal (precontingency) operating procedures: Operating procedures that are normally invoked by the system operator to alleviate potential facility overloads or other potential system problems in anticipation of a contingency.

Normal voltage limits: The operating voltage range on the interconnected systems that is acceptable on a sustained basis.

North American Electric Reliability Council (NERC):   A not-for-profit company formed by the electric utility industry in 1968 to promote the reliability of the electricity supply in North America. NERC consists of nine regional reliability councils and one affiliate, whose members account for virtually all the electricity supplied in the United States, Canada, and a portion of Baja California Norte, in Mexico. The members of these councils are from all segments of the electricity supply industry: investor-owned, federal, rural electric cooperative, state and municipal and provincial utilities, independent power producers, and power marketers.

Open Access Same Time Information Service (OASIS): Developed by the Electric Power Research Institute, it is designed to facilitate open access by providing users with access to information on transmission services and availability, plus facilities for transactions.

Operating criteria: The fundamental principles of reliable interconnected systems operation, adopted by NERC.

Operating guides: Operating practices that a control area or systems functioning as part of a control area may wish to consider. The application of guides is optional and may vary among control areas to accommodate local conditions and individual systems requirements.

Operating policies: The doctrine developed for interconnected systems operation. This doctrine consists of criteria, standards, requirements, guides, and instructions, which apply to all control areas.

Operating procedures: A set of policies, practices, or system adjustments that may be automatically or manually implemented by the system operator within a specified time frame to maintain the operational integrity of the interconnected electric systems.

Operating requirements: Obligations of a control area and systems functioning as part of a control area.

Operating security limit: The value of a system operating parameter (e.g., total power transfer across an interface) that satisfies the most limiting of prescribed pre- and postcontingency operating criteria as determined by equipment loading capability and acceptable stability and voltage conditions. It is the operating limit to be observed so that the transmission system will remain reliable even if the worst contingency occurs.

Operating standards: The measurable obligations of a control area and of systems functioning as part of a control area. An operating standard may specify monitoring and surveys for compliance.

Outage: The period during which a generating unit, transmission line, or other facility is out of service.

Planning policies: The framework for the reliability of interconnected bulk electric supply in terms of responsibilities for the development of and conformance to NERC planning principles and guides and regional planning criteria or guides, and NERC and regional issues resolution processes. NERC planning procedures, principles, and guides emanate from the planning policies.

Planning principles: The fundamental characteristics of reliable interconnected bulk electric systems and the tenets for planning them.

Planning procedures: The planning policies that are addressed and implemented by the NERC Engineering Committee, its subgroups, and the regional councils to achieve bulk electric system reliability.

Postcontingency operating procedures: Operating procedures that may be invoked by the system operator to mitigate or alleviate system problems after a contingency has occurred.

Protective relay: A device designed to detect abnormal system conditions, such as electrical shorts on the electric system or within generating planets, and initiate the operation of circuit breakers or other control equipment.

Rate: The authorized charges per unit or level of consumption for a specified time period for any of the classes of utility services provided to a customer.

Reactive power: The portion of electricity that establishes and sustains the electric and magnetic fields of alternating-current equipment. Reactive power must be supplied to most types of magnetic equipment, such as motors and transformers. It also must supply the reactive losses on transmission facilities. Reactive power is provided by generators, synchronous condensers, or electrostatic equipment such as capacitors and directly influences electric system voltage. It is usually expressed in kilovars (kVAr) or megavars (MVAr), and is the mathematical product of voltage and current consumed by reactive loads. Examples of reactive loads include capacitors and inductors. These types of loads, when connected to an ac voltage source, will draw current, but because the current is 90 degrees out of phase with the applied voltage, these loads actually consume no real power.

Real power: Also known as *active power*. The rate at which work is performed or that energy is transferred, usually expressed in kilowatts (kW) or megawatts (MW). The terms *active power* or *real power* are often used in place of the term *power* alone to differentiate it from reactive power.

Real-time operations: The instantaneous operations of a power system as opposed to those operations that are simulated.

Regional Reliability Council: One of 10 electric reliability councils that form the North American Electric Reliability Council (NERC). These NERC reliability council regions are East Central Area Reliability Coordination Agreement (ECAR); Electric Reliability Council of Texas (ERCOT); Mid-Atlantic Area Council (MAAC); Mid-America Interconnected Network (MAIN); Mid-Continent Area Power Pool (MAPP); Northeast Power Coordinating Council (NPCC); Southeastern Electric

Reliability Council (SERC); Southwest Power Pool (SPP); Western Systems Coordinating Council (WSCC); and Alaskan Systems Coordination Council (ASCC, affiliate).

Regional transmission operator (RTO): An organization that is independent from all generation and power marketing interests and has exclusive responsibility for electric transmission grid operations, short-term electric reliability, and transmission services within a multistate region. To achieve those objectives, the RTO manages transmission facilities owned by different companies and encompassing one, large, contiguous geographic area.

Regulations: Rules issued by regulatory authorities to implement laws passed by legislative bodies.

Relay: A device that controls the opening and subsequent reclosing of circuit breakers. Relays take measurements from local current and voltage transformers, and from communication channels connected to the remote end of the lines. A relay output trip signal is sent to circuit breakers when needed.

Reliability: The degree of performance of the elements of the bulk electric system that results in electricity being delivered to customers within accepted standards and in the amount desired. Reliability may be measured by the frequency, duration, and magnitude of adverse effects on the electric supply. Electric system reliability can be addressed by considering two basic and functional aspects of the electrical system: adequacy and security.

Reliability coordinator: An individual or organization responsible for the safe and reliable operation of the interconnected transmission system for their defined area, in accordance with NERC reliability standards, regional criteria, and subregional criteria and practices. This entity facilitates the sharing of data and information about the status of the control areas for which it is responsible, establishes a security policy for these control areas and their interconnections, and coordinates emergency opting procedures that rely on common operating terminology, criteria, and standards.

Resistance: The characteristic of materials to restrict the flow of current in an electric circuit. Resistance is inherent in any electric wire, including those used for the transmission of electric power. Resistance in the wire is responsible for heating the wire as current flows through it and the subsequent power loss due to that heating.

Restoration: The process of returning generators and transmission system elements and restoring load following an outage on the electric system.

Right-of-way (ROW) maintenance: Activities by utilities to maintain electric clearances along transmission or distribution lines.

RTO: *See* Regional transmission operator.

Safe limits: System limits on quantities such as voltage or power flows such that if the system is operated within these limits it is secure and reliable.

Schedule: An agreed-upon transaction size (megawatts), start and end time, beginning and ending ramp times and rate, and type required for delivery and receipt of power and energy between the contracting parties and the control areas involved in the transaction.

Scheduling coordinator: An entity certified by an ISO or RTO for the purpose of undertaking scheduling functions.

Seams: The boundaries between adjacent electricity-related organizations. Differences in regulatory requirements or operating practices may create "seams problems."

Security: The ability of the electric system to withstand sudden disturbances such as electric short circuits or unanticipated loss of system elements.

Security coordinator: An individual or organization that provides the security assessment and emergency operations coordination for a group of control areas.

Short circuit: A low-resistance connection unintentionally made between points of an electrical circuit, which may result in current flow far above normal levels.

Shunt capacitor bank: Shunt capacitors are capacitors connected from the power system to an electrical ground. They are used to supply kilovars (reactive power) to the system at the point where they are connected. A shunt capacitor bank is a group of shunt capacitors.

Single contingency: The sudden, unexpected failure or outage of a system facility or elements (generating unit, transmission line, transformer, etc.). Elements removed from service as part of the operation of a remedial action scheme are considered part of a single contingency.

Special protection system: An automatic protection system designed to detect abnormal or predetermined system conditions, and take corrective actions other than and/or in addition to the isolation of faulted components.

Stability: The ability of an electric system to maintain a state of equilibrium during normal and abnormal system conditions or disturbances.

Stability limit: The maximum power flow possible through a particular point in the system while maintaining stability in the entire system or the part of the system to which the stability limit refers.

State estimator: Computer software that takes redundant measurements of quantities related to system state as input and provides an estimate of the system state (bus voltage phasors). It is used to confirm that the monitored electric power system is operating in a secure state by simulating the system both at the present time and one step ahead, for a particular network topology and loading condition. With the use of a state estimator and its associated contingency analysis software, system operators can review each critical contingency to determine whether each possible future state is within reliability limits.

Station: A node in an electrical network where one or more elements are connected. Examples include generating stations and substations.

Storage: Energy transferred from one entity to another entity that has the ability to conserve the energy (i.e., stored as water in a reservoir, coal in a pile) with the intent that the energy will be returned at a time when such energy is more usable to the original supplying entity.

Substation: Facility equipment that switches, changes, or regulates electric voltage.

Subtransmission: A functional or voltage classification relating to lines at voltage levels between 96 kV and 115 kV.

Supervisory control and data acquisition (SCADA) system: A system of remote control and telemetry used to monitor and control the electric system.

Surge: A transient variation of current, voltage, or power flow in an electric circuit or across an electric system.

Surge impedance loading: The maximum amount of real power that can flow down a lossless transmission line such that the line does not require any kilovars to support the flow.

Switching station: Facility equipment used to tie together two or more electric circuits through switches. The switches are selectively arranged to permit a circuit to be disconnected or to change the electric connection between the circuits.

Synchronize: The process of connecting two previously separated alternating current apparatuses after matching frequency, voltage, phase angles, etc. (e.g., paralleling a generator to the electric system).

System: An interconnected combination of generation, transmission, and distribution components comprising an electric utility and independent power producers (IPPs), or group of utilities and IPPs.

System operator: An individual at an electric system control center whose responsibility it is to monitor and control that electric system in real time.

System reliability: A measure of an electric system's ability to deliver uninterrupted service at the proper voltage and frequency.

Thermal limit: A power flow limit based on the possibility of damage by heat. Heating is caused by the electrical losses which are proportional to the square of the *real power* flow. More precisely, a thermal limit restricts the sum of the squares of *real* and *reactive power.*

Tie-line: The physical connection (e.g., transmission lines, transformers, switch gear) between two electric systems that permits the transfer of electric energy in one or both directions.

Time error: An accumulated time difference between control area system time and the time standard. Time error is caused by a deviation in interconnection frequency from 60.0 Hz.

Time error correction: An offset to the interconnection's scheduled frequency to correct for the time error accumulated on electric clocks.

Transactions: Sales of bulk power via the transmission grid.

Transfer limit: The maximum amount of power that can be transferred in a reliable manner from one area to another over all transmission lines (or paths) between those areas under specified system conditions.

Transformer: A device that operates on magnetic principles to increase (step up) or decrease (step down) voltage.

Transient stability: The ability of an electric system to maintain synchronism between its parts when subjected to disturbance and to regain a state of equilibrium following that disturbance.

Transmission: An interconnected group of lines and associated equipment for the movement or transfer of electric energy between points of supply and points at which it is transformed for delivery to customers or is delivered to other electric systems.

Transmission loading relief (TLR): A procedure used to manage congestion on the electric transmission system.

Transmission margin: The difference between the maximum power flow a transmission line can handle and the amount that is currently flowing on the line.

Transmission operator: NERC-certified party responsible for monitoring and assessing local reliability conditions, who operates the transmission facilities, and who executes switching orders in support of the reliability authority.

Transmission overload: A state where a transmission line has exceeded either a normal or emergency rating of the electric conductor.

Transmission owner or transmission provider: Any utility that owns, operates, or controls facilities used for the transmission of electric energy.

Trip: The opening of a circuit breaker or breakers on an electric system, normally to electrically isolate a particular element of the system to prevent it from being damaged by fault current or other potentially damaging conditions. *Also see* Line trip, for example.

Voltage: The electrical force, or "pressure," that causes current to flow in a circuit, measured in volts.

Voltage collapse (decay): An event that occurs when an electric system does not have adequate reactive support to maintain voltage stability. Voltage collapse may result in an outage of system elements and may include interruption in service to customers.

Voltage control: The control of transmission voltage through adjustments in generator reactive output and transformer taps, and by switching capacitors and inductors on the transmission and distribution systems.

Voltage limits: A hard limit above or below which is an undesirable operating condition. Normal limits are between 95 and 105 percent of the nominal voltage at the bus (connection node) under discussion.

Voltage reduction: A procedure designed to deliberately lower the voltage at a bus. It is often used as a means to reduce demand by lowering the customer's voltage.

Voltage stability: The condition of an electric system in which the sustained voltage level is controllable and within predetermined limits.

Watt hour (Wh):   A unit of measure of electrical energy equal to 1 watt of power supplied to, or taken from, an electric circuit steadily for 1 hour.

Selected Bibliography

Adallah, Tareh, et al., "Control Dynamics of Adaptive and Scalable Power and Energy Systems for Military Micro Grids," ERDC/CERL TR–06–35, U.S. Army Corps of Engineers Construction Engineering Research Laboratory, Washington, DC (December 2006).

Aspen Institute, "Electricity—Who Will Build New Capacity?" 2005 Aspen Institute Energy Policy Forum, Washington, DC (2005).

Center for Building Performance and Diagnostics, "High Performance Sustainable Building Initiative," Carnegie Mellon University, Pittsburgh, PA (November 2007).

Brennan, Timothy, J., et al., "A Shock to the System— Restructuring America's Electricity Industry," *Resources for the Future*, Washington, DC (1996).

Brown, Dr. Marilyn A., et al, *Carbon Lock–In Barriers to Deploying Climate Change Mitigation Technologies*, Oak Ridge National Laboratory, Oak Ridge, TN (November 2007)

Chao, Hung-Po, and Hillard G. Huntington, *Designing Competitive Electricity Markets*, Kluwer Academic Publishers, Boston (1998).

Cicchetti, Charles J., and Colin M. Long, "A Tarnished Golden State: Why California Needs a Public/Private Partnership for Its Electricity Supply System," Pacific Economics Group LLD, Los Angeles (July 2003).

Cicchetti, Charles J., and Colin M. Long, "Restructuring Electricity Markets, a World Perspective Post-California and Enron," Vision's Communications, New York (2003).

Edison Electric Institute, "Key Facts about the Electric Power Industry," Edison Electric Institute, Washington, DC (2008).

Edison Electric Institute, *Statistical Yearbook of the Electric Power Industry*, Edison Electric Institute, Washington, DC (December 2006).

Electric Power Research Institute, "Electricity Sector Framework for the Future," Electric Power Research Institute, Palo Alto, CA (August 2003).

Electric Power Research Institute, "Electricity Technology Roadmap—Meeting the Critical Challenge of the 21st Century, 2003 Summary and Synthesis," Electric Power Research Institute, Palo Alto, CA (2003).

Electric Power Research Institute, "Electricity Technology Roadmap—Powering Progress, 1999 Summary and Synthesis," Electric Power Research Institute, Palo Alto, CA (July 1999).

Electric Power Research Institute, "Pathways to Sustainable Power in a Carbon-Constrained Future," *Perfect Power*, pp. 4–13, Palo Alto, CA (Fall 2007).

Electric Power Research Institute, "Technical Assessment Guide—Power Generation and Storage Options," Electric Power Research Institute, Palo Alto, CA (December 2006).

Electric Power Research Institute, "The Western States Power Crisis—Imperatives and Opportunities," Electric Power Research Institute, Palo Alto, CA (June 2001).

Faruqui, Ahmad, "2050: A Pricing Odyssey," *The Electricity Journal*, Vol. 19, Issue 8 (October 2006).

Fox-Penner, Peter, "Rethinking the Grid: Avoiding More Blackouts and Modernizing the Power Grid Will be Harder Than You Think," *The Electricity Journal*, pp. 28–42 (March 2005).

Galvin, Rohert W., *The Genius of a People*, Xlibris Corp., Philadelphia, PA (2008).

Gellings, Clark W., and Kurt E. Yeager, "Transforming the Electric Infrastructure," *Physics Today*, American Institute of Physics, Washington, DC (December 2004).

Giles, Ellen Flynn, *2008 UDI Directory of Electric Power Producers and Distributors*, Platts Division of McGraw-Hill, Boulder, CO (2007).

Goodell, Jeff, *Big Coal—The Dirty Secret Behind America's Energy Future*, Houghton Mifflin Company, Boston (2006).

Gralla, Preston, *How the Internet Works—Millennium Edition*, Que, McMillan Computer Publishing, Indianapolis, IN (1999).

Hardy, Charles, *The Age of Paradox*, Harvard Business School Press, Boston (1994).

Hewitt, Ben, "Plug-in Hybrid Electric Cars: How They'll Solve the Fuel Crunch," *Popular Mechanics* (May 2007).

Hyman, Leonard S., et al., "America's Electric Utilities—Past, Present & Future," Public Utilities Reports, Inc. Arlington, VA (2004).

InterAcademy Council, "Lighting the Way Toward a Sustainable Energy Future," InterAcademy Council, Amsterdam, The Netherlands (October 2007).

Isherwood Production Ltd., *World Power*, 2007 Edition, Isherwood Production Ltd., London (2007).

Jong, Jacques J. de, and Ed Weeda, "Europe, the EU and Its 2050 Energy Storylines," Clingendael International Energy Programme, The Netherlands Institute of International Relations, The Hague, The Netherlands (January 2008).

KEMA, "Dutch Electricity Technology Roadmap—Technology for the Sustainable Society," KEMA, Arnhem, The Netherlands (April 2002).

Kleit, Andrew N., *Electric Choices—Deregulation and the Future of Electric Power*, Rowman and Littlefield Publishers, Inc., Landham, MD (2007).

Kursunogles, Behrman N., et al., "Economics and Politics of Energy," *Proceedings of the International Conference on Economics and Politics of Energy*, Plenum Press, New York (1996).

Law, Cliff, "Saving Energy with Plug-in Hybrid Electric Vehicles," Institute for Electric and Electronic Engineering, Washington, DC (May 2007).

Lovins, Armory B., "Energy End-Use Efficiency" and "Transition to Sustainable Energy Systems," InterAcademy Council, Amsterdam, The Netherlands (2005).

Markoefer, Jay, *Re-Energizing America—A Common-Sense Approach to Achieving U.S. Energy Independence in our Generation*, WingSpan Press, Livermore, CA (2007).

Massachusetts Institute of Technology, "The Future of Coal, Options for a Carbon-Constrained World," an Interdisciplinary MIT Study, Cambridge, MA (2007).

Mintzer, Irving, and Peter Swartz, "U.S. Energy Scenarios for the 21st Century," Pew Center on Global Climate Change, Arlington, VA (July 2003).

Munson, Richard, *From Edison to Enron—The Business of Power and What It Means for the Future of Electricity*, Praeger Publishers, Westport, CT (2005).

Nahigian, Kenneth R., *The Smart Alternative: Securing and Strengthening Our Nation's Vulnerable Electric Grid*, The Reform Institute, Washington, DC.

National Commission on Energy Policy, "Enduring the Energy Stalemate: A Bipartisan Strategy to Meet America's Energy Challenges," National Commission on Energy Policy, Washington, DC (December 2004).

National Energy Technology Laboratory, "A Compendium of Modern Grid Technologies," Modern Grid Initiative, Pittsburgh, PA (June 2007).

National Research Council, *Electricity in Economic Growth*, National Academy Press, Washington, DC (1986).

Pande, Pete, and Larry Holpp, *What Is Six Sigma?*, McGraw-Hill, New York (2002).

Pansini, Anthony J., *Electric Distribution Engineering*, Second Edition, Fairmont Press, Lilburn, GA (1992).

Patterson, Walt, *Keeping the Lights On—Towards Sustainable Electricity*, Royal Institute of International Affairs, Earthscan Publications Ltd., London (2007).

Patterson, Walt, *Transforming Electricity—The Coming Generation of Change*, Royal Institute of International Affairs, Earthscan Publications Ltd., London (1999).

Pernick, Ron, and Clint Wilder, *The Clean Tech Revolution—The Next Big Growth and Investment Opportunity*, HarperCollins, New York (2007).

2008 Global Energy Outlook, Platts Insight, McGraw-Hill, NY (November 2007).

Rader, Linda K., "Century of Power—100 Most Influential People in Gas and Electricity," Hart Energy Markets, Houston, TX (2000).

Reviving the Electricity Sector; National Commision on Energy Policy: Washington, DC (2003).

Schewe, Phillip F., *The Grid—a Journey through the Heart of our Electrified World*, Joseph Energy Press, Washington, DC (2007).

Schurr, Sam H., et al., *Electricity in the American Economy—Agent of Technological Progress*, Greenwood Press, Westport, CT (1990).

Smil, Vaclav, *Creating the Twentieth Century—Technical Innovations of 1867–1914 and Their Lasting Impact,* Oxford University Press, New York (2005).

Smil, Vaclav, *Energy at the Crossroads—Global Perspectives and Uncertainties,* MIT Press, Cambridge, MA (2005).

Sustainable Development in a Dynamic World, Transforming Institutions, Growth, and Quality of Life, World Development Report 2003, World Bank and Oxford University Press, New York (2003).

Temin, Peter, *The Fall of the Bell System,* Cambridge University Press, New York (1987).

"The Energy Web," *Wired Magazine,* pp. 114–127 (July 2001).

United Nations Center for Human Settlements (Habitat), *Cities in a Globalizing World Global Report on Human Settlements 2001,* Earthscan Publications Ltd., London (2001).

United Nations Development Programme, *Human Development Report 2001, Making New Technologies Work for Human Development,* Oxford University Press, New York (2001).

United Nations Environment Programme Division of Technology, Industry and Economics, "Buildings and Climate Change—Status, Challenges, and Opportunities," United Nations Environment Programme Division of Technology, Industry and Economics, Paris (2007).

U.S. Green Building Council, "Building Momentum—National Trends and Projects for High-Performance Green Buildings," U.S. Green Building Council, Washington, DC (February 2003).

U.S.–Canada Power System Outage Task Force, "Final Report on the August 14, 2003 Blackout in the United States and Canada—Causes and Recommendations," U.S. Department of Energy and Canadian Ministry of Natural Resources (April 2004).

Vaitheeswaran, Vijay V., *Power to the People — How the Coming Energy Revolution Will Transform an Industry, Change Our Lives, and Maybe Even Save the Planet,* Farrar, Straus and Giroux, New York (2003).

World Energy Council, "Energy and Climate Change," World Energy Council, London (2007).

Yeager, Kurt E., *"Electricity for the 21st Century; Digital Electricity for a Digital Economy,* Technology in Society Series, Elsevier Ltd, St. Louis, MO (2004).

Yeager, Kurt E., "The U.S. Electricity Enterprise — Past, Present and Future Prospects," *Encyclopedia of Engineering,* New York (July 2007). Taylor & Frances Group

Zerriffi, Hisham, "Making Small Work: Business Models for Electrifying the World," Working Paper 63, Stanford University Program on Energy and Sustainable Development, Palo Alto, CA (September 2007).

Index

About the Authors

Robert (Bob) W. Galvin is the son of the founder of Motorola, Paul Galvin. In 1940, Bob began working for Motorola and was named president of the company in 1956. Two years later he succeeded his father as chief executive officer. In 1986, Bob Galvin gave up the title of CEO while remaining chairman of the board. Under his leadership, Motorola sales had grown from 216.6 million in 1956 to 6.7 billion in 1987 and cash flow per share had grown from 89 cents to 6.10. Bob also led the creation and implementation of the Six Sigma quality management system at Motorola. While guiding Motorola, Bob was instrumental in opening key international markets, including Japan and China, to competitive U.S. businesses and innovation. In 2005, Bob was awarded the Vannevar Bush Award for "his visionary leadership to enhance U.S. innovation, competitiveness, and excellence at the interface of science and technology with the Nation's industrial enterprise. In the counsels of government, industry, and academe, he unselfishly gave the Nation the benefit of his knowledge, experience and creative wisdom while leading his company in its great contribution to the computing and telecommunications transformation of society."

Kurt E. Yeager began his career in energy and the environment in 1968 with the Environmental Systems Department of the MITRE Corporation, after six years on active duty with the U.S. Air Force. From MITRE, Kurt joined the newly established U.S. Environmental Protection Agency (EPA) in 1971 as Director of Energy R&D Planning. Subsequently he was

EPA's representative to Project Independence, a federal initiative established in the wake of the first Arab Oil Embargo. Kurt joined the Electric Power Research Institute (EPRI) in 1974 and became its president and CEO in 1996. Under his leadership, EPRI expanded into the world's leading collaborative research and development organization for electric power, providing technical solutions to the electricity enterprise in over 40 countries as well as the United States. Since retiring from EPRI in 2004, Kurt has served as executive director of the Galvin Electricity Initiative, and chaired the World Energy Council's Study on Energy and Climate Change published in 2007. Kurt has authored over 200 technical publications on energy and environmental topics. In 2003, he was named Technology Policy Leader for Energy by *Scientific American*.

Jay Stuller has straddled the worlds of corporate communications and mainstream journalism for more than three decades. The author of seven books and nearly a thousand national magazine articles—including features in *Audubon*, *Smithsonian*, *Playboy*, and *Reader's Digest*—he also spent 25 years in public affairs and communications with Chevron Corp.